BRIDAL GAME CHANGERS

STRATEGIES TO
TURN AROUND
& TRANSFORM
YOUR BRIDAL BUSINESS

BY
JIM BUTLER
#1 BEST-SELLING AUTHOR OF
BRIDAL PROFIT EXPLOSION
AND
HOST OF THE
BRIDAL BUSINESS SUCCESS PODCAST

DEDICATION:

To my children:
Madeline, Mason, Lauren
Dallin and Miles
who each make life
with my wonderful wife Heather
so rewarding and full of joy

This publication is designed to provide accurate and authoritative information in regard to the subject matter covered. It is sold with the understanding that the publisher is not engaged in rendering legal, accounting, or other professional service. If legal advice or other expert assistance is required, the services of a professional should be sought.

Butler, Jim
Bridal Game Changers: Strategies to Turnaround and Transform Your Bridal Business
ISBN: 978-0692350225
   1. Business
   2. Success

CONTENTS

INTRODUCTION

The book you are reading contains the most important lessons I've learned about what it takes to turnaround or transform a bridal store or wedding business. I've observed and lived these lessons first hand through successes and failures both running my own bridal stores and coaching many of today's top bridal retailers in today's competitive environment.

Technology today is making it easier for customers to bypass traditional distribution channels. As a result, customers today are in charge and armed with information that can dictate what they will pay. Brides are coming into retail bridal stores today with much more information than their counterparts five years or ten years ago ever dreamed of having. As a result, smart retailers must learn how to better position what they sell in a way that helps them be more profitable. In this book, I want to teach you how you can sell more profitably in an unprofitable world and give you specific game changing strategies to help you achieve greater success in your bridal business.

Shortly after I began writing this book, I read a transformational book by Howard Schultz, the current CEO of Starbucks entitled *Onward: How Starbucks Fought For Its Life Without Losing Its Soul*. I've read and studied this book carefully and before I get into the game changing lessons I've learned at my stores and from coaching others, I want to share with you the eighteen lessons that Schultz explained in his book. Starbucks learned from the adversity it has faced during the recession as it made a remarkable turnaround. I think the lessons in this book are a great place to start if you are in a place where you want to grow your store even bigger or even if you want to turn it around if you have been struggling.

Here are the eighteen big lessons I got from this book that I think will be game changers for those who follow them and utilize their powerful principles in the midst of their own rapid growth or turnaround (whatever the case may be). As I share these with you, think about how you are utilizing these (or if you are not, how you could be utilizing them).

1. Grow with discipline.
Schultz stepped down as CEO of Starbucks in the year 2000 after helping the company achieve record growth. Yet, in the years that followed, many of the core principles were lost.

Growth is an interesting phenomenon. Most bridal store owners I talk to would love to have rapid growth and it is admittedly a great goal. The challenge in any kind of rapid growth is that you can get more caught up in the velocity of your increased revenues than actually focusing on what it is that you are selling. That focus is where the problem lies. When you care more about the numbers than the experience you are creating, you lose something.

This is what I believe the phrase 'grow with discipline' really means. You can never lose sight of what got you there in the first place. I have been the part of the rapid growth of several bridal stores. The big lesson I've learned is that growth brings its own set of challenges and distractions. Some of these distractions can lead you away from the core principles and products that helped you become great in the first place. I learned this lesson the hard way.

Schultz says this about Starbucks growth:

"We were opening as many as six stores each day, and every quarter our people were under intense pressure from Wall Street—and from within the company—to exceed past performance by showing increased comparative store sales, or comps, which are the year-to-year differences in revenue generated by a retailer's existing stores. Our answer had been to build more stores as fast as we could. Our strategy was to do more of what had worked in the past. But we were not pushing ourselves to do things better or differently. We were not innovating in lasting ways. We were venturing into unrelated businesses like entertainment. And we were pushing products that deviated too far from the core coffee experience. As one Starbucks partner expressed, it was as if we were running a race but no longer knew what we were running for." –*Onward*, p. 35.

There is a great lesson in that statement. When we become successful in the bridal business, it is easy to be seduced into expanding into other areas that aren't our core competency and where we think we see others doing well. These forays into new areas can create new revenues, but sometimes as Schultz mentioned they can slowly lead you away from the core business that helped you become successful in the first place. A few weeks ago I was talking with a successful bridal retailer who told me that she had seen this lesson first hand in her bridal store. She had built a very successful and profitable business, but thought that adding a few new lines (that didn't have the same margin) would help her appeal to a new customer she didn't already have. The reality was that she sold the new dresses, but at a lesser profit margin for the same amount of work.

It is so easy to be seduced by the persuasive power of NEW without thinking about how it really integrates with the successful OLD core parts of your existing business. New will always cannibalize old and allowing this to happen at the expense of what creates your core profitability can be a big mistake that may not be fully realized until much later. In the case of Starbucks, they were able to get back to the core before it was too late. Other businesses are not as fortunate.

Schultz says:

"The merchant's success depends on his or her ability to tell a story. What people see or hear or smell or do when they enter a space guides their feelings, enticing them to celebrate whatever the seller has to offer. Intuitively, I have always understood this. So when, in 2006 and 2007, I walked into more and more Starbucks stores and sensed that we were no longer celebrating coffee, my heart sank. Our customers deserve better." –pp. 34-35.

When Schultz returned as CEO in early 2008, he had three strategic initiatives that he launched:

1) "He knew he had to improve the current state of its US retail business since this drove the perception and business in other countries as well.

2) He knew he had to reignite the emotional attachment with customers. This meant that he would have to get back to the heart of the experience that customers had when they walked in the store (the aroma, the sense of community, the relationships with their local barista, and knowing that their purchases helped support high standards and socially responsible practices.

3) He knew he had to immediately make long-term changes to the foundation of the business. This meant he would have to carefully re-examine the organization and the leadership throughout the entire operation in ways that would reduce costs and improve customer service. He knew everything was up for overhaul except for two things (the employee health care program and the quality of their product). He would not cut there because he knew those two things were at the core of what made Starbucks work so well."

These three strategic initiatives were the basis of the Transformation Agenda that he would launch in the next few weeks.

In early March of 2008, Schultz had a meeting with all of his top leadership where he shared the Transformation Agenda. It began with a compelling strategic vision and was followed by their seven big moves (and specific tactics to accomplish each one). The plan was clearly articulated on one page so that everyone could refer back to it often.

I want to share with you their vision and plan and then talk about how you can utilize this in your business as well. My comments and questions will follow what Schultz and his team laid out in italics:

Our Aspiration: "To become an enduring, great company with one of the most recognized and respected brands in the world, known for inspiring and nurturing the human spirit.

Seven Big Moves:

1) "Be the undisputed coffee authority. Starbucks could not possibly transform the company if we did not excel and lead in our core business. We needed everyone to recognize the quality and passion we exhibit in sourcing, roasting, and brewing coffee. To accomplish this we would tell our story, as well as improve the quality and delivery of our espresso drinks, reinvent brewed coffee at Starbucks, deliver innovative beverages, and increase our share of the at-home coffee market."

I think Schultz is right on when he says that you cannot transform your company if you don't lead and excel in your core business. It is critically important to be perceived as the undisputed authority for what you do better than anyone else in your market niche. So, with that in mind, ask and answer these four questions:

What can you be the undisputed authority on to brides in your market?

What is your core business (what drives everything else)?

How can you better tell your story so brides seek you out and want to do business with you <u>before</u> they arrive at your store?

Are there other ways you can be in touch with the bride throughout the planning process that will reinforce your authority in the marketplace? Answering this question should help you realize how much additional value you could offer to brides through educational wedding planning resources to help you build trust in the marketplace.

2) "Engage and inspire our partners. Every partner should be passionate about coffee, from soil to cup, and possess the skills, enthusiasm, and permission to share that expertise with customers. Going forward, we would significantly improve training and career development for our partners at all levels of the business, and once again, Starbucks would develop meaningful and groundbreaking compensation, benefit, and incentive packages for partners."

Are each of your bridal consultants passionate about what you sell in your store from ordering through delivering the pressed dress (and their role in that process)?

How are you educating your bridal consultants so they are versed in things that can help solidify the impression that you are the undisputed authority of bridal gowns in your region?

What specifically are you doing to train them so they have the expertise that will enlighten and entertain the brides who shop at your store in a way that creates a more meaningful experience for them?

3) "Ignite the emotional attachment with our customers. People come to Starbucks for coffee and human connection. We would put our customers back in the center of the experience by addressing their needs, providing 'value' in a manner congruent with the brand, and developing programs that recognize and reward our most loyal customers. In our stores, we would achieve operational excellence, finding new ways to deliver world-class customer service and perfect beverages while keeping costs in line and our retail partners engaged."

What do people come to your store for? The answer is not just a dress or dresses. They come for the fulfillment of their wedding dreams. You sell dreams, not dresses.

Do brides feel like they are at the center of the experience in your store, or do they feel like they are just buying a dress?

In what ways specifically can you enhance the emotional connection they feel when they arrive at your store?

4) "Expand our global presence—while making each store the heart of the local neighborhood. We'd continue to grow our retail presence around the world—Starbucks had less than a 1 percent share of the global coffee market—but also strive to connect with and support the neighborhoods and cultures that each store serves. Enhancing our local relevancy would mean redesigning existing and new stores, offering new products that reflected the tastes of particular cultures, and reaching out by volunteering or fund-raising to support local programs and causes."

Is your bridal store perceived to be the anchor store in a bride's overall experience with planning her wedding?

In what ways could you become more of the heart of the experience the bride will have as she prepares for her wedding day?

How could you better connect with and support those demographic niches you have chosen to specialize in?

In what ways are you letting your community know that you exist and that you are giving back to them in ways that are meaningful and memorable?

5) "Be a leader in ethical sourcing and environmental impact. Starbucks has led the way in treating farmers with respect and dignity, working directly with organizations such as Fairtrade and Conservation International. Now we would expand our efforts, strengthen those partnerships, and forge new ones, as well as reduce each store's environmental footprint. We also had to do a much better job of sharing with others our extensive efforts on this front."

There is a limited amount you can do in this area that would even compare with what Starbucks does on a national or international level, but reflecting on and acting on this issue can help you stand out in relation to other bridal retailers who completely ignore this. Ask: In what ways are you or could you be perceived to be a leader in this area?

6) "Creative innovative growth platforms worthy of our coffee. Starbucks would grow not just by adding stores and selling coffee, but also by extending its brand and/or expertise to new product platforms expanding or complementing coffee, such as tea, cold beverages, instant coffee, food, and the booming health and wellness market. Innovation that was relevant to our core and values would be a hallmark of our transformation."

Starbucks expanded their new product creations into supermarkets for the at home market. Educational seminars that help brides better plan and save on their overall wedding costs could be a great way to promote your unique advantage in the marketplace.

What else can you offer to brides that complements the experience she'll have at your store?

Are there market niches that you could add that would complement what you are already doing and not distract from your specialization and focus?

7) "**Deliver a sustainable economic model**. Without a profitable business model, Big Moves 1 through 6 would not be possible. It was imperative that as we refocused on our customers and our core, we also improved upon how we operated our business by reducing costs and building a world-class supply chain, as well as creating a culture that drove quality and speed and managed expectations on an ongoing basis. Big Move 7 would likely be the most painful, least sexy, and most difficult part of transforming the company." –*Onward*, pp. 106-108.

This is obviously the most important thing in any business. You have to have a profitable AND sustainable model. Without this, you won't be able to grow or sustain what you are doing very long.

How often are you evaluating the profitability of the lines you carry at your store?

When a line you carry isn't profitable, do you have the courage to stop carrying it and replace it with something that is?

Schultz says this about what he launched at this meeting: "The Transformation Agenda was no quick fix. It was a mind-set dictating the company's primary focus until we were in a healthy position, ready to refocus on profitable growth. It was also a one-page road map designed to be willingly and creatively followed. More than a business plan, the Transformation Agenda gave us all something concrete to believe in." –p. 108.

Schultz coupled the Transformation Agenda he unveiled with a revised mission statement that specialized in the following areas (which I have adapted for our business): Our Product (Our Coffee), Our Bridal Consultants (Our Partners), Our Brides (Our Customers), Our Store (Our Stores), Our Wedding Community (Our Neighborhood), Our Profitability (Our Shareholders). This coupled what everyone needed to do with why. Having a clear outline of what to do each day and why you are doing it is a valuable exercise you should do so you can stay on task with what matters most and feel great about it at the end of the day."

As you go through this book, I invite you to assemble the ideas I'll share with you into your own transformation agenda to achieve success in your bridal business. Decide what you'll do and be clear about what every member of your team must do to make this new vision of success a reality.

2. Balance intuition with rigor.

Schultz says:

"In any well-run retail business there is, by definition, a maniacal focus on details. Especially in the beginning. Young companies must produce results everyday or risk closing their doors. Anything with the slightest potential to add or detract from sales or earnings—the quality of each item, every customer interaction, the attitude of each employee, every dollar spent—is attended to with steadfast concern."

He continues:

"In 2008 I felt very strongly that many of us at Starbucks had lost our attention to the details of the business....Like a doctor who measures a patient's height and weight every year without checking blood pressure or heart rate, Starbucks was not diagnosing itself at a level of detail that would help ensure its long-term health. We predicated future success on how many stores we opened during a quarter instead of taking the time to determine whether each of those stores would, in fact, be profitable. We thought in terms of millions of customers and thousands of stores instead of one customer, one partner, and one cup of coffee at a time. With such a mind-set, many little things dangerously slipped by unnoticed, or at least went unacknowledged. How could one imperfect cup of coffee, one unqualified manager, or one poorly located store matter when millions of cups of coffee were being served in tens of thousands of stores? We forgot that 'ones' add up." *–Onward*, pp. 97-98.

Now, as a bridal retailer and wedding professional you can likely only imagine what it would be like to have millions of customers and thousands of stores, but the lesson he shares here resonates. You can never get so caught up in the growth of your business that you forget about the experience you create for each individual bride and how she feels about the dress she buys from you in relation to her incredibly important and special wedding day.

In Chapter 2 of this book, I'll share with you the habits and behaviors of top bridal business owners and share with the critical success factors that are the essence of any turnaround or transformation. It is easy to be busy. It is much more difficult to be disciplined to be focused on what matters most.

3. Innovate around the core.

The first thing that Schultz did was get back to the basics. Stabucks had to play to win, not just play to lose. They had to create something unique that spoke to their customer base.

He says:

"For the past few years, Starbucks had been acting out of fear, mainly a fear of failure. So much of what the company had done was defensive, done to protect itself. Our primary goal had been to avoid missing our earnings projections rather than to actively engage our customers. As ceo, it was my job to reignite our partners' courage and to foster an aggressive desire to once again swing for the fences—as if our lives depended on winning." –p. 82.

His top coffee experts immediately went to work to help redefine the product they were selling—to make it an even richer experience.

One thing that has always amazed me about Howard Schultz is his ability to tell a great story. He is a master of this skill. He knows how to romance the experience through words--so he can explain how and why the coffee beans that Stabucks harvests and use from soil to cup are so much superior to any other coffee company you'll find. By doing this, he heightens the anticipation that people will have when they taste their product for the first time. He does so in a way that builds value and helps people sense what a rare feat is accomplished when someone buys a cup of coffee at one of their stores. As a result, the company is able to command premium prices.

He is also a master at explaining why his competitors can't compete with his company on the same level by discussing their process for harvesting the coffee beans instead of attacking the competitor directly.

Here is an example:
"Wherever the location, the best [coffee] beans—the ones with enchantingly complex flavors and compelling characters, known as Arabica—grow under some degree of stress, like high altitudes, intense heat, or long dry periods. Such harsh weather conditions can produce high-quality beans, but also fewer beans per tree. This makes arabica coffee more costly, which is why most mass coffee producers opt to buy cheaper robusta beans. Produced in more predictable and mild climates, robusta beans are less expensive because they deliver a higher yield per tree. But most robusta beans also taste harsh and rubbery, sort of like sucking on a pencil eraser. In its almost 40-year history, Starbucks coffee has never used a single pound of robusta beans in our products....Only 3 percent of the world's highest quality arabica beans are good enough to make it into one of our burlap bags."
–p. 83.

He continues:
"While most companies have access to the same high-quality arabica beans that Starbucks insists on purchasing, it is what happens to beans after they are harvested that further sets coffee companies apart from one another. No organization has the same combination of original technology and knowledge as Starbucks, and thus none can match the

uniqueness and consistency of the coffees that we roast, blend, and serve on a global scale." –pp. 83-84.

How are you telling your story? Do you let the brides you serve know what makes the dresses you select and bring into your store different than any other bridal store in the region?

Do you use percentages and analogies to help brides understand your value and exactly what you bring to them that really sets you apart?

These are important questions to ask and respond to as you become a better storyteller and get back to the heart of what makes you unique. To grow, you have to innovate around the core of what you do at your store and that means you must innovate around the products you sell in your business.

You have to have a good reason why brides should buy from you over any of your competitors and a story that communicates that difference is a great way to do it. If you haven't already articulated your new story, now is the time to do so.

Coming up with a new signature product was very important in Starbuck's strategy since McDonald's had recently beat Starbucks in taste tests. They went back to the testing laboratories and came up with a new signature product called Pike Place Roast (after their first store location). They set a launch date of April 8, 2008 after they developed the new product.

Schultz said:

"Strategically Pike Place Roast had the potential to be a powerful catalyst for and symbol of our transformation. For partners, the new brew was an accomplishment, the first in a while, to rally around, savor, and celebrate. For customers, Pike Place Roast ushered back in some of what had been missing in our coffee experience. Aroma. Freshness. A little theatre. And for our shareholders, Pike Place would be proof that the company was actively reclaiming its coffee authority. I was determined to demonstrate to our partners that Starbucks was going to push for self-renewal and reinvention. Pike

Place Roast was just the beginning." *–Onward*, p. 87.

A big part of making any kind of transformation or turnaround is to understand what is missing. Do you know what is missing? If so, what will you do at your store to put back what is missing?

How can you incorporate more theatre and experience into how you sell and educate brides coming into your store?

You can only do these things if you are committed to self-renewal and reinvention and you specifically work to innovate around the core of what makes your bridal store work. I'll discuss how you can do this in more depth in Chapter 4.

4. Don't embrace the status quo.

In tough economic times, it is much easier to hold on to what you have than to make changes that can get you back on track or to achieve rapid growth. It is easier to cower and hide than it is to face the music and do what needs to be done.

When Shultz took back over the day-to-day operations of Starbucks, it was in trouble. After 16 years of 5 percent growth or better, store traffic was decreasing and their sales had only gone up by one percent in the first three months of the fiscal year. Retailers such as Home Depot and Nordstrom's were announcing similar drops in revenue.

One of the first decisions Schultz made was to discontinue warm breakfast sandwiches, which at the time were accounting for approximately 3% of the revenue of each store. They were also getting in the way of their core competency as the smell of burnt cheese from the ovens overpowered the experience of the smell of their coffee. Stores had also added all kinds of products to sell that would help them increase their store numbers from quarter to quarter.

Schultz says:

"Once I walked into a store and was appalled by a proliferation of stuffed animals for sale. 'What is this?' I asked the store manager in frustration, pointing to a pile of wide-eyed cuddly toys that had absolutely nothing to do with coffee. The manager didn't blink. 'They're great for incremental sales and have a big gross margin.' This was the type of mentality that had become pervasive. And dangerous." –p. 90.

Are you selling things in your store that take you away from your core competency?

If you have products that take up space that account for a very small percentage of your overall sales, but detract from your mission of being the best bridal retailer in your area, you may need to make a decision similar to what Schultz did. He cut out what was cutting into his store's perceptions and experience and retooled the experience to get back to his core competency (coffee, in his case).

I think this is something all entrepreneurs must be honest with themselves about. I have been in stores that are literally cluttered with all types of wedding supplies (wedding invitations, etc.) that don't relate to the core competency of a bridal retailer. When we opened our first store, we carried wedding invitations for a short while because I thought it added to what brides could get from us. In reality, it took time to explain what to do and the profitability on the invitations was very low compared to how much time it took to explain, write, and place the order. We cut out the invitations and threw away the numerous books we had been sent by the invitation suppliers. You may need to make a similar decision to focus on your core competency. Many bridal retailers I know have chosen to focus on bridal gowns and don't even carry bridesmaid or prom dresses. Their businesses are very profitable and focused on what they do the very best.

The ups and downs of the economy have had an interesting effect on many businesses for this reason. Business owners have had to get back to the core of what *really* matters. Some have ignored these realities and they are really struggling. Those who have gotten back to what they do best and have gotten away from the status quo have seen their store sales rise as the economic outlook has continually improved and gotten better (but mostly, this has been because they have gotten better as a business owner first).

This is a mistake that many of the big box bridal retailers have made. I'll discuss more how you can beat them in Chapter 7.

5. Find new ways to see.

One of the first things Schultz did when he took over the company again as CEO was to shift his schedule so that he had more time to spend thinking early in the morning (either at home or at his office) preparing for his day so he could be as productive as possible. He eliminated all outside distractions (including resigning from corporate board positions). One interesting thing he did involved having an outside corporate retreat where he and other senior members of their staff asked themselves the question: "What does it mean to re-invent an icon?" This question along with an exercise that caused them to think about what The Beatles did with their music over time got them to think outside of their normal way of thinking about their current situation. These thought exercises opened up the creative forces of their own minds because they forced them to look at their business in a new way. It also helped them evaluate what they would need to do to change and apply those ideas and templates back to their own business.

There is a great lesson to be learned here. All entrepreneurs need to take time to think and plan out busy days before we begin. Thinking strategically about where you want your businesses to go is critically important to what you actually get done and where you will end up. Getting outside of the constraints of what you have always done and thought about can be freeing in a lot of ways.

Numerous questions came out of what was discussed which helped the management of Starbucks start thinking in a new direction. I've adapted three of the questions they posted below for you to consider and think about in your bridal business:

1) How is the bridal business changing online and offline and how are you reacting to it? What can you do to drive it?

2) With competitors breathing down your neck and bridezillas posting negative reviews (some of which may not even be true), how can you get out and tell your story to reassert your leadership authority to brides? How can you change the bridal industry as a whole?

3) How is what is going on in the national and international scene (with celebrity weddings) going to affect perceptions of weddings this year? What are you doing or will you do to capitalize on this?

The other thing Schultz did that helped him see better is that he asked for help from others to help imagine what the company's future would and should look like. He got perspective from a myriad of sources to think through issues on paper. Most bridal store retailers don't do this nearly enough. They react more to what is going on than proactively thinking about where they want to be. To see things differently, you have to change the way you look at your business and sometimes that might be through someone else's eyes.

Schultz made two immediate choices. One was to close all of the stores for an afternoon and evening and retrain all 135,000 baristas in espresso beverage preparation. He found the best way to do this was to close all of the stores for that period of time even though it cost him by his estimates around $6 million in revenue. The result was that customers talked about the difference in the experience of what they purchased (how it was prepared and tasted) and that resulted in higher sales and higher repeat visits. He announced on January 11 that the following month on February 26th, all of the stores would be closed for a "historic in-store education and training event." This helped get everyone back on board with the experience they were creating that led to a powerful transformation of the company.

The second thing Schultz decided to do was host the 2008 leadership conference for their 8,000 US store managers and almost 2,000 partners. He was confident that this meeting (even though at the time he wasn't sure exactly what he would do) would help infuse each of those people in his company with "the emotional capital they so desperately needed to reconnect with the company." –p. 78.

The biggest benefit that came from a renewed sense of vision was Schultz's belief that everyone at the company had to get back to asserting and demonstrating Starbucks superior product and authority in the marketplace. In his words, he says:

"One thing in particular was absolutely clear to me: Starbucks had to advance its position as the undisputed coffee authority. Without great coffee, Starbucks had no reason to exist. In the weeks ahead, I would intensify our focus on coffee quality and innovation." –p. 80.

I think this is an important point to amplify here. You can't grow your bridal business if you don't have a reason to exist in the minds of the brides you serve. If they think you are the same as every other bridal store they go to, they won't stay and they won't buy from you. The reality is they'll keep looking until they find a dress or a store they personally connect with that can help them realize the wedding of their dreams.

What is your store the undisputed authority on?

What can you do to capitalize on that strength?

How can you help brides see you with a new set of eyes and a new perspective?

You can only answer those questions if you take the time to think about and work on capitalizing on your strengths. If you want to make a turnaround in your business or grow rapidly, you have to know what you stand for and what makes you unique from any other bridal retailer in your area. If you are the same (or are perceived to be the same), you will never grow until you get past that hurdle. As Schultz discovered, it sometimes takes a new way of looking at things in order to get back on track to where you need to be.

6. Never expect a silver bullet.

One of the things that happens quite frequently in any business (and the bridal business is no exception) is that when things get tough, business owners look for a single silver bullet that will pull them out of the difficulties they are experiencing. For some store owners, it is often a single line of dresses that they feel if they have will bring in the customers they need or give them the margins they want.

Starbucks was no different. Shortly after Schultz took back over the company, they found an Italian-made beverage that was not ice cream or sorbet or a smoothy but when mixed with milk, fruit or yogurt tasted delicious. This new product was dubbed Sorbetto and Schultz believed it was the answer to increase revenues. Unfortunately, when they finally received the product from Italy to make the drinks, they found that their margins had shrunk. On top of that, the employees didn't enjoy the process that took nearly an hour and a half to clean the machines that made the drink each night. They lost enthusiasm even though they figured out how to reduce the process to 45 minutes. They ended up eliminating the product and cutting their losses.

Schultz says:

"I'd brashly embraced Sorbetto as a silver bullet. But there is no such thing. Not growing our store count. Not new coffee blends. Not loyalty or value programs. Not healthier food and drinks. Yes, opportunities to transform Starbucks for profitable, sustainable growth existed everywhere, but no single move, no product, no promotion, and no individual would save the company. Our success would only be won by many. Transforming Starbucks was a complex puzzle we were trying to piece together, where everything we did contributed to the whole. We just had to focus on the right, relevant things for our partners, for our customers, for our shareholders, and for our brand." –p. 169.

This is a common attitude amongst bridal retailers. I am often asked by bridal retailers after seminars I give what the one thing they need to do is that will help them be successful. There is no one single thing that will propel a store to be successful. It is a myriad of things that work together in concert to make the store work. It is a simultaneous approach of actions instead of a step-by-step sequential process. It is understanding and implementing great systems. In this book, I outline the factors I think are most important for success in the bridal business, but you can't look at them independently as if they are the only single thing that will make you successful. Schultz is right. There is no single silver bullet.

7. Get your hands dirty.

Schultz explained to a roomful of its top leaders one day early in the transformation:

"When you start a business, you do not operate from a lofty place, because you cannot afford to. It is so vitally important that we get back to the roots of the business, that we get back in the mud."

"'Get our hands in the mud!' I literally pleaded, holding my hands out in front of me. I held on to this analogy because it made so much sense, and from that day on I repeated it over and over and over, to people at every level.

"In fact, one day when I was walking through the offices of Starbucks' architects and designers, I stopped in my tracks when a poster caught my eye. A pair of dirt-smudged hands, palms up, framed the words 'The world belongs to the few people who are not afraid to get their hands dirty.' I asked to borrow the poster and marched it to the eighth floor, where I placed it on the wall of our boardroom so Starbucks' executive team would see it every time we met. The words—Get dirty. Get in the mud. Get back to the roots of the business—cascaded down through the organization." –*Onward*, p. 98.

Bridal retailers understand this better than any of the principles I'll cover here. When you work with brides on a daily basis and help them find what they are looking for, you are in the mud of the marketplace. You know what they are looking for, what you don't have, what you need and what is selling better in your area better than anyone else. As your business grows, you may find that you are not on the floor everyday selling. This is dangerous ground because you can lose your touch with what is going on in the marketplace very quickly if you are not careful. It is much better to get into the mud of the marketplace as much as you can so you can better understand what needs to be done and what is happening with the attitudes and preferences of the brides in your area. If you delegate this to someone else, you will never understand what is going on as well as if you get into the business yourself on a daily basis.

Schultz was able to effect a transformation at his business because he did precisely that. He got his hands dirty by visiting stores and roasting plants, by visiting with people who were working through their challenges, about what specifically was working, and how he could help them. This is important that you do the same and that you never lose sight of the fact that every bride in front of you or any member of your staff is critically important to the future of your business. Remember, the bride in front of you is funding your paycheck. Each member of your team needs to understand this truth. Knowing what each bride is looking for, what her concerns and fears are surrounding her wedding, and what will help bring her happiness and joy on her big day are things that you must never lose sight of. The moment you do, your business will start to decline.

Your bridal consultants are always watching you. They are watching and interpreting how you look, your facial expressions, and how you communicate with them and brides at your store. They can sense when you are stressed, when you are worried, and when you are unhappy with their performance. This affects their performance as well. It is so much better to project confidence (yet not arrogance), excitement, and enthusiasm in everything that you do. This will result in higher morale and improved performance amongst everyone on your team.

Be sure the experiences you are having on a daily basis are allowing you to get dirty in the mud of the marketplace. Keeping your ear low to the ground can help you anticipate where trends are moving. Acting on these observations quicker than your competitors can give you a big advantage in how you can help brides have the wedding day of their dreams.

8. Listen with empathy and over communicate with transparency.

One of the initiatives started by Starbucks during this period was a web site called www.MyStarbucksIdea.com. Within 24 hours of launching this site, over 7,000 ideas were posted online. Over 100 of the ideas that have been shared have been implemented since the site began.

Probably the toughest decision that Schultz had to make was to close 600 stores in July of 2008. It represented 8 percent of the company's US owned retail stores. 20% of them had been opened in the past three years when they were opening stores thinking that was all they had to do to be successful. The decision about which stores to close was financially based, but the way Starbucks went through the process is a great lesson in empathy and striving to communicate with transparency.

Schultz said when he made this announcement:

"Throughout the history of the company, we have always aspired to put our people first. This makes our decision to close stores more difficult.... At the same time, we recognize that we must make decisions that will strengthen the U.S. store portfolio and enable us to enter fiscal 2009 focused on enhancing operating efficiency, improved customer satisfaction and ensuring long-term shareholder value for our partners and customers. By far, this is the most angst-ridden decision we have made in my more than 25 years with Starbucks, but we realize that part of transforming a company is our ability to look forward, while pursuing innovation and reflecting, in many cases with 20/20 hindsight, on the decisions we made in the past, both good and bad." –pp. 157-158.

They received tremendous feedback from fans and customers who pleaded with them not to shut down their store locations. A web site called www.SaveOurStarbucks.com popped up online. This kind of outpouring is unique and in some cases, Starbucks listened to what was said. In the end, they evaluated the criteria a store needed to reach in order to be saved. It was a tough time for everyone involved, but they did their best to be open with which locations were closing and why, and gave severance and time for their employees who were affected to find new jobs.

I have had to make tough calls in business just like I know you have. I think the critical thing is to listen closely to your bridal consultants and get their feedback on what can be done before you make major changes and get the support of your leaders before moving ahead. John Maxwell talks in depth about how he has done this with his organization numerous times in his book, *The Success Journey*. If you have struggled with making changes in your store, this would be a great resource for you to get and study.

One message that Starbucks heard loud and clear from their customers was their desire for a rewards program that would reward them with free drinks with a certain amount of purchases over time. The rewards program when re-launched in June of 2008 (the first launch in April got lost in the shuffle of several new drinks and promotions that were running simultaneously). They invited those who already had gift cards to register them online in order to get a free beverage. Within a month, one million people signed up reloading $150 million onto their Starbucks cards.

Today, one in seven customers uses a Rewards card and they plan to take their referral program to the next level. Starbucks believes that the following five goals will happen. They will:

1) See an uptick in sales.

2) Reward their core customers.

3) Provide the value people seek in tough economic times without cheapening the brand.

4) Save money by reducing the number of credit card transactions, and thus some of the millions of dollars we paid in associated fees.

5) Strengthen the bond with customers inexpensively in combination with our evolving online presence." –*Onward*, p. 166.

If you don't have a rewards program or an incentive for brides who buy on their first visit, you really should put some thought into how you can launch this. Listen to what your brides have to say and implement ideas that you believe will work to help grow your store and your brand.

9. Tell your story, refusing to let others define you.

The essence of marketing is found in this phrase. By building your own brand and telling your own story you give brides a chance to hear your side of the story. There is a lot of concern these days about bridezillas or unscrupulous competitors who write nasty or untrue things online.

Protecting yourself from the misinformation that bridezillas feel compelled to share with the world is becoming more and more important. In addition, every bridal store owner I've talked to has at least one bridal competitor and sometimes more who are unscrupulous and downright mean-spirited about how they treat one another as fellow competitors.

I think it is important to evaluate the feedback that you receive from brides very carefully. In some cases, they point out problems in your systems and in how one of your bridal consultants handled a certain problem. Being open to criticism can be helpful to help you improve gaps or holes in the systems that make up your store.

In the case where brides are downright rude, nasty, and lie, this is a completely different situation. It would be nice to have a better consumer bureau (where we could report some customers who are downright rude to other business owners). In the case where people blatantly lie about something, I would recommend contacting the blog or web site where the negative review was posted and give your side of the story. Facebook has an option for every post where you can report someone who is spewing bad or malicious information. You are also in control so you can delete a post that may be negative. You have to be careful with this however. Don't ignore feedback that you get. You may find out things that can help you offer training to improve your store as well.

The important thing is not to just lay back and take abuse of bridezillas or competitors posing as brides. You have to protect your reputation.

The best way to do this is to focus on telling your story again instead of getting caught up in a back and forth mud slinging battle that doesn't do *anyone* any good. If you can constantly be out telling your story and the stories of brides you have helped, you can counteract the negative things with the positive things you hear as well.

If you find a negative comment online, I think there are at least three things you should do:

1) Determine if there is any validity to what has been said. Reach out directly to the bride who made the comment and see if you can resolve it yourself.
2) If the bride responds and you are able to successfully resolve it, ask the bride to update her post and post how you were able to successfully resolve the situation.
3) If the bride refuses to be cooperative, consider posting your response to how you tried to resolve the situation and help the bride out. Then, ask your Facebook network or other brides to post their positive experiences in the same area so that you can overwhelm the negative with lots of positive feedback.

10. Use authentic experiences to inspire.

In late October of 2008, Schultz brought 10,000 North American district, regional, and store managers together for a week in New Orleans for a leadership conference that helped galvanize the group together and better understand what needed to be done in the days that lay ahead for the transformation. The thing that inspired everyone there more than anything else was the community volunteer event where they rebuilt and refurbished some of the city's most devastated public spaces and neighborhoods. They bought

$1,000,000 of shovels, hammers and other supplies in two large rental trucks and spent a combined 50,000 hours of work working to do whatever needed doing in New Orleans as organized by nonprofit community and nongovernmental organizations. They were extremely productive and helped repair more than 86 homes and many community centers so families could move back in after being displaced for more than 3 years. Each worker wore a T-shirt that said "Onward."

Schultz says of this experience:

"All told, Starbucks volunteered approximately 50,000 hours of time in New Orleans. It was unprecedented, and I was beyond proud. Our partners were as well. Proud of the impact we were able to make during our visit in New Orleans, as well as even a little bit prouder of the company that we had come here to rebuild."

The remarks he gave at the general session are worth some study. He combined a harsh dose of reality and a vision of hope for what they would do going forward and how they would deal with their increased competition. When he spoke to everyone who had assembled, he said:

"We are here for a reason. We are here to celebrate our heritage and traditions and also to have an honest and direct conversation about what we are responsible to do as leaders.... We are not a perfect company. We make mistakes every single day. We put our heart and our conscience first, but we have lots of issues that we are trying to balance. Expectations are high from every constituent and we are trying our best, especially during this downturn and in this economy, to do the right thing... Now we can point to many things that perhaps are causing the issues that we have faced this year. Like many other companies, we are facing perhaps the most difficult economic situation since the Great Depression. It's real. It is serious. People do not have as much money as they once did, and Starbucks more often than not is not a discretionary purchase. So we have the economy. And we also have something else. Something new. We have competitors small and large who think we are vulnerable and not as good as we used to be. Not as passionate. And they are trying to take our customers away. Which is why one of the themes of this conference has been to make it personal. But what does that mean? What does it mean when approximately 50 customers a day are not coming into our stores versus last year? What does it mean when at eight o'clock in the morning the line is out the door and a customer peels off and leaves? What does it mean when you see a customer you recognize with a cup of coffee that is not ours? What does it mean when you know for a fact that the beverage you just handed over to the customer was not made to the standard of Espresso Excellence? These are serious questions, and what they mean, I have always believed strongly, is that we have to take accountability and responsibility for the things that we observe. The things that we experience. And the things that we learn." –p. 202.

He finished by saying:

"The power of this company is you. We need to recognize as leaders that, unlike any other time in our history, this is a seminal moment. This is a test. A crucible. A challenge for how we are going to respond. And my primary message is to share with you the pride that I have in being your partner. The faith that I have in you. People talk about the power of the Starbucks brand, but the power of the Starbucks brand is not some external force. It is you and the people you represent. You are going to restore it. People are going to be writing history books about the business of Starbucks, and the business of Starbucks is going to once again demonstrate that you can build a company with a conscience. Please remember what you have experienced here. Remember how you felt. And when you get back, please do not be a bystander. Change and refine behavior when you see it is inconsistent with the standards that we have all observed here this week. And all we ask is that you take all this emotion, the feeling, and the power of 10,000 that you have each experienced in the last few days." –*Onward*, p. 206.

Wow. What inspiring words. Do your speak with your bridal consultants on one hand about the difficulties ahead AND do they also hear you speak with hope about their role and the future they can help you create together? That is a great model to follow as you speak with and train your bridal consultants on what must be done moving forward with your store.

Use authentic experiences to do things with your bridal consultants when you achieve your goals. Take the time to honestly assess what must be done as you grow your store to be even more successful in the future. Then, communicate that vision with your key staff members and every member of your team who makes it happen day in and day out for the brides and prom customers who come into your store.

11. Hold people accountable but give them the tools to succeed.

A great example of this occurred at the company leadership meeting in New Orleans in October of 2008. After explaining the elements of the Transformation Agenda, Cliff, the head of Starbuck's US business, walked on the stage with a silver briefcase. Before opening it, "Cliff first reviewed the various new support tools coming to stores: a new, easier-to-use point-of-sale system (essentially, the automated cash registers) and labor scheduling software which would allow managers to better control staffing and expenses. A 'retail dashboard' would provide data and a common language to improve business acumen. Each announcement was followed by cheers from a stadium filled with store managers fed up with Starbucks' antiquated technologies.

'Okay, you've been wondering what's in this briefcase.' Cliff picked it up and placed the case on the podium. He flipped open the top and removed a black laptop computer. A roar of applause. There were whistles. High fives. Hoots.... 'The tools you need to do your job are on the way,' said Cliff...announcing that every store would soon be getting its own laptop. The volume and duration of our partners' jubilation exceeded anything we had heard or seen that day, providing proof of just how desperately our managers needed better resources and how hungry they were to do a better job." –pp. 205-206.

It never ceases to amaze me how bridal consultants respond to things that help them do their jobs better. As an example, anytime I've purchased new computers and updated our software, our team members love it because everything works faster and better.

I am of the same opinion of Schultz that people want to do a good job, and when you provide them with the tools they need to succeed, they will do extraordinary things for you.

Do you have the tools that can help your bridal consultants sell better and accomplish the goals you've set for your store?

What can you do to better assist each member of your team better accomplish their job?

A good way to determine this is to break down each person's job responsibilities and then ask what you could do to help make their responsibilities easier and more manageable. Being serious about helping each member of your team and empowering them with the sales tools they need will help them hit your sales targets better than they ever could without them. Don't handicap your team before they even start. Look for ways to help them succeed. I'll talk more about how you can better manage your team and stay productive on what matters most in Chapters 8 and 9.

12. Make the tough choices; it's how you execute that counts.

In tough times, you have to make tough choices. But sometimes those tough choices can prove to be a blessing in disguise. Leading up to the holiday season of 2008, the leadership team at Starbucks "began brainstorming ideas of how to breathe life into what was sure to be one of our worst holiday seasons on record. For inspiration, we considered our Rewards Card, our loyalty program that could be chugging along nicely since its June 2008 re-launch. What could we do with a card to provide even more value than the rewards program? We played with some numbers and eventually came up with the idea for a $25 Gold Card that would give cardholders 10 percent off on anything they bought at Starbucks for one year. Excited, we called the Rewards Card team from the plane to discuss benefits and pitfalls, and by the time we landed in Seattle I had given the Starbucks Gold

Card the go-ahead, assuming no major problems cropped up. Our goal was 25,000 cards in the first week. We surpassed that amount in the first *weekend*." –p. 232.

While those numbers are very impressive, I think the idea that got me thinking was how to create more value into a rewards program that can be used to generate revenue now.

What could you offer to brides in a Gold or Platinum Wedding Card that could help you boost your ticket sales and give more meaningful value to the brides you serve? Cards live in bride's purses and so they are seen more often and can be a powerful way to be transferred into referral cards. Perhaps you could bundle several cards together which a bride could buy as gifts for their bridesmaids that could then be redeemed for a special offer when they buy their bridesmaid dress from your store. Perhaps you could offer a special bridesmaid memory event at your store when they purchased a certain quantity of these cards.

You can also capture the email addresses of each of those who have the cards so you can build a database from which you could promote meaningful offers in cost-effective ways. Starbucks has used such programs to invite cardholders in for a free drink of new products that they create. Perhaps you could offer a private gown showing for cardholders and past brides where they can bring one engaged guest with them to an event highlighting a new season's arrivals.

Any database of brides and prom girls you can build can be a very powerful way for you to develop the hidden assets in your business.

13. Be nimble.

A great example of a time when Starbucks was nimble and acted quickly on their feet was during the lead-up to Election Day on November 4, 2008. They created and ran a television commercial on *Saturday Night Live* that said:

"What if we cared as much on November 5th
As we care on November 4th?

What if we cared all of the time
The way we care some of the time?
What if we cared when it was inconvenient
As much as we care when its convenient?
Would you community be a better place?
Would our country be a better place?
Would our world be a better place?
We think so, too.
If you care enough to vote,
We care enough to give you
A free cup of coffee.
Come into Starbucks on November 4th
Tell us you voted,
And we'll proudly give you
A tall cup of brewed coffee on us.

Then, the commercial finished with:
You & Starbucks.
It's bigger than coffee." –*Onward*, pp. 209-210.

They only paid for one commercial and then uploaded it to YouTube. They then invited their fans on Facebook and via Twitter to check out the YouTube video. The results really show the power of social media. According to Schultz:

"Every time someone clicked a response or watched the actual video, the action triggered a message to his or her Facebook news feed. For example, Facebook friends where notified when their friends RSVP's 'yes' to Starbuck's free coffee day, exposing his entire network to Starbucks' election campaign. This second-hand or 'viral' exposure added 14 million more individual impressions on top of the 75 million original impressions Facebook yielded, meaning that, all told 89 million people were exposed to the election campaign in some way." --*Onward*, p. 215.

People who voted where telling others that they should go and get free coffee. The opportunity to be nimble happened when the stores ran out of pastries and controversy erupted when some claimed that Starbuck's was attempting to influence voter turnout and how they voted. Schultz says:

"Then claims surfaced that our free-coffee promotion violated federal and some state election laws because it promised an incentive in return for voting. To avoid any legal tussles, we again turned on a dime and extended the free-coffee offer to any customer who requested it. Unfortunately, word of the shift often got to customers before our partners, and at times confusion reigned." --p. 216.

Even with the confusion and controversy, they served more than two million cups of coffee that day (two and a half times more than on a typical weekday) and more importantly a sense of community with people talking about the election were at the stores.

The campaign ended up being a big success in large part because of social media. The YouTube video was viewed 419,000 times on Election Day. On Facebook, 405,000 people replied 'yes or maybe' to their invitation. Someone tweeted about the promotion on Twitter every eight seconds.

By being nimble, Starbucks discovered powerful ways to drive traffic and positively engage with their customers (which has been utilized many times since then) to drive sales.

You have numerous opportunities to be nimble in your bridal store if you choose to take advantage of them. Bridal consultants sometimes make mistakes and you have to make up the difference. Responding quickly can earn new fans and prevent small problems from escalating into big ones. Social media also offers opportunities to promote what you do to your customers in big ways as well.

Five more lessons that Schultz talks about in his book *Onward* that are self-explanatory are the following:

14. Find truth in trials and lessons in mistakes.

15. Stick to your values, they are your foundation.

16. Be decisive in times of crisis.

17. Be responsible for what you see, hear, and do.

18. Believe.

At the end of the book, Schultz makes this observation:

"Starbucks has regained a healthy balance with a culture that celebrates creativity and discipline, entrepreneurship and process, as well as rigorous innovation. But perhaps the most vital thing that came out of the past two years has been the confidence we gained knowing that we could preserve our values despite the hardships we faced. Holding fast to those values steadied us throughout the tumultuous journey, and the ways in which we conduct our business will continue to bring our partners pride and fuel their engagement as we continue to grow." –pp. 314-315.

My hope is that as I've shared what Schultz did to turnaround Starbucks along with my perspective of how you can use these same principles to affect great changes for your bridal store that you've been renewed with a new sense of confidence and hope in the future.

The wedding business is a great business. You do a great work each and every day as you help brides find the most meaningful dress she may ever wear in her lifetime. The passion behind what you do everyday must never be diminished by the challenging experiences you go through and endure. Rather, you must use those challenging moments to reignite and redefine what makes your business great and what you will do daily to put more meaning into the lives of your bridal consultants and the brides you serve each day.

On the pages that follow, I'll outline a plan you can utilize in your store and share what I would encourage you to do if we were sitting down to discuss how to turnaround or transform your business face-to-face. It's your time to make this your best year ever. Let's get down to business.

CHAPTER 1:

TEN TIPS TO TURNAROUND OR TRANSFORM YOUR BRIDAL BUSINESS

"Your success in life isn't based on your ability to simply change. It is based on your ability to change faster than your competition, customers and business."-Mark Sanborn

The ten tips I'll share in this chapter are the essence of what I believe it takes to succeed and what must be done if you want to turnaround or transform your bridal business.

The thing I'll say at the outset is that it is important for you to question your assumptions. I invite you to read and study what I share with you with an open mind because sometimes what seems irrational or counter-intuitive can be your big breakthrough to success.

As an example, consider this fascinating statement made by Jim Cockrum in his book *FREE Marketing*:

"The positive impact of being irrationally generous has never been more evident than it is now. It clearly pays to have a highly ethical and customer-centered business approach.... If you don't believe that the irrational customer service approach can be applied to any business then go do some research on the customer service habits of zappos.com and you'll quickly see my point. Among their irrational policies is a 365-day return policy on any shoes. That's nuts, but it's working because of the viral power of their fan base that raves loyally and consistently online to an ever-growing network of contacts." –p. 21.

In the book, he identifies five irrational habits that supercharge your online reputation (followed by my comments):

1. Don't keep secrets; expose them.

Some businesses seem to thrive by keeping things a secret. Instead of taking this approach, instead write a special report that details the most important lessons or places that brides should go as they prepare for their wedding that will save them money and create fewer hassles for their wedding. If the information is helpful, the bride's view of you and her trust in you will increase.

2. Eagerly send customers to a competitor if it's best for them.

There are certain items that some bridal retailers don't offer such as mother's dresses or flower girl dresses. If this is the case with you, refer mothers to competitors who are specialists in those areas.

3. Sell only to your Mom.

Jim Cockrum says: "Your prospects are becoming increasingly irritated by self-serving, sales-pitch-sounding messages. The litmus test I use when writing advertising copy is quite simple and it has worked for me for several years. My guiding principle is to sell only to a friend or to my mom when writing copy. Talk to that one person and treat them like you'd treat a true friend."--26.

Identify the kind of customer you want and then write all of your marketing to her. When you write to an audience of one, your message comes across as more genuine, more authentic and most importantly, more believable.

4. Give stuff away.

Create amazing information and give it away. Use it to build your credibility and to begin the process of reciprocity with your brides. A great way to do this is with special reports.

Let me give you several places you can go:

Fiverr.com (place to find others to promote you or unique ways to get others to promote you)

Groupme.com (app that allows you to text a large list at the same time)

Fangager.com (Reward your fans and followers with points for interacting with you socially online)

5. Let your customers talk to each other.

Jim Cockrum says: "For many businesses the idea of allowing their customers to interact online together sounds like a complete nightmare. In my opinion the real problem isn't with the customers, but with the policies and services of the business they are discussing. In other words the real question is, what do you have to hide? The reality is that customers will discuss you, your products, and how they feel about them whether you like it or not. You would be wise to provide them a forum for these discussions. It's better to have a forum that you can easily monitor and use to reply to customer issues." –p. 28.

In today's economy, it is wise to do things that are completely different than what your competitors are doing so you stand out in the minds of the brides that you hope to attract to your store.

Before we get into the ten tips, I have an assignment for you as you're going through this book. I want you to get a notebook that you keep with you at all times when you're reading this book where you can jot down the best ideas that you're learning. Then, split your notebook into the following eight sections or pages:

1) *Implementation list* - list what you will implement in your store – the first and last page of my notebook contains my implementation list

2) *Examples of advertising that works* - When watching TV or listening to advertising of any kind (regardless of the industry it is), jot down the words you hear that cause you to feel persuaded (pay attention to how you feel and what you think)

3) *Examples of headlines that work* - Take note of the headlines used by successful print ads you see

4) *Powerful stories that move you* - When you hear a story that moves or inspires you, take note of where you heard it and list the names involved. Get more information online (collect great stories that can help you inspire the brides you work with)

5) *Examples of successful ads that sell other products to brides* - Study the headlines and ad copy that sells books or products that are marketing to brides. You can do this by studying what's being sold to brides on Amazon.com.

For example, study the copy that is selling Randy Fenoli's book, *It's All About the Dress*:

"Every bride wants to feel beautiful and wants to have her dress express the essence of who she is. Now choosing the perfect thing to wear on that special day is easier than ever! Drawing on his experience as fashion director at Kleinfeld Bridal, Randy Fenoli has written a guidebook bursting with insights and inspiration for helping brides-to-be determine what story they want their dress to tell. *It's All About the Dress* covers:

- Suggestions on flattering cuts, fabrics, and styles for every body type
- Price ranges and budget
- Trains, veils, headpieces, undergarments, and accessories
- Insider secrets on managing the bridal dress appointment
- Options for bridesmaids, mother of the bride, and more!
- Featuring 100 inspiring photos plus invaluable tips on how to deal with bridal dress 911's, IT'S ALL ABOUT THE DRESS is the ultimate sourcebook no bride-to-be should say "I do" without!"

6) *List of businesses to study and pay attention to*

- Follow what they are doing (what direction they're moving in)
- Use Google Alerts to track what they are doing
- Study qualities of leaders
- Force yourself to pay attention to industries that you would not normally pay attention to and learn from others

7) *A list of ideas of things you could do for others*. Here are two examples to get you thinking:

a) TOMS

TOMS is a great example of a company with a mission focused around helping others. For example, their shoe division promises "With every pair of shoes you purchase, TOMS will give a pair of new shoes to a child in need. One for One." This is a powerful message and story. Notice the power of story from their web site:

In 2006, American traveler Blake Mycoskie befriended children in Argentina and found they had no shoes to protect their feet. Wanting to help, he created TOMS Shoes, a company that would match every pair of shoes purchased with a pair of new shoes given to a child in need. One for One. Blake returned to Argentina with a group of family, friends and staff later that year with 10,000 pairs of shoes made possible by TOMS customers.

Why Shoes?

Many children in developing countries grow up barefoot. Whether at play, doing chores or going to school, these children are at risk:

- A leading cause of disease in developing countries is soil-transmitted diseases, which can penetrate the skin through bare feet. Wearing shoes can help prevent these diseases, and the long-term physical and cognitive harm they cause.
- Wearing shoes also prevents feet from getting cuts and sores. Not only are these injuries painful, they also are dangerous when wounds become infected.
- Many times children can't attend school barefoot because shoes are a required part of their uniform. If they don't have shoes, they don't go to school. If they don't receive an education, they don't have the opportunity to realize their potential.

b) Diane Cornelius and her Brides for Haiti Mission

A great example of linking cause to her bridal business is that of Diane Cornelius and her Brides for Haiti mission (http://www.usaweekend.com/article/20111125/LIVING03/31125 0007/Diane-Cornelius-brings-joy-weddings-Haiti)

8) *Quotes, pictures, or ideas that inspire you*

Now, with that framework in mind, let's get into the ten tips that will help you turnaround or transform your bridal business. You'll notice that each one is designed to get you thinking differently about your business and to shift the perceptions brides have about you as well.

1. Turn what you do into something extraordinary.

How do you turn something ordinary into something extraordinary? The best way to do this is to move up the fascination scale so that brides are attracted to you and what you do. In other words, it doesn't matter if you are the best bridal store in the world if nobody knows.

To help you answer this question, I have three assignments for you:

1) Make two columns on a sheet of paper. List all of the things that brides might perceive to be ordinary about your store on the left side. Then write ideas on the right side of the page about how you can romance these ordinary things up and make them more fascinating.

2) List all of the specific ways why you are different and better than your competitors. It is best if you have testimonials from your brides that back up each of your claims.

3) Focus on a key, core message that you can use to identify why you are the best. Craft a story that will help you communicate this message faster and in a way that brides can share with others they know.

The goal of these assignments is to help you move up the fascination scale in the mind of a bride by articulating a point of difference in a way that is meaningful for her.

Author Sally Hogshead explains the fascination scale in her book *Fascinate*.

"All fascinations sit on a spectrum. Some are mild; others, quite intense....Here's a way to visualize this spectrum of attraction, ranging from avoidance to compulsion." –pp. 9-10.

Avoidance	Disinterest	Neutrality	Mild Affinity	Interest	Engagement	Immersion	Preoccupation	Obsession	Compulsion

To make what could be perceived ordinary in your business into the extraordinary, you need to know where you fall on this scale. Ask: Where do brides perceive your store to be? Do they avoid you or do they feel compelled to do business with you?

Remember, the brain seeks fascination. You can cause brides to be more fascinated with you and your business by activating any or all of the seven triggers that cause fascination. According to Hogshead, these triggers are:

1) Power – the ability to take command in your words and actions

2) Passion – the ability to attract with emotion and provide sensory gratification

3) Mystique – the ability to arouse curiosity; you can do this by luring in a bride with a puzzle, a contest, or unanswered question

4) Prestige – the ability to increase respect; remember your customers can earn respect through the symbols of achievement that are meaningful to them. What are you doing to heighten your prestige?

5) Alarm – the ability to create urgency and cause a customer to feel threatened by what might happen with an immediate consequence if she doesn't take action.

6) Vice – the ability to change the game by tempting someone with what they perceive to be forbidden. This is a powerful trigger because it causes people to step outside of their usual habits or behaviors.

7) Trust – the ability to build loyalty and comfort with certainty and reliability.

Brands activate these triggers everyday. For example, people buy products from Apple because of an emotional trigger. Their best customers buy every new product or version of it that they offer because of the passion and prestige they feel from owning those products.

The question you must ask yourself is: What are you doing to increase your fascination so brides are *compelled* to do business with you?

Here are some questions for you to consider about how well you're utilizing these triggers in your sales and marketing efforts:

Does your store brand provoke a strong and immediate emotional reaction? Answer honestly. If you aren't generating a negative reaction from someone you're probably not fascinating *anyone*.

What reactions do brides have when they hear about your store?

Are your brides actively promoting you to their friends and family as the best place to get their dress?

Can you create ambassadors?

How will you inspire them, reward them, and support their communication with you?

Do you have customers posting videos of their experience with you and your product? (example: Apple customers posting videos of them unwrapping their iPad or new iPhone)

Does your store incite conversation amongst your competitors and brides in your area?

Let me share an example. Zappos.com changed the game for shoe retailers in two major ways: 1) they lowered the alarm trigger by offering free shipping both ways and 2) they give customers control to view the product they are considering from every angle before buying it (power and passion)

How are you changing the game?

Does your store *force* your competitors to realign themselves around you? Do they have to change *their* business to stay in business?

You will never be in a category of one and be a true game changer until you figure this out for your store.

2. Defy industry norms. Don't let others tell you how to run your business.

What industry norms have you defied? Here are five examples of norms the most successful bridal retailers have defied to become successful:

1) Margin (refusing to accept the industry standard, looking for opportunities to be more profitable)

2) Requiring 100% down for all special orders (instead of 50% like many stores)

3) Choosing to sell off the rack vs. only doing special orders

4) Incentivizing the bride to buy on her first visit instead of waiting for her to come back multiple times before buying.

5) Charging other wedding related businesses for promoting their brands to brides who enter the store.

Now, it is your turn. List five specific ways you've defied industry norms (or that you will):

1)

2)

3)

4)

5)

Are there any other industry norms that you could change or tweak to give you more of a competitive advantage?

Jay Abraham in his book *The Sticking Point Solution* identifies nine "sticking points" that are getting in the way of your store's success. I want to briefly cover these here because each of these sticking points (at their core) are the result of being stuck in the status quo and are the result of *not* defying industry norms:

1) Your store is stuck losing out to the competition.

Peter Drucker: "Since business owners are not constantly working to obsolesce themselves, they can rest assured that their competitors are."

2) Your store is stuck not selling enough.

In selling today, you must be much more covert. You must come across with a consultative approach that pushes for the sale without being pushy. If you're stuck not selling enough at your store, you need to change how you sell. My 8-Week Bridal Sales Blueprint course can help you learn what's working now to increase your closing ratios and be more effective working with every bride coming into your store. Please email me at info@bridaltrainingsystems.com if you would like more information about how you and your staff can utilize this valuable resource that is online at www.bridalsalesblueprint.com. Your ability to pre-sell the bride on why she should buy from you is another critical component to selling more at your store. I talk about this principle in depth in my book *Bridal Profit Explosion*.

3) Your store is stuck with erratic sales volume.

There are three ways to solve this problem. They are:

- Having and implementing a systematic solution for bringing in brides consistently throughout the year.
- Look for the business within your business so you have additional ways to generate new revenue (such as selling advertising to wedding vendors).
- Utilizing effective follow up so you can convert brides to buy more from you through a great follow up system.

Each of these three solutions revolves around systems. Remember, systems help you see and track what is going on in your business. Do you have systems in place that allow you to see and track what is happening on a daily, weekly, monthly and yearly basis?

Do you have a marketing funnel that is bringing brides into your store?

If you don't have one, you **must** put together a marketing funnel for your store so you and every member of your team understand the flow of your customers in and back into your business (not just in and out).

Your goal (as I explained on page 185 of *Bridal Profit Explosion*) is to:

- Create systems for every aspect of your bridal store.
- Set up your store to be run by those systems.
- Then, have your staff (manager, assistant managers and bridal consultants) run the system.

If you would like more detail on how to put together the sixteen most important systems for your business, I invite you to read, study, and apply what is in my book *The System is the Secret*.

4) Your store is stuck failing to strategize and prioritize.

It is difficult for many to plan and set goals for their business. Many store owners rationalize their inability to do this by saying they don't have time or they are too busy. As a result, they end up spending more time on non-productive and non-strategic activities that won't get them closer to their goals. Instead, focus on getting your business to work harder and harder for *you* instead of you working harder and harder for your business.

5) Your store is stuck with costs eating up all of your profits.

Now, more than ever you have to measure your return on investment. If it costs without producing results, you have to eliminate it, delegate it, or outsource it.

What are three of your biggest costs that are eating up your profits? What will you do to eliminate or reduce these costs?

6) Your store is stuck doing what's not working.

So much of success is breaking out of the status quo and the mindset that keeps you where you are instead of where you could be.

As Jay Abraham points out: "Most entrepreneurs are slaving away, sacrificing their lives with little to show for it. Why? Because almost all the work they're doing is increasing their potential and not their success. In essence, they're spending their time on false efficiencies." -- *The Sticking Point Solution*, p. 151.

Don't get caught in that trap. Stop doing what isn't working and start doing more of what does.

7) Your store is stuck being marginalized by the marketplace.

You have to be different. If you aren't, you will be commoditized by brides who will make the decision to buy from you solely on the basis of price (or who is selling what she wants for the lowest price). It is better to carry privately branded merchandise with protected territories than advertised merchandise that everyone has (including Internet vendors) for this reason. Think carefully about *how* you are different. Remember, you need to be different in at *least* three ways in order to be perceived as being different from something or someone else.

8) Your store may be stuck with mediocre marketing.

Jay Abraham asserts: "Most entrepreneurs fail to understand that the difference between mediocrity and making millions has more to do with effective marketing than with any other single factor.... Marketing is the bedrock of virtually every enduring dominant business in every field. You must be a superior marketer."-- *The Sticking Point Solution*, p. 23.

Are you developing the skills to be a superior marketer?

If you would like to master your marketing instead of being frustrated with lackluster results, I have created an online 8-week Bridal Marketing Mastery class. If you would like information about how you can enroll for these important and valuable classes, please email me at info@bridaltrainingsystems.com with the subject line "Bridal Marketing Mastery Course" and I'll email you all of the details so you can start flooding your store with brides and prom customers right away.

9) Your business may be stuck because you are trying to do it all yourself.

You can't do it all yourself. You must learn to delegate and leverage yourself through other A players on your team. I'll talk more about this in Chapter 8 where I'll discuss management mistakes that will hinder and stop your growth. Grade your bridal support team often with the checklist included on pages 237 and 238 of my book *Bridal Profit Explosion*. This will help you know where you can improve with training and when you may need to replace someone who isn't pulling their weight on your team.

3. Position your bridal store so you dominate a territory, niche, or market square. Then, be sure you market with the purpose of evoking an emotional response.

First off, you need to look at what market gaps exist or may exist in your market area. For example, you may choose to specialize in plus size, sleeved, or expensive, high-end couture gowns. Whatever area of specialty you choose, it should be an area where you've already had paying customers tell you: "I'm sure glad you offer this. No one else I went to did or could do what you just did…" or something to that effect.

Here are some questions for you to think about:

- What market gaps do you see in your area?
- What unmet needs or desires do brides have? How could you meet those needs?
- How could this set you apart from your competitors?
- How can you stretch the price pyramid at your store?
- What opportunities can be next? What if I couldn't continue as is?

Now, that you've identified these niches, **you need to evoke emotion**

as you market them. Without emotion, your message will fall on deaf ears.

One of the greatest examples of this principle in action was P.T. Barnum. P.T. Barnum once wrote: "The great secret of success in anything is to get a hearing. Half the object is gained when the audience is assembled."

What are you doing to create excitement and build drama for the brides in your area through your pre-sales efforts?

Are you persuading them that you are worth the time and effort to come see (and to come see first) so you can position your competitors in a way that highlights your best differentiating point and that is most favorable to you?

If not, you are missing the entire essence of the magic of marketing.

Here are some suggestions for how you can stand out, be unique, and grab attention in your store:

- At your next bridal show, have something that grabs the attention of the brides who go by your booth (the chance to win a free dress, win prizes with a spinning wheel, etc.). What makes this idea work so well is that other brides see brides interacting with you and having a great time. They will then leave your booth excited knowing that they have the chance to win something they can redeem when they arrive at your store. Listen to episode #2 of my Bridal Business Success Podcast (www.BridalBusinessSuccess.com) to learn the best way I've discovered and taught bridal retailers to utilize to capture and convert leads at bridal shows. You can subscribe on iTunes or via the Stitcher Radio links that are on that site.
- Put banners and signs in your windows that create interest

and excitement. If you can create curiosity to find out what is going on inside, brides will stop to check it out.

- Have a referral program that gets brides talking about you. When a bride buys a dress, have a contest between her and other brides to see who can get another friend into your store to buy another dress. The winner will get some prize, which she has to post on her Facebook page to all of her friends (telling them what she did—bought her dress from your store—and what she got as a result). You can't ignore the power of creating excitement through social media.

- Create displays or information on the home page of your web site that create curiosity and interest for brides who are coming online to check you out. A countdown clock is one great way you can do this.

- Create displays in the front of your store when brides first come in that they have to ask about. You can do this by putting a sign on the display that says, "Ask me how you can save $100 on your wedding dress purchase today." This can help the walk-ins who haven't been properly prepared with the pre-sale sequence to decide to buy from you before they even try on any dresses.

Take the ideas I've given you above and brainstorm how you can expand on these to create excitement and an emotional response that will get brides thinking about and coming to your bridal store. Then, you can focus on finding out what they're looking for and helping them to find it. I'll talk more about how you can do this in Chapter 6.

4. Improve and change your processes so they consistently deliver results.

The secret sauce in any business is made up of the processes and systems that are designed to deliver results. In selling, there are six areas where systems can be put in place to deliver better results. These are:

- The Pre-Sale
- Setting Appointments on the Phone or Online
- The Approach
- The Presentation of Gowns
- The Close (Do your bridal consultants know at least five ways to ask for the sale? This is important because the majority of brides are buying today once they have been asked at least three times to get their dress in the course of an appointment.)
- Follow Up Sequences to Get Brides Back into the Store

When considering this set of systems (or any set of systems in your store), you should ask yourself the following questions about each area:

- Are you effectively communicating your difference?
- Where are you dropping the ball?
- Are you getting the results you really want? If not, where are you dropping the ball?

When I go into a bridal store and consult with them, I typically look at the following processes that can be improved. What I see here and the changes I suggest are in large measure what allow these stores to make the changes that will shift their entire performance and put them on a path to greater success. Some questions you should ask to help you improve the processes at your store include:

- How is the phone answered?
- How are orders processed?
- What do brides experience during the first 30 seconds after they walk through your doors?
- What do brides experience on their first visit?
- How can you better target brides who don't buy from you in

the first visit?

- Do you have and implement a marketing sequence?
- What bait will entice brides to come back?
- What new event or process are you inviting your brides to experience at your store?
- Do you have follow up rituals that include at least two outbound phone calls/day?
- What email sequence do you have in place to remind brides why they should return and do business with you?
- How are you providing information to brides so they are prepared for the next step of planning for their weddings?

The most important process you should be thinking about is how to create more memorable experiences that brides want to be a part of. If you aren't marketing an experience (even if you create one) at your store, you are making a mistake.

Pay attention to your processes. Once you figure out what works best, duplicate it as often as you can without diluting the experience the bride will have.

The most successful bridal retailers I know are constantly tweaking what they are doing at their stores to have better offers and plug leaks in the holes of their processes. You should do the same.

5. Raise your price and your margin on private label gowns on which you have exclusivity.

This seems like such a simple thing, but it is one of the hardest things to get bridal store owners to do. Profit is a good thing. It pays the salaries of you and your team; it provides jobs to countless individuals who benefit from your ability to stay in business. You aren't doing anyone any good if you aren't making money. You may already carry private line gowns in your store. If you don't, it is time to invest in some that will allow you to make the profits that will help you stay in business. If you already have private gowns in your store, you should go through every private labeled gown in your store. There are some gowns you are selling well that you could make a greater margin on. If that is the case, make the change. No, ifs, ands, or buts about it. Just do it. If you truly have exclusivity, there is no reason you can't do this. If you would like to be able to go direct to the largest bridal gown manufacturer in the world and have exclusive dresses, email me at info@bridaltrainingsystems.com with the subject line "Direct Bridal Alliance" and I'll email details about how you can do this for your store. The bottom line is that you figure out the most profitable area of your store and look to enhance it. What could you do to enhance the experience in your most profitable area and make buying a dress an even more valuable proposition for a bride who comes into your store?

6. Put systems in place at your store that can function perfectly if you're not there.

In the bridal business, a system is a way of doing things to produce a marketing and sales result. The system is the solution to get the results you want.

To make this game changer a reality and achieve success in your bridal business, you need to constantly be asking and thinking about how you can improve your store so that it is systems dependent rather than people dependent.

We all like order. Order is the basis of having and executing a great system. When brides come into your store, they can sense how orderly you are by how you act. When they sense that your store is orderly and organized, their sense of risk disappears, and they feel they can trust you.

This allows you to utilize your system of selling to help the bride find exactly what she is looking for and help her have an incredible experience in your store.

When you refine operations to improve how the systems in your store work, you are working *on* your business, not just *in* it. These are the sixteen absolutely critical areas of systems you should have at your store:

1) Goals / Mission / Vision Systems (how you set your goals, mission, and vision for your business and how you will reward yourself for their accomplishment)

- Do you and every member of your team know your minimum, target, and optimal goals for each department of your store?

2 and 3) Inbound and Outbound Marketing Systems

- How is your story helping attract brides into your business?
- Do you have a marketing flow chart that shows what should happen to each bride coming into your store?
- Do you have a systematic way in which you are capturing and following up with leads?

4 and 5) Your Pre-Sales and Marketing Systems

- What are you doing to prepare brides to buy from you *before* they enter your store?
- Do you have a marketing calendar for next year in place and are you following it?
-

6) Your Sales & Persuasion Systems

- Are you training and rehearsing the information that will help you sell more now?
- Do you have systems in place to help you review performance and replace employees who aren't selling?

7) Organizational and Internal Business Process Systems

- When a bride buys something at your store, do you have an organized system that shows how the paper and the product flow through your business?

8) Follow-Up Systems

- Do you have a systematic process for following up if your prospects don't become buyers on their first visit to your store?

9) Leadership Development Systems

- Do you have systems in place to help you develop leaders around you at your store?

10) Hiring, Staffing, and Training Systems

- Do you have a mandatory meeting that every employee must attend on a weekly basis?
- What are you doing to ensure that these meetings are effective and help increase performance?

11) Financial Systems (Inventory and Buying)

- Do you have systems in place to monitor what is selling on a weekly or monthly basis?
- Are you using this information to make sure your buying is informed and effective?

12) Customer Service Systems

- Do you have a written plan for any and all customer service situations that come up that your assistant managers and bridal consultants can refer to in case you aren't in the store?

13) Crisis Management Systems

14) Productivity Systems (Personal and Team)

- Do you measure what you are doing on a daily and weekly basis to ensure that you are being as effective as you could with your time?

15) Creativity and Business Reinvention Systems

- What are you doing to anticipate, prepare, and deal with the changes that are happening in your business as the result of technology and competitors?

16) Systems for Balancing Your Work and Family

- Are you planning and actually taking breaks that help you rejuvenate yourself?

I've written a book entitled *The System is the Secret* that goes into great depth about how to develop each of these systems in your business. If your business systems have room for improvement, this resource will be very helpful to you.

7. Little hinges open big doors. Look for the micro and macro changes that can yield powerful dividends in your business.

One of my mentors, Bill Glazer, taught me that "little hinges open big doors." The basic concept of this principle is that the little things you do have a big impact on the results you have. For example, when we've used "What special occasion brings you into our store today instead of "Can I help you?" we've found we open up a dialogue with our brides instead of hearing the predictable "I'm just looking" phrase.

Another important change is to ask brides when they get in the dressing room, "Of all of the dresses *you've* chosen which one do you like most?" This question allows the bride to pick the one she is drawn to first (which is often the dress she ends up selecting). Then, you say: "Great, let's try that one on first."

In my Bridal Sales Blueprint online training course, I explain the questions and sequences we've found help you open a bride's mind to a bigger budget (and the four considerations that make up the price of a dress) when she comes in with an unrealistic expectation of what she wants to spend.

If you want to find the hinges that will open bigger doors at your store, you should always be asking questions that will help you improve and get better. Be willing to ask the questions others won't. These kind of questions will help you shake up and make significant improvements to your store.

Luke Williams talks about three such questions in his book *Disrupt: Think the Unthinkable to Spark Transformation in Your Business* that every business owner should ask as they think about creating their own disruptive hypothesis to shake things up in their market area. According to him, these are:

1) What do you want to disrupt?

To successfully think about this question, it is a good idea to 'hover above your world' and think about the realities that face brides today and how you could change these. Williams says: "One of the major hurdles facing today's executives and business leaders is how to meaningfully differentiate themselves from everyone else who's operating in the same space. To do that requires that you define the situation in the industry, segment, or category that you want to challenge. And by 'situation,' I mean the broad view from 10,000 feet. Here's what this might look like:

- "This is an area in which everyone seems to be stuck in the same predicament and nothing has changed in a very long time."
- "This is an area where profit performance is average—it really should be more successful than it is."
- "This is a category where growth is slow and everything seems the same."

Williams continues:

"Once you have a situation to focus on, describe it in one sentence: 'How can we disrupt the competitive landscape of [*insert your situation*] by delivering an unexpected solution?' –pp. 20-21.

The goal here is to start thinking in terms of specific problems that brides have that you can come up with a way to solve. When you can solve the problem that a lot of people have, you have a much more persuasive marketing message and you stand out head and shoulders above your competition.

As an example, when Netflix originally began, they asked the question: What would it be like if you didn't have to pay late fees when renting movies? This question caused them to figure out a solution to a problem that was a big problem for many individuals. Netflix built a very big business out of offering their solution in a way that sidestepped a problem that many people had with an unexpected solution.

Are you thinking hard enough about the problems brides are facing and how you can solve them?

2) What are the clichés?

Williams says:

"Now that you've defined your situation, the next step is to identify the assumptions that seem to influence the way insiders (and often outsiders) think about an industry, segment, or category. In other words, what are the clichés—the widespread, hackneyed beliefs that govern the way people think about and do business in a particular space. If you pay attention, you'll notice that clichés are everywhere."

The best example of a business that went against clichés in their marketing was that of Nintendo in its battle with Sony with its Playstation and Microsoft with its Xbox. Williams says: "Both were driven by several clichés. First, that the world is split into 'gamers' and 'nongamers.' Second, that gamers mostly care about faster chips and more realistic graphics. Third, game consoles are expensive. And, fourth, that people play video games sitting down, barely moving anything but their fingers."

"Then, along comes Nintendo, a distant third player, which turned the gaming industry's clichés on their head. Nintendo's Wii is relatively cheap, has no hard drive, no DVD, has weak connectivity, and comparatively low processor speed. But, within weeks of its launch, Wii became a hit with consumers, thanks to its innovative motion controller, which integrates players' movements directly into the game."

"With the Wii, you can play tennis, baseball, golf, and even bowling. You can sword fight and box, too. Nintendo opened up the console world to a huge demographic of people who never considered themselves gamers." –p. 23.

Today, Microsoft is trying to capture some of the massive market share that Nintendo has carved out with its Kinect device. The story has yet to be written about how this battle will all work out, but there is no question that Nintendo has achieved the success it has because it thought about how to remove the clichés in their marketing approach. They also dominated the landscape of the video game consoles through a carefully crafted scarcity strategy that helped propel the desire for these devices into the stratosphere.

My question for you is: How carefully are you dissecting the clichés that brides have about the bridal industry? How are you looking to capitalize on your growth by how you market your store to avoid the clichés that brides are tired of and that no longer work for them?

Your careful analysis of these clichés can give you some opportunities from which to attack with your marketing collateral and showcase your true differences. Take the time to think as a team at your store about the numerous clichés that brides see when they come into you and your competitor's stores. Your willingness to list and attack these clichés can help you overcome the status quo and rise in importance to the brides in your market area.

3) What are your destructive hypotheses?

Williams says:

"Now that you have a list of the clichés that are influencing the business situation you're focused on, your next goal is to start provoking the status quo. To do that, you'll take those clichés and twist them like a Rubik's cube and look at them from the inside out, upside down, backward, and forward. You're trying to find a way to rearrange the pieces, which in turn will provoke a different way of looking at the situation. Specifically, you're looking for something (or things) that you could scale up or scale down, move in the opposite direction, or completely do without." –p. 27.

In other words, by looking at things in a new way (and through the eyes of the bride), you can resist what most of your competitors are already doing and truly break out. Most bridal retailers will never do this because the resistance is too great and they aren't willing to do the work necessary to break free from the self-imposed limitations that they put on themselves.

Williams suggests that you can take action and create your 'What if?' hypothesis through three methods:

1) Inversion – brides usually receive some information from their bridal consultant when they leave the store; inverting this idea would involve giving a gift to the bride when she shows up, thus completely changing the dynamics of the relationship and the expectations that might go with it.

One way to look at inversion is to ask: *Is there something that is successful and big that could be successful and small or vice versa?*

You can better visualize this and how it will apply for your business if you think about it with other industries. Think about White Castle and Burger King on both extremes of size of hamburgers or how compact cars are now overtaking SUVs in overall sales.

A great question you should ask is: *Are there any attributes of your bridal store that you could minimize in the bride's mind?*

Or: *Are there any attributes of your bridal store that you could maximize in the bride's mind?*

Could you offer a special bonus to brides who actually buy their dress more than a year before their wedding?

Inversion can help you look at a common situation from a completely different perspective and often will give you answers to how you can position and market your store in ways that others may not have considered or thought about.

2) Denial – traditionally, brides have paid 50% when they placed their order; denial involves asking, "What if brides paid the entire amount when they purchased their dress?"

One way to look at denial is to ask: *Is there something that other bridal stores don't give to brides that you could?* For example, the first time incentive or First Visit Advantage Program that many bridal retailers offer at their stores at my direction and coaching is really the answer to this question.

Here's another question you could ask: *Is there something that brides can have replaced each month as they prepare for their wedding? Is there something that your store can replace for them?*

3) Scale – this is looking at one thing someone offers and looking to see if you can scale it up or down on one side of the equation or the other.

Good examples of this in other industries include: shifting small TVs to big scale TVs and then scaling them back again on mobile phone devices, McDonald's successful campaign of super sizing their meals changed the process of how they took orders at drive through windows by asking an up sell question. Today, you also see many infomercials that offer "double your money back guarantees" to ramp up the stakes with scale.

How can you use scale to let brides know that you do more than any of your competitors? Here are some other examples of "what if" questions that you could answer to help you stand out:

- What would happen if brides knew there was a specific experience they could have that would help them find their dress easily and without stress?
- What would happen if brides could design their own wedding dress?
- What would happen if brides didn't have to wait to get their wedding dress (they could buy right out of stock)?
- What would happen if brides could find dresses at your store that they won't find at any other bridal salon around your region, state or country?

Think carefully about how you can shift the perceptions of what brides expect when they shop at bridal stores and do so in a way that is both profitable and unique. By doing this, you can stand out from your competitors. It will also help you get out of your comfort zone and do something unique that brides will never forget.

In tough economic times, it is much easier to hold on to what you have than to make changes that can get you back on track. It is easier to cower and hide than it is to face the music and do what needs to be done. Remember, getting out of your comfort zone keeps you on the edge of your fear which can help you channel that energy into growth and excitement that can set you apart from those around you who are content to just remain with the status quo.

8. Focus on the little things that will have the biggest results. Don't get caught up in activities that don't reward you with accomplishment. Successful business owners work on activities simultaneously, not sequentially.

To successfully turnaround or transform any business, the business owner must first give up his or her excuses and focus their efforts and priorities only on what really matters.

Most unsuccessful bridal retailers get caught up in activities that make them feel busy, but in reality are doing little to nothing to help them prosper and succeed. Here's another way to look at this: It is easier to make an excuse than it is to do what really works. If you want to succeed in this, or any business, you must find a way when others see a wall.

Thomas Carlyle, an English writer and philosopher once said: "The block of granite which was an obstacle in the pathway of the weak, became a stepping-stone in the pathway of the strong."

Tony Robbins once said: "The truth of the matter is that there's nothing you can't accomplish if (1) you clearly decide what you're absolutely committed to achieving; (2) you're willing to take massive action; (3) you notice what's working or not, and (4) you continue to change your approach until you achieve what you want, using whatever life gives you along the way."

This statement really gets to the heart of this principle. You've got to focus on the little things. A decision to focus on the priorities at your store that really matter, that only you can do, may seem like a little decision, but what a difference it makes!

The decision to pay attention to what's working and eliminate what's not could be viewed as a little thing, but it's not! Most importantly, the decision to implement and to take massive action is absolutely critical to turning around or transforming any business.

When Lee Iacocca took over Chrysler he simultaneously began doing multiple things to turnaround the company. He didn't sequentially do one thing and then another thing. He began massive action in numerous areas of the company that needed to be fixed. In other words, he worked on things simultaneously, not sequentially.

This all gets to the big question: What little changes can you make at your store that will have a big effect?

As an example, consider the power of a new concept or idea on how someone perceives why he or she needs what you sell (and that you are the only one they can get it from). Is the way that you are presenting the gowns you sell in your store allowing you to present yourself in the context of being truly unique and in a category of one (as a new idea)? If not, you should carefully think about what it is that you are actually selling.

Create the perceptions you want brides to have about you and your store. There is no excuse for letting someone else brand you or be in a situation where brides are walking or driving by your store and have no idea *who* you are or *why* you are so important to them as they begin and conclude their wedding gown search. Be unique. Stand out. Present yourself and your store in a category of one. When you do that, you'll truly stand out and the financial rewards will be much greater to you and your business as well.

9. Implement quickly.

I love this statement from author and business improvement speaker Warren Greshes:

"You have 24 hours to act on a good idea. If you do nothing about a good idea within 24 hours, rest assured, it's dead. Now, I'm not saying you have to do everything about a good idea within 24 hours, but you have to take at least one action step, if for nothing else than to keep the excitement going.

"You know as well as I do that we're most excited about our good ideas when we first get them. The longer we wait to do something about an idea, the less excited we get. In fact, we probably spend more time talking ourselves out of it or letting other people tell us why it's a lousy idea." – *The Best D--- Sales Book Ever, p. 94.*

He continues with his seven-step action plan:

"1. First, make a copy of the page where you wrote down all your goals and make a copy of the three forms where you created action plans for your three most important goals."

"2. Take these pages and post them someplace where you can see them every day. If you don't want anyone else to see them, a good place is the inside of your closet door at home....Posting [your goals] up where you can see them every days keeps the goals fresh in your mind and makes them dominant in your thoughts. Napoleon Hill, author of *Think and Grow Rich*, stated, 'We are what we think about all day long,' and 'We move toward our most dominant thoughts.'"

"3. I believe in posting goals up where anyone can see them because 'you never know.' In fact, if you want to get to your goals even faster, tell everyone you know, even people who you would never expect to be able to help you, because you never know, help can come from some of the most unexpected places."

"4. Once you have your plan posted up, it's important to review it on a regular basis. I suggest you review your plan every quarter, if for no other reason than to make sure the goals you set for yourself are still important to you. Let's face it, people change and priorities change. What's important to you today might not be important a year from now. If that should happen, what do you do about the goal? Change it, of course, or get rid of it. Remember, this plan is yours; it can change. It was written in pen or pencil on a sheet of paper. It wasn't carved into a block of stone with a chisel. It can change."

I think it is important to review your goals much more often than this. It is a good idea to at least look at them weekly and prioritize what you will work on at your store. You can change your goals, but I believe it is best to be solidly committed to the achievement of a few goals than have a lot of ambiguous goals that aren't really your priority or your focus.

"5. What do you do if you get to reach your deadline and you haven't yet reached your goal? Kill yourself, of course! No, of course not—just move back the deadline! Remember, it's yours! It can change. Believe me, the goal setting police are not going to bash in your door, grab you by the neck and say, 'Okay pal, you're coming with us.' That's not going to happen....The deadline is there to give you a frame of reference and to give you the incentive to get started. It's not there as a punishment, something to flog yourself with should you not achieve your goal in time."

"6. What do you do if you happen to achieve all the goals you set for yourself? Stop right there, your life is now over. No! Set some more goals! Create an action plan for each one. Do the same thing to set the new goals that you did to set these."

"7. Here's a guarantee for you: I guarantee that if you shove this plan into a drawer and never look at it again, it will never work." –Warren Greshes, *The Best D--- Sales Book Ever*, pp. 94-96.

I think the key to successful goal setting and their achievement is that you've got to stay hungry. You've got to stay motivated and understand what it is that you really want. Then, and only then will you do what it takes to succeed.

T. Harv Ecker makes this point in his book, *Secrets of the Millionaire Mind*:

"During the 2004 Olympic Games, Perdita Felicien, a Canadian and the reigning world champion in the hundred meter hurdles, was heavily favored to win the gold medal. In the final race, she hit the first hurdle and fell hard. She wasn't able to complete the race. Extremely upset, she had tears in her eyes as she lay there in bewilderment. She had prepared for this moment six hours a day, every day of the week, for the past four years. The next morning, I saw her news conference. I wish I had taped it. It was amazing to listen to her perspective. She said something to the effect of 'I don't know why it happened but it did, and I'm going to use it. I'm going to focus even more and work even harder for the next four years. Who knows what my path would have been had I won? Maybe it would have dulled my desire. I don't know, but I do know that now I'm hungrier than ever. I'll be back even stronger." –p. 99.

That attitude is impressive. It is what it takes to do the work necessary to turnaround or transform a struggling business. To be and stay successful, you've got to stay hungry. You've got to know what you want and what you will do to make it happen. This means massive action and implementation.

Garrison Wynn makes this statement in his book *The Real Truth About Success*:
"Willingness to use an advantage is just as important as discovering it. Cross that line from knowledge to implementation, and be willing to act! Not everybody is. Many need to be coaxed into utilizing their distinctive edge to their advantage. Most people tend to draw a line in the sand or create a boundary they're unwilling (or afraid) to cross.

Many of these are not based on ethical or legal bounds; they're rooted in personal fears of how others will perceive us. Can you step back and look beyond the conventional business culture? Are you willing to take a chance? Can you create a plan for yourself? Can you adapt your beliefs in order to utilize your advantage?

"Creating that willingness to actually utilize your edge is how you achieve greater success. The funny thing about willingness is that it's like opening a door. If you just crack it a little, you'll find it's relatively easy to move forward from there. But you first have to turn the knob and push. If you start with a little willingness to change or improve in certain areas, you'll soon find it easier to tackle other areas of your life or business relationships. But if you aren't willing to look at all or if you try to avoid delving into some particular area, you'll wind up getting stalled. Any advantage that gets you noticed is worth pursuing. Opening a door just a little bit is much easier than worrying about all the closed doors in life you'll have to go through to become successful. Knowing something and doing it have very little in common!" –p. 206.

To help you determine what you should be implementing at your store, consider the following questions:

- Who do I need to *be* in order to get what I want?
- What are the behaviors that I actually do day in and day out at my store?
- What are the behaviors that others do that I would like to do?
- What are the behaviors that I do that I don't have to do?
- When I start working on a priority, do I have a beginning and end time? What prevents me from procrastinating or taking longer on a task or activity than I should?

10. Focus on doing only things that cause money to flow towards you and your business.

According to Dan Kennedy, there are four big factors that cause money to move. These are:

1) Decision and clarity about what you want.
2) Subconscious programming, which attracts money to you.
3) Your ability to ask and be persistent until you get what you want, especially when asking for the sale.
4) Being a celebrity and promoting what's new.

Are you doing what's necessary to have money move towards you and your life? Are you clear about what you want?

Are you writing down your goals?

Are you asking others for help to get what you want?

Are you building your celebrity?

Are you constantly focusing on what's new so that brides are attracted to you and your business?

The unfortunate reality is that many bridal store owners aren't doing the things that cause money to move towards them and their business. Instead, they are doing things that are repelling money. They have adopted habits in their lives that prevent them from attracting money and success to them.

Kenneth Foster makes this observation in his book *Ask and You Will Succeed*:

"I am amazed by the number of times I meet with clients and we're discussing what they think is holding them back from really creating success in their lives and they tell me it is because they are overwhelmed. But once we dig in, there is often one common denominator at the root of what is holding them back: Clutter!"

"Clutter in the workspace, clutter on the kitchen table, in the closets, clutter underneath the bed, in the car, clutter in the basement…clutter everywhere! Do you know where clutter starts? In your mind. It is a symptom of an unruly mind. What is showing up in your environment starts first in your mind. And it starts many times with the questions you ask and choices you make."

"Many people keep clutter in their lives because they ask poor questions. Questions like 'Should I save or keep this magazine, file folder, picture, discount coupon, and so forth, or not? Remember, the answer is in the question you ask. So, if you ask a poor question like the one just asked, you will get answers like 'Maybe, I don't know, or let me think about it,' or the most classic answer of all, 'You never know, I might need this some day.'"

"These answers lead to confusion and indecision, which is the main reason people can't get rid of their clutter. They don't have a clear understanding of what to do with it. So, to clean up a messy environment, you will have to take back control of your thinking by asking questions that will direct the focus of your mind to come up with an empowering answer."

"Try asking questions like 'What is the system I can come up with to always have a clutter-free environment?' Or 'What has to happen for me to live clutter-free?' Or 'What three steps can I take daily to live clutter-free?' By asking these types of questions you will be getting answers that will solve your problems rather than increase the clutter."

"Consider this: If you haven't used something in a very long time, if you haven't worn that shirt, opened that book, or spent that coupon, chances are it has outlived its usefulness to you. You no longer need it. It's time to let it go."

"The social scientists tell us that the subconscious mind keeps track of every piece of paper and every object in your environment. Have you ever had an uneasy feeling or maybe the feeling of being overwhelmed when you looked at a messy office or house? If so, then you have experienced the results of clutter."

"It's so easy to let clutter pile up. In fact, in the short-term, it seems easier to just let it build, rather than taking the time and energy to do something about it. Did you know that the number one reason that clutter builds up is from the inability to make a quick decision? That's right. When you are consistently uncertain or doubtful, the result will be clutter. So clutter is actually a mirror of the places in your mind where you are struggling with doubt. Instead of tossing one more magazine onto the pile, start by asking yourself, 'Where in my life am I feeling uncertainty, and what has to happen to move past it?'"

"Think about it. Have you ever sorted through the mail and couldn't make a choice of whether to throw out a piece or save it, so you set it aside for later? Or you come back from a meeting with a folder full of notes but don't have a good place to file it, so it sits? Or you hold on to old items that no longer serve any purpose, but you are afraid to let them go because you think you will need them someday in the future? And then all the stuff seems to somehow multiply, until you've got yourself...a pile of clutter!"

"While just letting things pile up might seem like the easy way in the moment, in the end, you will need a lot of energy to get rid of the junk. It has been said that our environment is more powerful than our willpower. If you don't believe this, then try to be upbeat and filled with positive energy on a consistent basis in a cluttered room."

"Set your intention to create a clutter-free environment and watch your creativity and energy soar. Clutter needs to be dealt with right from the start—before it takes over. It's important to be in charge of clutter, rather than it being in charge of you! Holding on to the clutter is like carrying around a 50-pound weight. Is this the way you want to go through life?"

"Remember that whatever clutter you might have in your life didn't build up overnight, so it will take some time to deal with it once you decide to roll up your sleeves and dig in. You may want to try using this acronym: F.A.D. When a new piece of mail or information comes in, 'File it,' 'Act on it,' or 'Discard it.'" –Kenneth D. Foster, *Ask and You Will Succeed*, pp. 54-55.

That is great advice. Don't let clutter dominate your thoughts or your business. Open up your mind to implement what I've taught you in this chapter and that I'll teach you throughout this book. Do the things that attract and cause brides and money to flow to you. Stop doing what repels them and their money. Throughout this book, I'll be giving you tips on how you can focus on what really matters.

Now, that I've given you these ten tips, I'd like you to think through the following questions:

Current Reality:

1) Where in your business do you feel you need a big breakthrough?
2) In what areas of your business are you feeling stuck?
3) What is it that you want to achieve, but feel like isn't happening for you?
4) What drives you to persist and strive to get what you really want?

Your Future:

1) What would your life and business look like if you released all of your self-doubt?
2) Where can you find the answers you need to get what you want?
3) What goals will you set to make a quantum leap in your business this next year?
4) What goals are the most important ones?
5) What priorities will you act on everyday to help you get what you want?

Your Limiting Beliefs:

1) What limiting beliefs do you believe about yourself that cause you to doubt your ability to succeed?
2) What one belief could you change right now that would change your daily reality and help you get what you want?
3) What story have you been telling about yourself that you need to change?

Your Actions:

1) What actions do you need to take right now to create more create more abundance in your life and in your business?
2) What areas of your business do you intend to change forever in the next two weeks?
3) What is one thing you can do right now that will help you move a big door and create a profound long-term positive result?

Think carefully through these questions. Reflect on your answers often. Think about which of these ten game changers will make the biggest impact on your business and then launch into the pages that follow for a comprehensive approach of what you can and should do to have success in the bridal business.

CHAPTER 2

ADOPT HABITS AND BEHAVIORS OF TOP BRIDAL BUSINESSES

"It is our choices, that show what we truly are, far more than our abilities."
-J.K. Rowling

In Jim Collins' book *Great by Choice*, he makes the following statement:

"We cannot predict the future. But we can create it. Think back to 15 years ago, and consider what's happened since, the destabilizing events—in the world, in your country, in the markets, in your work, in your life—that defied all expectations. We can be astonished, confounded, shocked, stunned, delighted, or terrified, but rarely prescient. None of us can predict with certainty the twists and turns our lives will take. Life is uncertain, the future unknown. This is neither good nor bad. It just is, like gravity. Yet the task remains: how to master our own fate, even so."—*Great by Choice*, p. 1.

Anthony Robbins once said: "Success leaves clues." You can choose to be great and create what you want by the habits you employ. So, here are the 10 habits and behaviors I've observed that top bridal businesses have so you can have them in your life and your business:

1. They are highly ambitious and extremely resistant to the status quo.

Most business owners are committed to preserving a status quo as long as possible. They want to set up a system or a series of systems in their business and then leave it alone and keep taking money from it for years. This is done without looking for ways to expand, improve, or change what is already working. Why fix what isn't broke, right? The problem with this philosophy is that it is not really possible anymore. Change is happening too fast. If you want to multiply and expand your business, you have to force yourself and your business to change for the better. You can't be reactive to the changes around you.

The top professionals in any industry that I know never permit themselves a moment of mental rest. They are always simultaneously working on implementing what is working now and working on a replacement for it when it is no longer working. This requires that you become resistant to anything that would cause you to be happy with the status quo.

Charles Darwin once observed: "It is not the strongest of the species that survive. It is those most responsive to change."

Your ability to resist complacency is a key component of why you will take the actions I'll describe in this book to turnaround or transform your bridal store. There are three ways you can beat the resistance of complacency. Each of these things allow you to diversify your knowledge and your action so you can get more done. These three actions are:

1) Continually educate yourself. Leaders are readers. The most successful people I know read voraciously. They study successful business owners and study what they do or have done to grow their businesses. If you are not now a reader, I encourage you to become one. The fact that you are reading this book is a great start! If you read one book a week for 10 years, you will have read 520 books. If you repeated this habit for 20 years, you will have read more than 1,000 books and be one of the most educated individuals in your area.

Another great way to educate yourself is to network with other individuals in other businesses and other industries. This allows you to understand their marketing methods and business systems. Many times, I've gotten ideas for my business processes from watching friends in other industries and how they deal with specific challenges. I've learned a lot from my friend Grant Miller, who owns a number of tanning salons named Sun Your Buns. He and I talk and share what we are doing to attract new customers and some of the specific promotions we're doing that are working now. The reason why networking is such a powerful way to learn is because it allows you to become familiar with marketing methods and media beyond what you are currently familiar with and use.

2) Look for new ways to attract and bring in brides to your store. This can't be something you'll get around to someday, it must be something you are constantly working on, testing, and implementing.

3) If you've been dependent on one source to bring in new brides, you must diversify since being reliant on any one single method to bring in business is a recipe for disaster. This is critical because media that once worked to bring in brides no longer does. You can also invest a lot of time into developing social media that may not be around in the future. As an example, in the early days of our store, we spent a lot of time developing a great MySpace page. Now, the media isn't relevant any more. Now, MySpace is trying to make a comeback and is combining elements of Facebook and Pinterest. With Facebook's constantly changing the rules for how you can advertise and market to your brides, there is no guarantee that it will always be what it is now.

This is again why it is so important to develop systems at your stores to attract brides into your store. If you would like to see my system for how I attract brides into my store, you can see my entire marketing funnel and more than 120 promotions we've used, you can do so by enrolling in my 8-week Bridal Marketing Mastery course. Email me at info@bridaltrainingsystems.com if you would like to see my powerful and very successful marketing funnel and program. I also share many of these ideas with bridal stores who are a part of my coaching programs.

2. Think with big, bold ideas. The biggest players in any business are the biggest thinkers.

Some bridal businesses hope to be bigger and more successful someday. They aren't really serious or committed to what it takes to achieve greater success.

Walter Isaacson's book on Steve Jobs is an excellent resource to see the power of big, bold ideas and big thinking. In the introduction to the book, Isaacson talks about how Jobs has revolutionalized seven industries (including retail). He was able to do this because he spent a lot of time thinking about where the market was heading.

Isaacson says:

"[Steve Jobs] and his colleagues at Apple were able to think differently. They developed not merely modest product advances based on focus groups, but whole new devices and services that consumers did not yet know they needed." –*Steve Jobs*, p. xxi.

It takes commitment and focus to think big. It takes courage to act on these bold ideas. I believe that Apple is one of the most valuable companies in the world today because of the big thinking that went into it first. Your bridal business will only become as big as you think it can.

You have to be 100% committed to whatever you set out to accomplish. Ken Blanchard once observed that "there is a difference between interest and commitment. When you're interested in doing something, you do it only when it's convenient. When you're committed to something, you accept no excuses, only results."

Stephen King, a best-selling author with over 40 books in print, many of which have been made into movies said: "Talent is cheaper than table salt. What separates the talented individual from the successful one is a lot of hard work."

Here are some big, bold ideas that can help you achieve more in your business:

- Become a celebrity and brand your own business.
- Make more and better follow up calls than your competitors.
- Have a bigger and better referral program that enables your best clients to become your biggest sales team.
- Have a sales system in place that ensures that each member of your staff is well trained and can close at a 75% or higher close rate with qualified prospects.
- Specialize and be unique so prospects and clients can't get what

you offer anywhere else except from you.

- Sell experiences and stretch what you do so you can sell to more affluent clientele.

These are big, bold ideas that can transform your business. Such big ideas become reality by thinking big. Many aren't able to think big, bold ideas because their own negative and limiting self-beliefs prevent them from doing so. If you want to be more successful at your store, you've got to think differently. A big part of changing where you've been to getting to where you want to be is based on changing your story.

Werner Erhard once observed, ""If you want to be successful in life and in business, you have to give up *your* story and change it to a *different* story." If you are to succeed at thinking bigger, you must change the story that you are telling to yourself and oftentimes that discussion revolves around your beliefs about money and wealth.

Here are eleven examples of stories that bridal store owners and wedding professionals tell themselves that hold them back in this business:

- Thinking your business is different.
- Allowing yourself to be controlled by the opinions and beliefs of others.
- Allowing yourself to be controlled by past experience ("I tried that and it didn't work...")
- Being a slave to industry norms ("I can only get a certain margin on what I sell because...that's what everyone else does...etc.")
- Fear
- Indecision

- Lack of clarity and focus – continually distracted by new, shiny objects instead of focusing on the areas that will bring you success.
- Having a strategy that is incongruent with your goals (For example, if you have a goal to sell $1,000,000 at your store, you've got to have a strategy that matches up with your goals. In other words, you have to figure out how you will sell at least 3 dresses at an average of $1,000 a day and bring in enough brides at your current closing ratio to make that happen. If you are at a 50% close ratio, that means that you must bring in six brides each day to reach that goal. If you are only bringing in three brides and your close ratio is 50%, your strategy is inconsistent with your goals and you won't hit them.)
- Small thinking
- Incorrect thinking about money and margins
- Thinking that you have to sell dresses for the same or lower price in order to get the sale.

Get over the stories you have been telling yourself. Start thinking bigger and develop the habit of big, bold thinking.

One of the most important big, bold ideas you must implement at your store is that of doing the things necessary to be viewed as a celebrity and authority by brides in your market region. Here are some tips on how you can do that:

1) Take a position and make a stand. Your market needs clarity about you. Are you going to provide it, or will you let someone else do it for you? In your marketing ask questions that help position you as a solution to a challenge a bride or prom girl is facing.

What question should you pose to your brides that will help her **sense a problem** she is facing and show how you can help her with the solution?

2) Shift your marketing / selling philosophy from being product-centric to customer-centric. You should be asking: "How can I best help my target brides get what they want—and be perceived as doing so?.... NOT: how can I sell the dresses I have at my store?"

3) Promote yourself courageously through as many mediums, methods and media as possible to get your message out to your brides.

What are ways you are currently doing this?

What could you / should you be doing to promote yourself in this way?

4) If you want to grow your celebrity rapidly, follow these five steps:

- Advance a clear, focused and shocking, radical, or contrarian position.
- Create a deliberate controversy.
- Be about something and be known for something specific (specialization).
- Exploit your created personality and celebrity through every possible media you can get in front of your target audience
- Don't just use media, seek to own it.

If you study the lives of any celebrity who has made it big and done so quickly, they have followed these five steps. I would especially encourage you to look at how Dave Ramsey and Dr. Robert Atkins used these principles to grow their brands. If you are to be well known in your market area as the best wedding professional in your niche, you must follow these steps as well. They will help you position yourself and get the attention of brides.

5) Remember, brides accept you as you present yourself.

How are you presenting yourself to brides? As I look at the advertising for many bridal stores each year, I marvel at how few really understand how to present themselves and market themselves so they stand out and have more authority, credibility, and celebrity. These same stores wonder why others seem to be getting more business than them. Brides accept you as you present yourself so you should talk up your accomplishments in this business. If you don't, who will?

6) Position yourself into a category of one.

What category of one can you position yourself in?

You want to be able to stand out in a way that differentiates you. Here are five ways you can do that:

- Be more fascinating. Stop doing things that cause brides to avoid you and do more things that attract brides to you.
- Focus on building your value so that it is more intangible, personal, and unique. I discus this in great detail in Chapter 8 of my book *Bridal Boosters and Breakthroughs.*
- Educate the bride better. If you aren't educating her about why and how you are different, how will she know?
- Have a better and more irresistible offer.
- Promote yourself as an expert and do things that celebrities do to attract brides to your business. Chapter 5 of my *Bridal Boosters and Breakthroughs* book goes into detail about how you can do this for you and your store.

3. They are extremely self-confident. They believe in what they do.

If you look at most successful individuals in any business or field, you will see that they are extremely confident in themselves and what they are doing.

They believe they can make things happen, conquer any difficulties that come in their path, and do what others can't or won't. This attitude and belief comes from confidence in what they know and what they have already done or accomplished.

Unsuccessful individuals never launch ideas or projects or fully commit to implementing ideas because deep down, they lack confidence in their own ability to follow-through with what they start. If you are to become one of the best in your field, you must believe in yourself.

Here are ten ways you can develop extreme self-confidence:

1) Change your associations (what you read and who you associate with).
2) Do something well.
3) Be and act better than your competition. When brides notice the difference, your confidence skyrockets.
4) Develop new skills and competencies.
5) Surround yourself with A players who you have confidence in and who you know will hit the goals you need to hit every day.
6) Do what you say you will do.
7) Expect and anticipate great things at your store and live into the picture / vision you have for yourself.
8) Reward yourself and your team when you accomplish extraordinary things.
9) Be immune to criticism.
10) Take the responsibility to create your own story. Don't listen to

what others have said about you in the past.

You have greatness within you. There is no reason why you can't go out there and make it happen in your business now. If you haven't been confident in yourself up to this point, that's okay. You can change today by changing the way you talk to yourself. Remember, change begins with language. Choose to say, believe, and act in accordance with what you want.

Have more confidence in yourself and the journey that you are on. You have great things to contribute to the brides in your area. It is up to you to make a difference by believing in yourself first.

4. They protect profit margins at all costs.

It doesn't take much imagination to cut prices, discount and discount more so that you have a slim to non-existent profit margin. To succeed, you must go to work on protecting your profits, not sacrificing them. If you can't figure out a way to sell what you sell profitably, you won't be in business long.

With the increased cost of running your business on almost every front (shipping, health care, salaries, etc.) and with clients expecting more today than they ever have, you must be profitable if you are to stay in business. Brides today feel entitled to a lot because that is what they've seen and what they've gotten from other businesses. This means that you have to get better at building more and more value into what you sell in ways that don't increase your expenses. If you don't do this and your sales revenues remain flat, you will fall behind very quickly with the rising cost of everything.

In order to protect your profits, you must:

1) Know and pay attention to the critical numbers in your business. You can't control costs if you aren't carefully watching what is increasing and looking for alternative options.

2) Alter the source of your customers (get better and less price sensitive customers). In the future, the most successful bridal businesses are those that do a much better job of attracting and acquiring more affluent customers.

3) Offer new and different products and services (that have high profitability). The choice to sell what is not profitable is a choice that will limit your growth and could jeoparidze your future.

4) Force higher transaction size by bundling products and services. You can add more value and avoid comparison shopping when you bundle products and services together. Create new names that differentiate you and highlight your strengths and differences when doing so.

5) Elevate the value of what you sell beyond easily comparable dresses that are commoditized. The higher you ascend the pyramid I discussed in Chapter 10 of *Bridal Profit Explosion*, the more you are paid for **who** you are than **what** you do. Having unique offerings and promoting your own uniqueness in the marketplace allow you to truly differentiate yourself from your competitors.

When bridal retailers become stressed out, they often use quick and easy fixes like offering discounts, sales and other promotions to increase their cash flow. Unfortunately, the continued use of these types of promotions without regard to how it affects overall profitability leads downhill. When each of your competitors offers discounted products or continuously has sales and you try to match them to win in the marketplace, you have to trade away more and more profit to succeed (especially if you are selling the same exact products as everyone else is selling).

Settling for decreased profits means that you will have less money to spend to advertise and get brides into your business, less control over the future growth of your business, less ability to pay others and yourself with, and the inability to bring in new, profitable inventory.

What are you actually selling? Determine if you should keep or discard a line based on their overall profitability and contribution to the revenues of your store. As you think about what is selling in your business now, please consider the following six questions that follow so you can make some decisions going forward about what will be best for you and your store.

1) What is the most profitable line I have?
2) What would happen to my profitability if I invested more of my inventory resources into my most profitable product line (instead of diluting it with less profitable offerings)?
3) How much money did I really make from the line I am selling the most of?
4) What profitability am I giving up by what I keep in my store?
5) Does the product turnover of each line justify its continued presence in my store?
6) Will increased costs allow me to continue to be profitable with this line?

As the owner or manager of your store, only you can control what you choose to sell. I love what Dan Kennedy says about this. He says: "Control equals responsibility and responsibility equals control; and anybody adept at making excuses is usually inept at making money." Are you in control or are you making excuses?

5. They continually work at improving their ability to persuade and look for new opportunities to sell more and better.

Any prosperous business revolves around solid salesmanship. I've talked a lot about this principle in previous books. The very best bridal store owners pay close attention to how each of their consultants is doing with each of the brides they work with. They help and train them to succeed by understanding the right kinds of questions they should be asking to find out the concerns of brides and help them to overcome them in the quest for the perfect dress.

As the owner or manager of your store, you may have mastered the skills of selling. To succeed on a larger scale, you've got to train those on your team to sell as well or better than you do.

Here are seven questions you should think about as you consider the bridal consultants you currently have on your team.

1) What are the closing percentages of your current bridal consultants?
2) What are you doing to move those who are under 50% to be above 50%?
3) By what date will you eliminate those who are at 30% and under?
4) What are you doing to get your team to 70-75% close ratios?
5) Ask yourself: 1) Who should I continue investing in, 2) who should I replace with someone else who can help me get where I want to go?
6) What selling processes do you need to focus on to provide better training at your store?
7) What impact will that have for you and your business?

When you are selling, it is not about you. It is about the bride. Everybody would rather talk about themselves because we all have a selfish tendency to look at things ONLY from our own perspective.

To be more successful in selling, you must ask brides questions about themselves. You've got to begin the process of looking at what you're offering with trust and rapport. The easiest way to persuade or influence someone is to find out what they want and give it to them. In order to find out what a bride is looking for, you've got to ask questions.

Are your questions prepared in advance or are you winging it? If you are winging it, you will get wing it results, which means that your sales results will be much lower than you really want them to be. With a selling system, you are able to get predictable results because human beings make buying decisions in patterns. The questions you ask should help you determine a prospect's buying fingerprint. When you understand a bride's buying pattern, you can help her lower her resistance and be excited about the decision to own the dress you are offering.

The first time a bride buys from you is because there is a tangible benefit that she sees that outweighs the cost. The second time she buys from you is because she likes you and your business. The better your relationship, the more likely the bride will buy from you again and again.

To sell more, you need to help brides see all of the benefits of choosing to buying now as well as all of the consequences that will happen if she chooses not to take action. If you haven't been selling as well as you would like (and especially if you don't have a sales system in your business), it is easy to make excuses instead of focusing on what needs to be done to get results.

Author Robert Johnson says: "I can imagine a cave-salesperson somewhere selling a whole lot more wheels and fire than the competition, while the underperformer was blaming his poor sales record on dinosaur attacks, evolution, floods, fires, and meteor strikes."—*This is Harder Than it Looks*, p. 22.

He continues: "Sales success doesn't just come simply from the execution of sales skills. Rather, it's an amazing journey wherein you develop the ability to manage the will, the skill, and drill of selling."

He defines these as:
"The *will* is the required mental preparedness: the drive to persevere and to face and overcome fear, procrastination, constant adversity, and rejection. Your will sets you in motion, and can also stop your momentum. This quality is the toughest to diagnose and handle since so much of our internal struggle is masked by excuses and our positive external voice.
"The *skill* is rooted in a vast foundation of knowledge of product, industry, competition, and selling skills. It is the mastery of these four basic areas that enables you to successfully guide prospects through a sales process.
"The *drill* is the process of setting goals, creating strategic and tactical plans, planning territory, and executing the key leading indicator activities that create sustained superior results on a daily basis. The 'drill to sell' is possible only by engaging the 'will to sell.' –*This is Harder Than It Looks*, p. 28.

You prepare for success by hiring those who already have the will to sell. You ensure success by training your sales team the skills of selling. And you maximize success by practicing the skills again and again through focused and effective training systems.

6. They have an unrelenting focus on the setting and achievement of goals.

Jim Collins calls this habit fanatic discipline or the 20-mile march in his book *Great by Choice*. He says: "The 20 Mile March is more than a philosophy. It's about having concrete, clear, intelligent, and rigorously pursued performance mechanisms that keep you on track. The 20 Mile March creates two types of self-imposed discomfort: (1) the discomfort of unwavering commitment to high performance in difficult conditions, and (2) the discomfort of holding back in good conditions." –p. 45.

Collins lists seven major components of these types of goals:
- "You must have performance markers." *I think these should be your minimum, target, and optimal goals.*
- "You must have self-imposed constraints. You have to decide what goals you will march towards every day and do so consistently.
- You must tailor your goals to your business and its environment.
- You must set goals that are largely within your control to achieve. In other words, work on the critical success factors that lead to success instead of shooting blanks in the dark. You've got to aim and focus on your target.
- The goal should be just right for you and your team. He calls this a Goldilocks time frame (where the goal is not too long or too short, but just right).
- Your goals should be designed and self-imposed by you, not set by someone who doesn't understand your business.
- Your goals must be achieved with great consistency."— Jim Collins, *Great by Choice*, pp. 48-49.

Here are five rules that I've found are very important when setting your goals:

1) Goals must be in harmony with one another, not in contradiction.

2) Your goals must be challenging. They must make you stretch without being overwhelmed. Set goals that stretch you, but that are not completely out of reach. Goals that are motivational are incremental goals. Stretch a little bit beyond your current capabilities. Motivate yourself with incremental goals until you are able to surpass these with another incremental goal. This is a very important point with growth. If you try to grow too fast without the proper foundation and framework, you will frustrate yourself, instead of motivate yourself.

3) You should have both tangible and intangible goals, both quantitative and qualitative. Theodore Roosevelt once said: "Do what you can with what you have, right where you are."

4) You need both short-term and long-term goals.

5) Break down your goals into yearly, monthly, weekly, daily, and hourly targets.
Set your goals throughout the year based on your minimum, target, and optimal goals. Once the goals have been set, you should set rewards for their accomplishment.

Let's take a minute to talk more specifically about your goals. I hope you've taken the time to figure out your goals so that you are absolutely clear about what you want. If not, you need to do that within the next week and determine what targets you are going to strive for and hit in the weeks, months, and year ahead. If you don't, you'll be stuck with what you've always been doing.

For example, you could set goals for a specific month and then looking at growth targets based on your minimum, target and optimal goals. I've found it helpful to have a minimum goal (which should be at least a 3-5% increase over the previous year just to keep up with inflation). You can set your target and optimal goals at whatever percentage increase you desire. This chart gives an example of a 6-9 percent increase for target goals and a 10-15% increase for optimal goals.

Once you've set your own goals, you can actually track how well you've performed in the last column. The worksheet also allows you to see on paper how you will be able to reach your goal based on the numbers you'll actually need to be able to hit to reach the goal. Thinking in specifics like this will help you be much more effective than just setting a goal. You've got to have a thought out process that allows you to determine exactly what must be done to reach your goals. Once you have set your goals, you can figure exactly what you must do in revenue by month, week, day, and hour to reach your goals by breaking this down as follows:

1) Total # of _____ Dresses Sold / Month: _____
2) Total # of _____ Dresses Sold / Week: _____
3) Total # of _____ Dresses Sold / Day: _____
4) Total # of _____ Dresses Sold / Hour: _____

Clarity is the key. When you are clear about your hourly, daily, weekly, and monthly targets, you can evaluate what you are doing at any moment to see whether it is moving you towards or away from your goal. In this way, your goals system will keep you on track towards the accomplishment of your goals and you can make adjustments when necessary.

If you have set goals in the past, but haven't achieved them, let me offer you three suggestions:
1) Don't emotionally throw in the towel.
Virtually all people who have accomplished anything have thought about quitting when they've been discouraged. The difference between those who succeed and those who end up failing is that the successful ones don't act on those thoughts.

I once read an interesting statement about former Green Bay Packers coach Vince Lombardi. He was widely recognized as one of the greatest motivational and optimistic coaches in the history of the game. Yet privately, he once considered quitting coaching and becoming a bank teller. Think about how many would have never benefited from his tremendous wisdom if he had decided to throw in the towel and give up. You have greatness within you as well. You have a mission you are here to fulfill. Don't let discouragement prevent you from making your goals happen.

I suppose that there will always be those willing to promote their attitudes of pessimism and doom and gloom. You may have thought these thoughts before. However, I've found that even when you have discouraging days in business, a shift in perspective can help you start thinking differently and acting decisively towards putting together marketing promotions and sales training that will help you get better results. Choose to focus on what you do want and be absolutely clear about it.

There is an interesting statement in Napoleon Hill's classic *Think and Grow Rich* that addresses this. He said: "Fears are nothing more than states of mind. One's state of mind is subject to control and direction. Man [or woman] can create nothing which he [or she] does not first conceive in the form of an impulse or thought.

He continues: "Face the facts squarely. Ask yourself definite questions and demand direct replies. When the examination is over, you will know more about yourself. If you do not feel that you can be an impartial judge in this self-examination, call upon someone who knows you well to serve as judge while you cross-examine yourself. You are after the truth. Get it, no matter at what cost even though it may temporarily embarrass you." –p. 225-226.

Fear can mean different things to different people. It can mean *F*alse *E*vidence *A*ppearing *R*eal, *F*orget *E*verything *A*nd *R*un or it can mean *F*ace *E*verything *A*nd *R*ise. Fears can be controlled through your decision to manage them. As Ralph Waldo Emerson said: "Do the thing you fear and the death of fear is certain."

2) Pay attention to the critical numbers. Focus on the fundamentals. Don't let yesterday's successes or failures prevent you from doing what must be done today.
Tennis champion Chris Evert once said: "If I win several tournaments in a row, I get so confident I'm in a cloud. A loss gets me eager again." That is great perspective for how you should react to both the day's successes and failures. Sometimes you win. Sometimes you lose. When you win, briefly celebrate your victory. When you lose, focus on what you will do differently the next time. Celebrating too long can cause you to be complacent. Beating yourself up for too long will cause you to become despondent. Either behavior causes you to take

your eye off of the fundamentals. Don't let this happen to you. Focus on the now and increase your sales with the prospects and clients in front of you.

3) Intensify your marketing.
One of the biggest mistakes entrepreneurs make during periods of economic slowdown is to cut back on their marketing. Intensifying and focusing on better marketing will help you be busier when other businesses in your industry may be slower.

If you don't have an effective marketing system and plan, it is easy to stop promoting yourself and get into a mindset where your behavior shows little to no action that is not healthy.

Looking for new ways to improve is so critical and important. Ask questions of others to find out what is working. Don't be content with how things are. Constantly seek to be learning and improving your marketing. There is one constant with today's buyers: The expectations of what your prospects and clients expect when they go into a business of any kind are changing. Clients are experiencing new and exciting opportunities and offers everyday. Simply standing still will ensure that you get left behind in a hurry.

You should set rewards for yourself if you achieve the target and optimal goals. Don't have rewards associated with the minimum goal, since that is what you should do as a bare minimum to stay up with the rising costs of running your business.

7. They have the habit of choosing and prioritizing opportunities and manage their daily schedule around them.
Robert Kiyosaki defines focus as: Follow One Course Until Successful. He says: "My favorite two words of that acronym are these: until successful. Focus...is power measured over time. For example, it is easy for me to stay on my diet from breakfast to lunch. But to stay focused for years on the diet is the true power of focus. I have gone on

diets, lost weight, gained it back, and had to lose the weight again. That is the lack of focus over time." —*The Midas Touch*, p. 51.

Here are some questions for you to reflect on:
1) What are your most important priorities?

2) Are you focused on them? Does your daily schedule reflect those priorities?

3) What are the things that you do well that you and only you can do at your store?

4) How is what you are presently doing, helping you build the future you desire for yourself?

5) List three areas where you are most productive. In what area of your business are you currently best using your time? Is this the right area of focus?

6) Are you using your time at your store in a way that allows you to work on your greatest opportunities *or* do you find yourself bogged down dealing with your greatest challenges?

7) What opportunities do you see now that you didn't see last year that you could focus on (and that are really worth developing)?

8) What can you do daily to stay focused on new opportunities?

Too many wedding professionals focus solely on their biggest problems instead of their future opportunities. Here are ten opportunities and some suggestions for you to consider that you could adopt to increase your sales.

1) Develop an advertising business within your business - this can be selling ads in a catalog or a bridal rewards package where vendors pay you to have access to your brides

2) Have your own catalog and sell full page or half page ads in any promotional literature or catalogs that you produce.

3) Develop a bridal rewards package that has a coupon program that you sell to other wedding vendors to offer additional incentives to brides in your local area.

4) Offer online advertising through apps where you can sell video or promotional web links from your online catalog for brides to download and view.

5) Sell commercials that you broadcast inside of your store on a television to your audience of brides.

6) Have a promotion through special reports for specific vendors where they pay to have coupons included in your marketing sequence.

7) Feature online links to vendor commercials of other wedding vendors in You Tube videos as you educate brides.

8) Have better follow up sequences to sell more and more often to the brides who have already purchased something from you.

9) Host educational classes or a bride's breakfast club for brides where you can sell vendors the opportunity to speak in front of that targeted niche of brides.

10) Have a bride's insider's club with monthly package that continually promotes what you sell - You can also sell ads within your monthly newsletter to brides as well as do profiles on certain wedding vendors to help brides see the benefit of advertising with them.

Here are five important questions for you to consider about the opportunities at your store:
1) What is generating the majority of your revenue now?
2) What is the most profitable area of your business?
3) What opportunities do you see now that you didn't see last year that you could focus on (and that are really worth developing)?
4) What do you believe would be a hit for your store, but can't prove...and would be worth a test for a home run?
5) What can you do daily to stay focused on new opportunities?

Follow one course until success. Your daily schedule is yours. Schedule it to focus on your most important priorities or someone else will.

8. The habit of utilizing leverage points and multipliers in your store to maximize productivity and results.
I talked about this principle at length in Chapter 7 of my book *Bridal Boosters and Breakthroughs*.

Here are twenty-two questions for you to consider as you evaluate how well you are doing with utilizing leverage points in your business.
1) How have I better leveraged unused capacity at my store (times when I'm not usually busy)?

2) Is my pre-sales process more effective than my competition? What am I providing to brides before they come into my store?

3) Are brides commenting on the experiences they're having at our store? What specifically is driving our focus on selling experiences, not just dresses at our store?

4) What game changing elements have you introduced at your store (different payment offers, incentives, fractional ownership, all-inclusive packages)?

5) Do brides perceive that you have additional value above and beyond just a place to purchase their wedding dress as they prepare for the wedding of their dreams?

6) Are your brides loyal to you once they've purchased their dress from you (or are other competitors more persuasive in their marketing to pull these brides into their businesses)? How do you know?

7) What recurring problem do you solve that brides have been talking about today? How specifically are you solving it?

8) Do brides feel that what you do is extraordinary or ordinary? What have brides told you that you are doing that is new or that they have seen as they've shopped that is new? How could you better leverage this?

9) Do you feel that you've re-invented the experience that brides have at your store? How specifically have you re-invigorated your processes, systems, and staff?

10) What industry norms has your store defied? What are you doing to stand out and be different? How could you better leverage this to your advantage?

11) What territory, niche, or market square are you now dominating? Are there market gaps that no one is really addressing in our area?

12) What unmet needs or desires do brides have? How could you meet those better than your competitors?

13) In what ways have you stretched the price pyramid at your store (are you selling high margin, lower price dresses or selling to more affluent brides)?

14) Do you have relationships with individuals in specific niche channels that your competitors don't have that you are able to monetize?

15) What processes are you leveraging at your store to have more success (how the phone is answered, how orders are processed, what brides experience in first 30 seconds and during their entire experience at your store)?

16) What have you done to increase your margin on the products you are carrying in your store? What leverage points or advantages has this given to you?

17) How much time are you spending thinking about where you want to be in the future? What leverage does this give you?

18) Are you copying your competitors or are they copying you? Are your competitors aggressively pursuing your brides? How do you know? What will you do about it?

19) How does your web site compare with that of your competitors? Does your web site leverage your business and help brides see why you are the best choice?

20) How do your sales closing percentages compare with those of your competitors? Do you have a sales training regimen that you use to keep your consultant's sales skills sharp?

21) How well are you implementing what you are learning? Are you where you want to be? What are you doing to ensure that you'll be in a different place six months from now than you are today?

22) What is extraordinary about your business as compared with your competitors? Do brides perceive this difference?

To grow your business, you need to better leverage the assets you have. Your own individual assets aren't enough. Taking the time to reflect on these questions will help you see opportunities to better leverage the assets you *already* have.

9. They plan and stick to systems. A big part of this is evaluating what's working and continually looking for better ways to improve them.

The very best bridal businesses have a plan for how they will attract brides into their business. It is best to have a marketing calendar scheduled a year in advance. Then, you can make adjustments based on what is happening in your business.

In the 8-Week Bridal Marketing Mastery course, I created I go through more than 120 examples of specific marketing strategies you can use to grow your business. If you would like to go through this course, please email me at info@bridaltrainingsystems.com and I'll send you the details of the course.

As a part of your marketing plan, you should also track what your biggest competitors are doing throughout the year and then put this on your calendar as well. Big box retailers typically follow the same marketing plan year to year, so this will allow you to anticipate and predict with certainty what they will do next so you can have your own counter to it.

10. They are implementers. They get things done and insist on things getting done.

Pay those on your team for results, not excuses. You don't stay at the top for long by being easy on yourself. The leaders in any field are those who expect superior, on-time, on-target from themselves in every setting. This can cause stress and unhappiness because you are always working to implement and know you must continually do more than you are.

Jim Collins calls this habit "productive paranoia" or being obsessed on implementation. One of the interesting observations he makes in *Great by Choice* is that "leaders remain obsessively focused on their objectives *and* hypervigilant about changes in their environment; they push for perfect execution *and* adjust to changing conditions..."—p. 114.

Be one who implements quickly. Remember, the top earners in this business or any other are those who have adopted the habit of implementation.

I hope this discussion of habits has been helpful for you. I'm reminded of something Robert Kiyosaki said in his book *The Midas Touch*. He says: "Leaders have vision, which is nothing more than the ability to see into the future. Entrepreneurs are different. They need more than vision. Entrepreneurs must have vision plus the power of focus."—*The Midas Touch*, p. 65.

My hope is that you will take these ten habits seriously and adopt each and every one of them into your life. You can choose to be great by what you focus on. I would encourage you to pick at least four of these habits and decide to adopt them and have them be a major part of your life by this time next year. Then, once you've mastered those habits, move on to the next set of habits you will master. My question is simply this: Which of the ten we've discussed will be the habits you will master in the coming year?

If you will work on one habit every quarter (3 months or 13 weeks) – if you will work on that habit at least 20 minutes a day for the next 13 weeks, it will be yours for life.

Put up signs around your home or your business to remind yourself of the habits employed by the most successful entrepreneurs that you are going to develop and make a part of your life. Then, you will employ the behaviors and skills necessary to build a great bridal business with systems that will propel you to new heights.

CHAPTER 3

DEFY THE FORCES, SHIFTS, AND CHANGES IN TODAY'S COMPETITIVE MARKETPLACE

"If you're not making mistakes, you're not taking risks, and that means you're not going anywhere. The key is to make mistakes faster than the competition, so you have more chances to learn and win." – John W. Holt, Jr.

In this chapter, I want to cover five big lessons from successful entrepreneurs that show how you can defy the shifts and changes that are happening today. My hope is that these lessons will help you think about and renew your commitment to succeed in your business. With that quest in mind, here are five important lessons I've learned from top business owners who once had very small businesses.

1. **To succeed, focus and simply. It is much easier to market a simplified message to a specific target market instead of trying to be all things to all people.**

A great example of the power of this marketing principle can be found with the company Gap. "Gap started life as a hippie style jeans store in San Francisco. Founder Donald Fisher went to exchange a pair of Levi's he'd bought at a department store that turned out to be an inch too short, but was told he could not. He decided there was a need for a store that stocked a comprehensive range of sizes, so in 1969 he and his wife Doris opened a place they called Gap, after the generation gap (this was the hippie era, after all), advertising 'four tons of Levi's.' By the end of 1970, there were six Gap stores in California, and in 1976, the company went public though it immediately found itself in a price war with competitors slashing their margins on Levi's. *Sound familiar? Discounters selling branded merchandise for less?*

"Gap responded by diversifying into more directional lines under such house-brand labels as Foxtails and Fashion Pioneers *(private labeling and private lines)*. But poor fashion sense forced Gap to sell too much stock at a discount, and Gap began to smell suspiciously like a bargain basement.

"In 1983, Fisher hired Mickey Drexler, a New York retailing whiz who had just revamped Ann Taylor, another clothing company that had been in similar trouble. Drexler's vision was single-minded: at meetings with Gap executives, he handed around plaques with just one word on them: 'Simplify.' Like any experienced spring cleaner, his first move was to eliminate all the 'junk'—the cheap-looking clothes stacked ten deep across the stores. In its place, he emphasized 'essentials': good-quality jeans and T-shirts in a wide ranges of sizes and colors, designed and manufactured by Gap so it could boost quality while keeping costs low.

"Under Drexler's hands-on approach, stores were redesigned to emphasize space and light—the beginning of what would become Gap's trademark look of elegant shelves, polished timber floors, and white walls. Drexler, who became company president in 1987, put new styles on tables in the center of the store, where customers were encouraged to pick them up and try them on, and he developed a list of directives that made sure his sleek, streamlined stores stayed that way...."

"As Gap jettisoned other brands to focus on its own single house label (a range of upmarket basics that appealed to middle-class buyers reminiscing about the preppie look of their college days), Drexler and Fisher built lines of distribution that enabled stores to react almost daily to fluctuations in demand, which gave them the flexibility to pull items that weren't selling well. It also meant stores could carry less floor stock; if shoppers saw just two or three sweaters in the same style, they carried an air of exclusivity—even though there were thousands more just a phone call away."

This is such an important marketing principle. Tell brides in your store that you only have one style in each size that she can buy for her wedding day. Even if you have extra stock in your back room of your best-selling styles, it is true that each bride will only buy one style, one size and one dress for her wedding day. Such an approach will brides sense the exclusivity of her gown and make the decision to buy now, so she doesn't miss out on the dress she really loves.

"Gap used a similar technique in its advertising to make its basics seem more exclusive. In 1988, it ran a campaign called 'Individuals of Style,' a series shot in black and white featuring celebrities wearing their favorite Gap piece. Dizzy Gillespie transformed a basic black turtleneck into the epitome of cool. It was such a successful campaign Gap has relied on carefully chosen celebrities, from actress Kim Basinger to Madonna, to 'individualize' its mass-market clothing every since.

"By 1990, Gap had 965 stores, including GapKids, BabyGap, and Banana Republic, making it the second-largest clothing retailer in the United States, behind Levi Strauss. In 1993 Drexler successfully flirted with more fashionable lines to combat complaints that Gap was becoming boring, and also to fend off competitors who were now copying its line of basics.

"When Gap launched another brand, Old Navy, in 1994, Drexler reworked the old formula once again, this time offering a line of simplified cotton classics to the masses, often in warehouse-style stores in working class neighborhoods. Old Navy, named after a sign on the side of a building in Paris, became the first retail chain to reach $1 billion in sales in the first four years of operation.

During the late 1990's and the early 2000s, Gap lost its focus. This is an important lesson for bridal retailers as well. When you become successful because of simplifying, it is easy to think that if you had more options, you would be even more successful. As a result, many bridal retailers who have reigned in their spending to a handful of lines have then gone back out to explore carrying many lines and trying to be all things to all people again. A good example of what happened with Gap can be found in their numbers.

"In 2001, Gap suffered what Drexler described as its 'most difficult year ever:' it had made $877 million in profit in 2000, but actually lost $7.7 million in 2001 prompting Drexler and Fisher to write in the annual report that Gap had forgotten one of its basic maxims: always keep it simple. The following year, Drexler attempted to spark some of the old magic, once again hiring stars, including Dennis Hopper and Christina Ricci, to promote denim and khaki. Sales lifted a little, but the company had lost its confidence in Drexler, and he stepped down." --*100 Great Businesses and the Minds Behind Them*, pp. 94-97.

This is such an easy lesson to state, but a hard lesson to remember and live. In my book, *Bridal Profit Explosion*, I make this statement: "Beware of dresses that look attractive but have no proven market for you. The temptation is to have an invest a little and see approach. This may work but it ties up capital and everyone wants you to do this. After a few seasons, you find that you have more lines that you need and you don't have any capital left to invest in lines that can make you money until you sell off what you already have. The most successful stores I know limit how many lines they have and the majority of what they sell goes through one, two, or at the most three profitable lines. Be careful to focus on your area of exclusivity instead of trying to be all things to all people."—*Bridal Profit Explosion*, p. 139.

Focus. It pays big dividends.

2. Never delegate the marketing functions of your organization. *You* are the brand and *you* are in charge.

A great example of this marketing secret can be found in the story of Gert Boyle, who is the chairwoman of Columbia Sportswear, an international outdoor apparel, footwear and equipment manufacturer. At age 13, Gert Boyle and her family fled Nazi Germany and moved to Portland, Oregon. Her parents, Paul and Marie Lamfrom, founded what was then called Columbia Hat Company in 1938. After attending the University of Arizona she and her husband, Neal Boyle, returned to Oregon and joined the family business.

After the death of her father, Neal became president. Six years later at the age of 47 he died of a heart attack. Gert found herself at the helm of a financially struggling company. Her son Tim, while still in college, helped run the business. After a year they were advised by a banker to sell Columbia, but they were only offered $1,400. Her stubbornness kicked in and she refused and decided to fight for her company. The bankers gave her six months to turn around the company and she went to work. She took over the marketing for the brand, cut costs, and focused the company in a direction with the products that proved most promising. They decided to focus on outdoor wear.

"In the 1970s, outdoor wear became fashionable, it became more functional, and new products and materials, such as lightweight, waterproof, and breathable Gore-Tex, became available and sent outdoorsmen into the stores wanting to update their casual wear. Columbia was the first to use Gore-Tex in its outerwear clothing *(another reminder about the importance of being first and capitalizing on your difference)*.

"Columbia Sportswear designed the innovative Bugaboo, a two-jacket-in-one parka with a waterproof outer shell with a fleecy jacket layer underneath. Skiers loved it, sales were in the millions, and the company's fortunes were reversed.

"With stronger sales, there were now funds available for advertising, one of the key ingredients, believes Gert, in the success of Columbia Sportswear. She often cites a saying she heard as a child, 'Early to bed, early to rise, work like hell and advertise.' Initially Columbia could only afford specialized niche publications. Brand awareness skyrocketed after Gert was persuaded to star in a series of advertisements as 'one tough mother,' making son Tim test out Columbia gear with the catchphrase: 'Before it passes Mother Nature, it has to pass Mother Boyle.' Gert has been putting her face out there ever since. She likes it that way, not in the least because the company doesn't have to pay anyone else to do it.

"The public couldn't get enough of Gert. And their campaign offered a real point of difference....Gert's recipe for success, which she delivers in her autobiography, *One Tough Mother*, is simple. Don't give up. Be prepared to change strategy. Tap into the wisdom and experience of others who know about what you are trying to do. Listen to your customers. Be a team player. Focus on what makes you unique. Don't spend money you don't have. Walk before you run. Always tell the truth. Do your best every day." – *100 Great Businesses and the Minds Behind Them*, pp. 140-142.

Today, the hard work of Ma Boyle, her son Tim and their staff of employees have made Columbia a leading global seller of outdoor apparel, footwear and equipment with annual sales of more than $1 billion. Gert Boyle has become an industry icon and she is a well-respected leader in Portland and around the world.

There are a lot of great lessons you can learn from this industry leader about what it takes to be successful in business. The most important one is how she took charge of marketing the business and let her face be the brand. She stood out and built her brand around her and people have responded very favorably. Too many bridal store owners are content to let the manufacturers of the dresses they sell take over and do the advertising and marketing for their stores instead of taking charge and making it happen on their own. You'll grow a lot quicker and get a much more responsive public when your brides and prom customers know *you* and sense that you care about them and their special event.

Another big lesson from Ma Boyle is that they decided to focus and stand for something instead of trying to be all things to all people. If you try to be all things to all people, eventually you will stand for nothing. Trying to extend your store brand may bring you short term sales, but long term you will end up weakening your brand and weakening the depth of your offering. You may have everything, but you will likely be weak in many categories as it is nearly impossible to stock deep in every single product category in the bridal industry and remain profitable.

Remember when you stand for something, you become unique.

3. Focus on sales. Motivate your sales force and recognize them for what they do well. Be a true sales professional and learn to master the skills of selling. Remember, each sale is the lifeblood of your business. When the sales stop flowing, your business stops growing.

No one better embodies this marketing principle better than successful entrepreneur Mary Kay Ash. She suffered tremendous heartache and disappointment in her life, but always focused on selling.

"She was born in 1918 in Hot Wells, Texas. By the age of seven she was caring for her invalid father, who suffered from tuberculosis, while her mother worked fourteen-hour days managing a restaurant. By seventeen, she was married and went on to have three children.

Her first husband filed for divorce after he returned from serving in World War II (turns out he had been in a relationship with another woman), and Mary Kay was left a single mother with three children to support. She had wanted to study medicine but realized it was not possible with her responsibilities. She began selling child psychology books door to door, and her natural talent for sales blossomed. She then worked in direct sales for Stanley Home Products for eleven years (also a training ground for Brownie Wise, who would lead the Tupperware revolution).

"At her company, recognition was a critical part of the success of the business. Her way of showing it was through pink Cadillacs, luxury holidays, and all manner of jewelry from diamond bumblebee stick pins and little ladders through to flashy designer watches. She wanted her independent sales force to be the highest paid women in the U.S. Hundreds of Mary Kay representatives have earned commissions in excess of a million dollars. 'She always focused on putting the honor in selling,' says Rogers (her son).

Do you see the honor in selling? Do you love selling enough to learn to master it?

I love this statement by Brian Tracy:
"You have one of the most important jobs in our society. Nothing happens for your company until you make a sale. Every other person in the company, from the president down to the janitor, is completely dependent upon you for their employment and their income. Your ability to generate sales is the absolute prerequisite for the success of your business. Your effectiveness as a salesperson is crucial to determining whether your company will succeed or fail.

"Selling is an honorable profession. Salespeople are the forerunners of progress, development, and growth throughout the entire economy. It is salespeople who ultimately generate the markets for almost all other skills. When you make a sale, it has a domino effect that provides employment up and down the line for everyone else in society. Where there are no sales, there is no domino effect....According to Dun & Bradstreet, the number one reason for business failure is lack of sales. The number one reason for business success is abundant sales. And the effectiveness of your activities determines which of these it is going to be." –*Advanced Selling Skills*, p. 166.

Mary Kay has grown to the stratospheric height is has because Mary Kay herself loved to sell and loved to help others learn this vital business skill as well. She was in many ways a woman ahead of her time.

I really like what author Darcy Andries had to say about her: "Being ahead of one's time is difficult enough, but the experience can be especially frustrating for a woman surrounded by men who are stuck in the past. Still, Mary Kay Ash managed to work her way to the top rung of the career ladder—no small feat for a woman in the 1950s. She even earned a position as the sole woman on the board of directors of World Gift Company. Yet whenever she expressed an opinion, the other board members accused her of 'thinking like a woman.' Considering the sales force was almost entirely women, Ash thought 'thinking like a woman' was an asset, but her suggestions were continually rejected. Finally, out of frustration, she retired.

"Ash didn't enjoy retirement, and she decided to open her own cosmetics business. Both her accountant and her attorney told her that she would be better off throwing her savings into a trashcan. She went ahead with her plans anyway. With her husband's help and support, she designed the packaging, wrote the training materials, recruited consultants, and prepared the products. Then, a month before she was to open her new business, tragedy struck: her husband suffered a fatal heart attack.

"Rather than postpone things, Ash enlisted the help of her twenty-year-old son and opened on schedule in 1964. As part of the marketing plan, she took her products to a beauty show—but sold only about two dollars worth. Still she refused to give up. By encouraging her sales force of women and awarding pink Cadillacs to top sales directors, Ash and her company soon achieved astounding success. During its first year, Mary Kay Cosmetics earned almost $200,000; at the end of the second year, that figure had grown to $800,000. By the time the company went public in 1968, only four years after it began, sales had reached more than $10 million. Today, annual sales exceed $1.6 billion, and Mary Kay products are available in more than thirty markets worldwide." –*The Secret of Success is Not a Secret*, pp. 84-85.

Have you ever been to a bridal show and been frustrated with the lack of results you had?

When we attended our first bridal show, we had no idea what we were doing. We took dresses to the show and sold several, but it was complete chaos and we were completely exhausted. I had stayed up nearly the entire night preparing for the show, but what I spent my time on didn't really matter in the end. We learned a lot from that first show. At our second show, we hired some temporary workers to help, but they didn't know what they were doing and the show turned out to be a disaster. Not only that, all of our help left at the end of the show except for one girl who helped Heather and I pack up our rental truck and put the store back together until nearly one in the morning. We ended up hiring her as our second employee.

This helped me develop a comprehensive system to run bridal shows that I've taught to hundreds of bridal retailers. It is a lot of work, but everyone knows their place and it works together very well.

The big lesson I learned from those first two bridal shows is that you have to take responsibility for how you will market yourself at the show and be sure everyone else understands that clearly as well. Because I didn't completely understand what to do at the show, no one else did either. You have to be the Chief Marketing Officer at your store. You have to see your store as a marketing organization and take responsibility for what must be done.

I think Mary Kay said it best:
"Every failure, obstacle, or hardship is an opportunity in disguise. Success in many cases is failure turned inside out. The greatest pollution problem we face today is negativity. Eliminate the negative attitude and believe you can do anything. Replace 'if I can, I hope, maybe' with 'I can, I will, I must.'"

4. Market what you sell in terms of what matters most to whom you are selling. The ones who market best win the battle of the marketplace.

Charles Revson mastered this marketing principle as he created the beauty empire Revlon. His story is inspring because of how he created a huge company from so little, simply by learning how to successfully market his products. There is a lot we can learn as bridal retailers from this brilliant entrepreneur.

"In 1932, Revson was twenty-five years old, with a canny eye for color and a background in sales for a fabric and a manicure product company. He wanted to run his own business, and, at possibly the worst time in the twentieth century, Revson had the nerve to step out on his own. He started his manicure product business just before the Great Depression struck. He began selling nail enamel made with pigments instead of dyes, which meant that he had a much broader range of colors to market than the competition.

"The Revlon Nail Enamel Company was a partnership between Revson, his brother Joseph Revson, and Charles Lachman. It's generally acknowledged that Charles Revson was the brains and brilliance behind Revlon's success, with the others just coming along for the ride. In 1939, a Revlon advertisement referred to Charles as the 'spark plug' for the business. Charles Lachman did little more than add the "L" to the Revlon brand name and reclusive Joseph

Revson sold his share in the business in 1955 to Charles and proceeded to live his life as a hermit.

"Revson and his partners had just $300, no lines of credit, and no backers. Yet the company had something new for the women of the world that they didn't know they wanted yet—opaque nail enamel. At the time, polish was worn only by prostitutes; but Revson wanted to change all that and make it an essential fashion item.

"Funds were desperately short in the early days and Revson relied on pawnbrokers to keep the business afloat, often paying 2 percent a month in interest. By 1933 sales were more than $11,000 with a modest profit around $2,800 (not bad for Depression times). He began a series of ads promoting his glamorous product, making links to society women through his advertising copy. In 1939, Revlon introduced lipstick when he realized that there should be matching lips and fingertips available. By 1940, sales had increased to $2.8 million.

"Revlon created not just a product, but a fantasy of an impossibly glamorous woman who wore Sun Rose on her nails and transcended the everyday. Perceptions of who wore nail polish were changed by Revson's advertising juggernaut. Revlon upped the stakes in its advertising campaigns and charged five times the price of other nail enamels for the privilege.

"There are conflicting stories as to how Revson developed the nail enamel that would make the company viable. In her book *War Paint*, author Lindy Woodhead attributes the product to a man known simply as 'Perrera,' who would give manicures to society ladies in Venice, including the future Vogue editor Diana Vreeland, who took the polish back to New York and showed her manicurist, who happened to be dating Charles Revson.

"Revlon's version of the opaque nail enamel was far from perfect in its early stages. Sometimes it would turn yellow, it took too long to dry, and did not last long. In an effort to improve his cornerstone product, Revson was indefatigable about personally following up all complaints and trying to iron out quality control problems. He also oversaw all aspects of product development.

"Revson was also hands-on at cultivating his sales network of wholesale distributors and salons and department stores. He spread word-of-mouth about the nail enamel through beauty salons with the 'ask your manicurist' tag line on many advertisements, thus giving it a sense of exclusivity.

"With increasing competition in the marketplace, things got dirty. Revlon sales representatives were known to hide 'competitors' stock, offer 'sell-up' bonuses to manicurists who sold Revlon product, and sabotage other firms' point-of-sale material. Revson tapped his staff's phones, eavesdropped on his competitors, and cultivated a culture of encouraging anything to beat off competitors (down to unscrewing tops of other nail polishes so they would dry out in the stores).

"Revlon's 1952 'Fire and Ice' campaign is seen as pivotal in the history of cosmetics advertising. The Fire and Ice woman was awash with sexy contradictions and caused a sensation, with the advertisement asking American women a list of risqué questions ('Have you ever danced with your shoes off? Do you close your eyes when kissed?'). The campaign was backed up with heavy store display and point-of-sale promotion, and produced sales that blew competitors out of the water." –*100 Great Businesses and the Minds Behind Them*, pp. 239-242.

Revson once famously observed: "In the factory we make cosmetics; in the drugstore we sell hope." It was this philosophy of marketing to what his customers wanted that helped him grow his business. In the bridal business, I don't think most bridal retailers do this enough. They focus on selling the dress, not the dream. It is so critical to focus on selling the wedding dream and the experience the brides wants (with the dress being a part of that dream) instead of just focusing on selling the dress. It is all about selling experiences, not dresses as I've mentioned before. Live by the mantra: In our store, we *have* dresses, but to the brides we serve *we sell the dream wedding* she's always wanted.

Brides today are so consumed with the negativity around what is happening in the economy that in many cases they've given up on the dream wedding they've always wanted. Instead, they have adopted a "settle for" mentality that is discouraging to them. Because this isn't what they really want, they are spending more time shopping and looking, while hoping that things will improve to help them have the wedding they want. Unfortunately, this waiting longer and procrastinating the decision to buy has resulted in them being even more stressed out as the timeline to their wedding draws closer. Don't ignore this important lesson that Charles Revson figured out decades ago. You must market and sell what the prospective bride wants before you'll ever create enough momentum to make the sale.

5. Wedding dresses don't sell themselves. It takes a dedicated staff of sales professionals to consistently make sales day in and day out.

Brian Tracy asks this question in his book *Advanced Selling Strategies*:

"If you worked at McDonald's behind the counter and a customer came up to you on the other side, what would be your probability of making a sale? The answer is that it would be about 100 percent! If a person drives to McDonald's, parks his car, goes inside, gets in line, and works his way up to the cash register, the chances of his buying something are 100 percent.

"Now, how much can you earn working behind the counter at McDonald's? The answer is that you can earn the minimum wage, or perhaps a little more. That's all. When the sale is guaranteed, all the company has to pay for an order-taker is the minimum amount required to get someone in the current labor market. No matter how good a person becomes working behind the counter at McDonald's, he can never earn any more than the very lowest amount that McDonald's needs to pay to replace him.

"As a salesperson, the reason you can make a wonderful living for yourself and your family, achieve your goals, and fulfill all of your aspirations, is because making the sale is difficult, often extremely difficult....You should get up every morning and give a silent prayer of thanks that selling is so difficult. If it was easy, the field would be flooded by amateurs and the amount you could earn would be greatly reduced." –p. 353.

I've always thought that was a very interesting perspective on the complexities of selling. Fortunately, you can study selling and systematize it so that you can get very good at it and sell the majority of the brides who come into your store. The sales training system I've developed to teach bridal consultants contains a comprehensive approach to how to overcome objections and get to the heart of every sale. If you have it and haven't listened to or studied it for a while, it is time to get it back out and study it again. If you don't have it, you can purchase it online at www.bridaltrainingsystems.com. In addition to that resource, I have an online eight week Bridal Sales Blueprint sales training course that you and your bridal consultants will be able to attend online without having to leave your store. Please email me at info@bridaltrainingsystems.com if you would like more information about this training resource.

Dan Kennedy recently made this statement about why sales people don't sell better and there is a big lesson here. He says:

"Most aren't professionals, but amateurs in their fields. When I use the term 'sales professionals' as synonym for salespeople, I'm being politically, overly generous. Most are not professionals at all. They do not study the history or science or art of their craft, they do not practice and rehearse, they do not watch film to improve, they do not work at being as highly skilled as possible—but this is what real professionals in every field do. As example, there is reason that fully grown, seasoned veteran, highly paid NFL players spend a week between games studying film of their performance, having it critiqued by coaches, scheming to be better and practicing. How many salespeople do you think practice at night, between days of selling? – *G.L.*, Nov. 2010, p. 2.

It takes commitment to get good at selling. Wedding dresses *don't* sell themselves. You and your bridal consultants have to take charge and offer attractive bait to draw brides in now and also give them the incentive to make the purchase on their first visit. It takes a lot of effort to break down the resistance to buy, but if you are consistently persistent, you will get the sale. You and each of your bridal consultants must be trained and patient enough to ask for the sale multiple times throughout the bride's visit or you will not get the sale. Why be content to warm her up 75% of the way to the purchase, only to find out that she ended up buying a dress at the next place she went to? Instead, learn the proven ways to ask for the sale multiple times without putting outside pressure on the bride and helping her to make the decision she really wants. This is so critical today.

One of my favorite stories about the persistence and hard work required to get good at sales is that of the founder of Kentucky Fried Chicken, Harland David Sanders. You probably know him as Colonel Sanders. He once said: "Hard work beats all the tonics and vitamins in the world." He started Kentucky Fried Chicken in his sixties and faced hundreds of rejections as he tried to find investors. In fact, for two entire years, he traveled across the country and met with thousands of business owners trying to develop his franchise. After two years, he only had five restaurants signed up.

Can you imagine how heartbreaking that would be? To work for two entire years, and only have five customers? The reason his statement about tenacity is so meaningful to me is because he kept at it. He persisted when things were difficult. He figured out what wasn't working and rethought his marketing approach. He tested new ideas until over the next four years, he had persuaded an additional two hundred restaurant owners to buy franchises. Three years after that, he had over 600. At the time of his death in 1980, Colonel Sanders had become the owner of one of the largest fast food chains in the

United States. Today, more than sixteen thousand stores in one hundred and six countries serve the Colonel's chicken. More than twelve million people each day are served at KFC restaurants around the world. --http://www.numberof.net/number-of-kfcs-in-the-world/

I hope you've found inspiration by reading and thinking about these important marketing lessons from these successful entrepreneurs. Their determination and persistence by focusing on the right things, embracing the responsibility to take charge and *market* their *own* businesses, learning to sell effectively, marketing in terms of what their target customers *really* wanted, and accepting the role of mastering the art of selling (understanding that sales don't happen by themselves) helped each of them to become very successful in their market niches and grow their businesses to stratospheric heights. My hope is that you will follow these important marketing and sales lessons at your bridal store and think carefully about how you can apply them.

There is constant change in bridal retailing. This doesn't come as much surprise to anyone who has been in this business for a while, but the big lesson I hope to share with you here is found in what you have to keep doing to defy the forces, shifts and changes that would drag you back to where you were or worse and how you can beat them to make more sales and more money.

One of the big challenges today is that you must shift with what your competitors do and what your employees don't or won't do to beat the gravitational forces that constantly seek to pull you down and prevent you from soaring to new heights and accomplishing what you really want.

Before we get into the strategies and actions you must take to rise above these challenges, I'd like to first discuss some of the forces that pull you back from what you could be. These forces are serious threats that you must adapt to in order to survive and thrive in the ever-changing marketplace.

There are six of these that I want to focus on in this chapter. They are:

1) The changing nature of the bride.

The mindset of brides has changed a lot over the years. One of the biggest challenges with brides today revolves around the way she gathers information and is influenced about the fashions she sees and considers for her wedding. These decisions happen largely before she ever sets foot in a bridal store. This means that you must better understand what she is looking to buy and insert yourself into the dialogue of the conversation long before you used to. It isn't enough anymore to start this dialogue when the bride arrives at your store. In most cases, she has already made the decision about a dress or a particular style *before* she arrives at your store.

The reality is that big box retailers shrink the available pool of brides before many bridal retailers are even aware that these brides are in the market for a dress. You can't succeed in today's marketplace by reactively waiting for disappointed, disaffected and unhappy brides who weren't pleased with another store's customer service to come into your store.

Remember, brides are so skeptical in today's marketplace that a mere marketing message (no matter how good it is) and whether it is a postcard, email, phone call, or contact at a bridal show will do little by itself to persuade. Brides aren't likely to drop everything in their very busy lives simply because we invite them to come into our stores. With all of the commotion of the marketplace, it is easy to see why your marketing message is getting buried in the clutter and ignored.

According to Daniel Seeburg in his book *The Digital Diet*, the average online user now visits 40+ web sites a day, checks and updates Facebook, email, texts, and is distracted by other online content more than 100 times a day. His thesis is that "human beings are being neurologically re-programmed by their tech addiction" to the point that they are constantly distracted. With all of the distraction consumers experience today, it is no wonder that your message isn't getting noticed or getting through to the brides you're trying to reach.

On top of that, you aren't the only one who is trying to contact brides. All of your competitors are marketing to the same narrow niche of customers and every other wedding vendor in your market region is trying to convince them why they are the best wedding vendor out there. Fortunately, most wedding vendors and bridal retailers aren't very good marketers and don't have a consistent message that draws brides into their businesses.

2) The changing nature of the perception of the need for marriage.

There is no question that the perception of marriage has declined over the past fifty to sixty years. Consider some of the findings of a study released in November of 2010 by The Pew Research Center on the topic of marriage and family titled "The Decline of Marriage And Rise of New Families". My comments follow in italics.

In 1960 72% of adults were married (and 85% had ever married), compared to only 52% in 2008 (and 73% had ever married). Part of the difference is the higher divorce rate in modern times.

In the past fifty years, the number of adults who are married has shrunk by 20%. That doesn't bode well since there are more competitors fighting for their share of a shrinking market. Yet, the amount the average couple spends is higher (so there is definitely opportunity if you can get in front of brides and grooms as they're making decisions).

Among unmarried adults 46% want to get married, 25% don't, and 29% aren't sure. Unmarried people in the South are most likely to want to get married (71%), followed by the Midwest (60%), West (53%), and East (49%).

This again is a little bit of a depressing statistic. This also shows what a difference where you live makes on the beliefs individuals have on marriage. Stores in the Midwest and the South and a distinct advantage over those stores on the east and west coasts. There is typically a larger population on the east and west coasts though, so opportunity is still present for those who get good at promoting their differences to the brides they serve.

People are putting marriage off longer. In 1960, 68% of 20-somethings were married vs. 26% in 2008.

Since brides are waiting longer to get married, they typically have more to spend on their wedding, but as societal perceptions about marriage continue to shift and change, this is a trend that you and I must pay attention to.

Even with the decline in marriage, Americans have one of the highest marriage rates of developed nations. In 2006 the U.S. experienced 7.4 marriages per 1000 people. Compare this to France and Italy with only 4.2 marriages per 1000 people in 2005.

Some good news! Yet, the statistical percentages of brides have definitely shrunk over the past several years. Where are you placing your focus to grow your business as these trends continue to decline?

39% of Americans think marriage is becoming obsolete, up from 28% in 1978. Interestingly, college graduates have the most hope for the future of marriage (71% vs. 52% of non-graduates). Unsurprisingly, those who are married have the most positive outlook for the future of marriage, followed by unmarried adults, single parents, and cohabiting parents.

This is a growing trend that should cause some concern as well. As the market for those who feel the need to marry shrinks, the business we are in is likely to be affected as well. Yet, those who specialize in market niches where they can get a dominant hold will be the ones who prosper and succeed in the years ahead.

Marriage used to be nearly as common among the uneducated and poor as among the educated and non-poor (76% vs. 72% in 1960). Now, marriage is much more popular among the educated and non-poor (64% of college graduates are married vs. 48% of those without a college education). Part of the reason for this change is that Americans have come to view economic security as a precondition for marriage, rather than a major benefit obtained through marriage (as it was in the past). 2007 also marked the first time that college graduates were more likely than non-college graduates to be married by age 30.

This trend of a decline in available good customers has been steadily shrinking. I think this emphasizes the need to focus on more affluent markets as well so you can be profitable with fewer customers.

Why do people get married? 93% of married people said they did so for love, 87% did so for a lifelong commitment, 81% did so for companionship, and only 59% did so for children, and 31% did so for financial stability. Unmarried adults order the reasons for why they would get married the same way. I find this interesting because in days gone by, the order would have been reversed for most individuals. Financial stability and children were the primary reasons for marriage." --http://pewsocialtrends.org/files/2010/11/pew-social-trends-2010-families.pdf

With numerous celebrities downplaying the need for marriage and the dramatic shift in cohabitation amongst couples today, these numbers will likely continue to decline in the future.

There are a couple of other interesting statistics about cohabitation from the study: 1990 was the year "unmarried partners" was added as an option to the Census Bureau form. Since then, the number of cohabiting couples has doubled. In 2008 there were 6.2 million cohabiting couples (12.4 million individuals) (565,000 of these couples were same-sex couples). This rose to 6.7 million in 2009 and 7.5 million in 2010. *If the percentage of couples who cohabitate continues to increase (nearly 12% in the past year and there is no indication that it won't continue to increase), the pool of available brides who have wedding dates will also likely decrease. The shifting perceptions about cohabitation and marriage definitely affect your business and indicate the importance of improving the experience you deliver to brides (since the pool of eligible brides is shrinking. This means that by necessity, you must better deliver amazing experiences if you want to persuade brides to buy from us.*

This report, which is 114 pages long, makes for some interesting reading about the state of marriage in society today. I encourage you to read it, yet I've discussed what I feel is the most pertinent information as it applies to bridal retailers from the study. The first paragraph of the report makes this interesting analysis:

"The transformative trends of the past 50 years that have led to a sharp decline in marriage and a rise of new family forms have been shaped by attitudes and behaviors that differ by class, age and race, according to a new Pew Research Center nationwide survey complemented by an analysis of demographic and economic data from the U.S. Census Bureau."

"A new marriage gap in the United States is increasingly aligned with a growing income gap. Marriage, while declining among all groups, remains the norm for adults with a college education and good income but is now markedly less prevalent among those on the lower rungs of the socio-economic ladder. The survey finds that those in this less-advantaged group are as likely as others to want to marry, but they place a higher premium on economic security as a condition for marriage." --http://pewsocialtrends.org/files/2010/11/pew-social-trends-2010-families.pdf

A more recent study (September 2014) indicated that "after decades of declining marriage rates and changes in family structure, the share of American adults who have never been married is at an historic high. In 2012, one-in-five adults ages 25 and older (about 42 million people) had never been married, according to a new Pew Research Center analysis of census data." The report continues:

"The dramatic rise in the share of never-married adults and the emerging gender gap are related to a variety of factors. Adults are marrying later in life, and the shares of adults cohabiting and raising children outside of marriage have increased significantly. The median age at first marriage is now 27 for women and 29 for men, up from 20 for women and 23 for men in 1960. About a quarter (24%) of never-married young adults ages 25 to 34 are living with a partner, according to Pew Research analysis of Current Population Survey data. In addition, shifting public attitudes, hard economic times and changing demographic patterns may all be contributing to the rising share of never-married adults." --http://www.pewsocialtrends.org/2014/09/24/record-share-of-americans-have-never-married/

What does this mean for bridal retailers? Simply put, you have to get better at marketing to the shrinking crowd who is getting married from year to year. If you aren't standing for something and are trying to be a generalist, you will *not* be noticed. Your business will decline. However, if you focus on niche markets that you can become the best in the world at, you will rise in prominence and power. Ignoring these trends is a recipe for certain disaster. It is easy to throw up your hands and say, "What's the use?" But here is the important point: there is opportunity when others feel this way. Your job is to find out where you can make your stand and be more aggressive in marketing to that niche of brides.

The passage of gay marriage by a number of states may be an area of opportunity for you and your bridal business. These brides and grooms are very adept with social media and will likely promote businesses that support them aggressively to others in their community.

2) The effect of the Internet on brides shopping for their wedding attire.

There isn't a very efficient way to track what the effect of the Internet on shopping for their wedding attire really is on a nationwide basis. In my opinion, most of the statistics about brides who buy online are under-reported. This is a significant concern to bridal retailers. You must brand your store instead of relying on manufacturers (who are also sold online) to do it for you. If you don't, you will be at the mercy of brides who decide to shop for the best price since in her mind there is no difference between a dress purchased from you or the same dress bought online except for an overall better price, since she doesn't have to pay sales tax and usually gets a free premium when she buys from these Internet retailers as well (although recently proposed and passed laws look to level the playing field in the future).

An interesting statistic in a 2014 *Brides* survey was reported as follows:

"Social media has become the number-one way for brides-to-be to connect with wedding brands/products during planning, with 75% doing so vs. 56% in 2012. Pinterest leads the pack, with 67% pinning content (up from 43% in 2012)."

The number of brides shopping online and using online resources to help them shop (which wasn't even on anyone's radar screens several years ago) will increase. Those bridal stores who position themselves well with social media and mobile applications will be the ones who funnel the brides into their stores.

Those who ignore these trends or downplay them (since they aren't sure what to do about them) will suffer declining revenues and shrinking numbers of brides who come into their stores.

3) The reality about what brides are actually spending on their wedding (according to *Brides* magazine).

According to a recent *Brides* magazine survey (2014 BRIDES American Wedding Study:

KEY COSTS
* The average wedding cost is $28,202, an increase of slightly more than $1,213 since 2012.
* The reception accounts for 43% of wedding costs, with an average price tag of $12,343.
* Outside of the reception, the largest chunks of money are going to engagement rings ($5,002), photography and video ($3,378), music ($1,297), and wedding rings ($1,727).
* The average wedding cake costs $461.
* The current average cost of an engagement ring is $5,002, down $229 from 2012's average cost of $5,229.
* **The average wedding dress costs $1,380, up $25 from 2012's average cost of $1,355.**
* The average bridesmaids' dress costs $134, consistent with the cost in 2012.
* Since some items were more expansive than expected, 79% rework the budget.

* To save for the wedding they want, 62% of couples say they are willing to have a longer engagement.
* Social media has become the number-one way for brides-to-be to connect with wedding brands/products during planning, with 75% doing so vs. 56% in 2012.
* Pinterest leads the pack, with 67% pinning content (up from 43% in 2012).
* After telling close friends and family 71% of brides-to-be changed their social-media status to "engaged."
* After receiving an engagement ring, 59% posted a picture of it to social networks.
* To spread the news about their engagement to friends, 46% relied on social media.
* While 64% pin content on Pinterest to come back to, purchase or execute for their wedding, another 54% show their wedding vendors their Pinterest boards.
* To keep their guests informed throughout the planning process, 37% of brides-to-be post photos and updates from cake tastings and vendor visits.
* Some brides issue a social media ban; 11% ask guests not to post photos of their wedding day on a social-media site.
* To plan/shop for the wedding 63% use a social-media app."--
http://www.marketwired.com/press-release/brides-reveals-trends-of-engaged-american-couples-with-american-wedding-study-1928460.htm

If, you noticed, the average cost of a wedding dress keeps going up. In 2014, the average cost of a wedding gown was $1380. This compares with $1355 (2012), and $1,289 (2011). By comparison, in 2009, the average cost was $1,072. That means in the past five years, the cost of a wedding dress has gone up nearly 30%. Yet, many brides seem determined to find an even better deal than this.

Other interesting statistics from the study show:

"* Today's bride is also spending another $617 on wedding-day accessories like jewelry, a headpiece, and a veil.
* White and off-white still dominate with 92% of brides selecting either color for their wedding dress.
* Veils are not seen as frequently; only 55% of brides are choosing to wear one.
* A small portion of the population is choosing to break from the traditional gown with 11% wearing cocktail length, separates,

jumpsuits, or a color other than white.

* Multiple dresses have become 9% purchase a second wedding dress for the reception, with another 8% buying another dress or outfit for the after-party.

* Most brides -- 84% -- are still incorporating something old, new borrowed and blue into their wardrobe for their wedding day.

* Tuxedos are most popular with 61% of grooms wearing one for their big day, while 33% choose to wear a suit.

* While renting remains the most popular option, more than one of three grooms purchases his attire."-- http://www.marketwired.com/press-release/brides-reveals-trends-of-engaged-american-couples-with-american-wedding-study-1928460.htm

The average cost has gone up in large part due to inflation and also bridal retailers who have focused on selling to more affluent brides (who have the money to buy dresses today and aren't as concerned about budget or price). The cost of dresses will continue to rise as inflation takes its toll. The purchasing power of the dollar is declining quickly and this is already being seen in higher prices across the board for fabric and construction. On top of that, new labor laws in China have caused the average worker's salary in China to double twice in the past three years. This trend will continue and the bottom line is that we will all pay higher prices for the dresses we buy and sell.

I also think the number of brides buying from a national bridal chain is closer to 50% (since the study admits that one in two purchase from an independent bridal salon) and I'm not sure how they arrived at the 29% who buy from a national bridal chain unless they are factoring the Internet sales in at 11%, which I think is too low as well.

The bottom line is that if you want to increase your sales and maintain your profit margins, you must market to more affluent markets who will be able to afford these price increases and you must get better at selling to the brides that you attract into your business on the first visit. Trying to wing it when you sell will result in declining close ratios. You have to continually train and support your bridal consultants so they are getting better at selling.

4) The lingering effects of the Great Recession that are and will continue to affect the bridal industry for years to come.

The rising cost of inventory is not the only concern bridal retailers have going forward. There have also been increases in postage costs, shipping costs, and increased costs with nearly everything in business including health care. With costs rising rapidly, sales must also rise too or your business will be in trouble very quickly. With all of the sales brides have seen over the past couple of years for virtually every product they buy, they expect more today than they ever have. This means that you have to get better at building more and more value into what you sell in ways that don't increase your expenses. If you don't do this and your sales revenues remain flat, you will fall behind very quickly with the rising cost of everything.

Entire industries were completely decimated by the Great Recession (real estate, mortgage brokers) and generalist retailers like K-Mart and Sears have been severely affected as well. Restaurants struggle with increasing costs but they aren't able to typically charge more because of the proliferation of discount menus and numerous competitors who are all trying to get individuals to eat at their place of business.

The bridal retailers who do the best in the new economy are those who can focus on niche markets where they have exclusivity (thus protecting their profit margins) and who focus on increasing their celebrity and specialization so they are better known through referrals and recommendations as the best place to get a wedding dress.

5) The changing nature of your inventory.

One of the forces that weighs and presses down every bridal retailer is bad inventory. You can't rise above the duds you've got that you keep and hold onto. Fashions change from year to year and if you are still holding onto inventory that clutters up your store that brides no longer even try on, you have got to get rid of it. I personally believe that every product you have and sell in your store should be put on trial for its life. If it isn't creating a profit, it has got to go. I recently spent time with a bridal retailer and while we studied her numbers, the decision to drop a line was made. You must make such difficult decisions in your business as well.

Continuing to market and sell old and decaying merchandise will not help your store stay or get on top.

Bill Gates, the second wealthiest business owner in the world, made the following statement: "In 3 years every product my company makes will be obsolete. The only question is whether we will make it obsolete or someone else will." This statement really got my attention. This should get your attention too. Parenthetically, every time a very successful business owner makes a statement that seems to contradict what most people in any industry think or do, I think it is critically important to pay attention to what they are saying. Peter Drucker reinforced what Gates said by saying: "Every 3 years, each product and process should be put on trial for its life, otherwise the competition will pass you by."

Imagine for a minute that a judge comes to your store and sets up his courtroom in your store. The trial has been set up to analyze every single piece of inventory in your store. One by one each dress style and sample you currently have in your store is brought before the judge and analyzed. Witnesses (the brides who have purchased these gowns) are called to make statements about the validity of your claim that the dress in question is actually selling and creating a profit for you. There can be no faking here. The truth will be discovered and inventory items that aren't producing profits or selling will be immediately eliminated.

If this scenario happened at your store, would you have any inventory left? Or would the judge and the brides who are called to testify announce the verdict that your store is relying on dress samples from 3 and 4 years ago to make the bulk of your sales when in most cases they aren't what brides in your market are even looking for any more?

The harsh reality is that if this scenario played itself out in bridal stores across the country, there would be a lot of guilty verdicts pronounced and countless items of inventory condemned. You should convene your own court and act as the judge, jury, and executioner eliminating stock that should no longer be there. Dead items should be priced to move and proven inventory that is selling should be brought back into the store as quickly as possible. Even if you are a sample store, you should carry multiples of your best sellers.

If you will have the discipline to put each product and process on trial at your store for its life, you'll be able to prune back dead and dying areas and make room for proven and promising products that will propel your growth to the top of your market niche.

General George S. Patton adopted this philosophy of constantly advancing during World War II. He never wanted his subordinates to inform him that they were holding their positions. "Let the Germans do that," he said. "We are advancing constantly and we are not interested in holding onto anything" other than what they could wrest from the enemy. "Our basic plan of operation," he said, "is to advance and keep on advancing regardless of whether we have to go over, under, or through the enemy." -- *The 21 Irrefutable Laws of Leadership: Tested by Time*, p. 216.

Remember, you are in business to make a profit. If you aren't currently making a profit with a product or a dress line (regardless of how successful it has been in the past), you are digging a slow grave, one loss at a time. Don't let the force of bad inventory hold you back from soaring to new heights. Mark it down and get rid of it. I cover several suggestions of how you can move bad inventory in my book *Bridal Profit Explosion* in Chapter 6.

6) The slow leaks in the skills of your bridal consultants.

Even if you don't have much turnover, you must continually develop and help your bridal consultants improve their skills. You can't remain static. You must continually train and help your best bridal consultants hone their skills so they become unstoppable.

I view training as a way to plug the slow leaks that develop in the skills of your bridal consultants. If you are continually training up your bridal consultants with the best ways to overcome the objections they're facing, your consultants will get better and your sales will increase. I've received great feedback from the stores who are utilizing the weekly sales training classes I've created and posted online. These 15-20 minute classes are utilized by many bridal retailers and contain helpful information designed to help your consultants increase their sales. If you aren't currently taking advantage of these weekly classes, I hope you'll start. Stores who are using these tell me that not only is the training invaluable, but it gives a great starting point for discussions about ways their consultants can improve.

On occasion, I have fired bridal consultants who have had high close ratios in the past. Such decisions are difficult. You don't want your top performers and 'A' players to feel like they are being pulled down from reaching your sales goals by those who aren't consistently selling. When such a decision is made, you show those on your team that you are serious about results.

My question for you: Are you aware of the consultants who need to be pumped up with more training whose skills have been slowly leaking out over time?

What are you doing to ensure that your consultants are always prepared and full of the best sales strategies and techniques to ensure high closing ratios?

It is wise to periodically take inventory of your bridal consultants. Ask yourself the questions I outlined earlier in this book about each of them. Then, think about where you are going. Will you be able to get there with the staff you currently have or will you need to make adjustments?

Once you've asked yourself those inventory questions, determine whether you should invest more resources into developing that bridal consultant or whether you would be better off to channel your attention and focus into a different consultant that can help you get where you want to go. When you ask yourself these types of questions, you'll find out what really matters. Then, have the courage to act on what you've discovered.

Now, I've just shared with you six of the biggest forces, shifts and changes that are going on in the bridal business today that you and I must be concerned about. Some of them are depressing and discouraging. Others are areas that you have to be vigilant about so you don't lose ground that you've worked hard to gain.

When you consider all of these shifts and changes and what's happening in the marketplace, it is no wonder that many bridal retailers feel like going crazy every now and then. So, what do you do about all of these forces, shifts and changes that are dramatically affecting the way you do business? That is what we'll cover in the rest of this chapter.

The reality is that all of these challenges can cause us to question what we are doing more often and many succumb to what Cameron Herold calls a crisis of meaning in his book *Double Double*. He says:

"When you start feeling yourself sliding into this Crisis of Meaning stage, you really do have to reach out for help....We all need to understand the feelings we're having as we're moving down the roller coaster. For women entrepreneurs, this can be a little easier since they know how to tap into that emotional intelligence and intuition from years of practice, and, frankly, it's more socially acceptable for them to do so. They're also more likely to talk to others about their feelings, whereas guys tend to think through stuff silently from our little caves. The bottom line? We all need to listen to our bodies and brains more." –p. 172.

He continues:

"When you're moving toward Crisis of Meaning, you need to be able to communicate. Say, 'Hey, I'm feeling stressed, terrified, completely anxious.' And don't feel ashamed of it; every single business owner out there goes through this stuff. I promise!"—p. 173.

Here are five BIG strategic approaches that I think you must make if you are to make more sales and more money today.

1. Add additional revenue streams within your business that strengthen your financial position.

This doesn't necessarily mean that you need to add new product lines or new product categories. When you introduce a new product category (bridesmaids, prom, tuxedos, etc.), you have another set of challenges within the business you already have and usually a learning curve as well.

One category that every bridal store should have is an advertising business within their business. This can be selling ads in a catalog or a bridal rewards package. You can even have a bride's university educational classes or bride's breakfast club where you can sell vendors the opportunity to speak in front of that targeted niche of brides. You can also sell ads within your monthly newsletter to brides as well as do profiles on certain wedding vendors to help brides see the benefit of advertising with them.

A big revenue stream that most bridal retailers miss out on is the one that comes from good follow-up. There is a cost for acquiring qualified brides who are ready to buy on their first visit. There is also a big opportunity cost that results from bridal retailers who refuse or resist marketing to brides who have already purchased one thing (that could purchase another). Since costs of acquiring brides and doing business will rise in the future, you need to have ways to have others help you defer these costs.

In years past, many bridal retailers would advertise wherever an advertising salesperson recommended that they advertise. As a result of the Great Recession, many of these same retailers have had to rethink what and where they are spending. Unfortunately, many have gravitated to only doing the cheapest things (such as spending a lot of time on social media sites) that don't always translate into a proportionate amount of sales for the amount of time that is being spent there (your time is money after all). Using it in ineffective ways decreases the amount of time you can spend in more productive and profitable ways.

2. Look for ways to expand your skills into new boundaries and market segments within your current business.

In order to sell more today, you may have to expand your boundaries to how and what you sell. Two areas in which you can expand your boundaries are:

1) Geographic and cultural expansion into different demographics

Every store has the opportunity to pull in customers from a larger geographical area. Attracting brides to come from a larger driving radius can help you achieve this goal. Another way you can gain competitive advantage in your area is by looking at completely different cultural segments of your business. There are likely cultural segments in big cities near your store that aren't being served that you could tap into and do well within.

You may be hesitant to get into different geographic or cultural niches of your are that you may not be familiar with, yet many of these sub-niches have very affluent populations within them that you can tap into. If you can meet the right connector within these niches, you can create new revenue opportunities for your business that you might not have ever considered before.

New areas of opportunity within new demographics could turn out to be a big profit center for you. My encouragement to you is to always be on the lookout for new niches you can dominate in your business.

2) Creating better experiences within your current niche that can help you reposition your store into a category of one (so brides don't want to go anywhere else).

The focus on creating new and better experiences to your current niche markets can help you grow new and better revenue opportunities within your current business and may be valuable for you to consider.

One way this can be done is by enhancing the experience brides will get at your store when they buy their dress from you by selling them or including a special membership package that allows special discounts or experiences that they'll only get at your store.

Carefully consider ways in which you can reposition what you are selling within such a new context as well. For example:

- Could you host bridal showers, bridesmaid parties, or other events at your store where you can sell additional items to the wedding party?
- Could you host a mother/daughter night out at your store?
- Could you host a father/daughter night out experience at your store?
- Could you host a wedding planning seminar where brides have the opportunity to win prizes from other local wedding vendors that you ask to be a part of your program?

Analyze your business and look at areas where you are making the most net profit in your business and look for ways within those niches where you can create enhanced or better experiences that you can expand and develop. Going into depth in these profitable areas can help you counteract some of the forces, shifts and changes in today's marketplace so you can make more sales and more money in these profitable niches.

If your business is located in one of the states that has legalized gay marriage, you may want to look at ways you can promote yourself to this emerging market.

The goal with this niche (as with all niches) is that you want to look at ways you can move up the pyramid of influence to focus on the most affluent groups who can help you expand and increase your profitability.

3. Look for ways you can align yourself and have the wedding professionals you align yourself with promote you to their list and their markets.

Each wedding professional you align yourself with has their own list to which they can promote your business to their customers. If you have them signed up as a preferred vendor at your store, are you leveraging that relationship to have them promote that they are now working with you to all of their customers? These wedding professionals all have Facebook fans, Twitter followers and other ways they stay in touch with their customers (newsletter, blogs, etc.). You can ask these vendors to share an article about your store with their customers and draw business from this.

The question to ask yourself is simply this: When you pay to promote your business, can you look for ways to get paid as well? Can you get any and all advertising venues you currently spend money with to promote your wedding gown and evening wear business to each of their customers?

What incentive could you create for these other wedding professionals so they are incentivized to promote you and get their list of brides into your store? Some serious reflection on this could create new opportunities for you to grow your current business. Don't just be content to pay others for advertising. You should also be looking for ways to promote yourself to others who pay that advertiser as well in ways that can help you capitalize on their customer lists as well. You can reciprocate the favor for them and help each other's businesses grow (especially since you aren't directly competing).

4. Find hidden money in your business.

Look for ways that you can find the hidden money in your business and bring it out so you can convert those items into cash.

You can easily bundle in-stock items together to help you move them faster. Another way to do this is to incentivize your bridal consultants when they sell certain items. Do you have discontinued gowns that you need to get rid of?

Can you bundle these types of dresses with other in-stock items you have to help you move them faster and move them out of your store?

Are there other alliances you could form with other wedding related businesses that could help you increase your sales and profits?

Every business has hidden money in it. Some thought about the assets of your business can help you uncover opportunities where you can convert them into cash.

Cameron Herold tells this story in his book *Double Double* about how they found hidden money in their business that is very instructive. He said:

"Years ago, one of my sales teams was working with a large client called Public Storage. We were doing about $180,000 of business with them annually. When we asked them how much total spending they did with us and with competitors of ours, they said they'd have to check. The following week they came back and reported that overall, company wide, they spent about $2 million. Wow! And we were getting a mere 9 percent of that!

"Imagine how the conversation changed at that point to this: 'How can we get more of your business? What do you need to see from us to spend 50 percent of that figure with us?' We knew they had the money because they told us they were spending it! Now we just had to work closely with them to have them spend it with us instead of our competitors."

He continues:

"Figure out which of your clients or prospects are doing well. Do you research, really focus on those prospects, and you'll land them without any problem. Ask your clients how much of their current business you are currently getting. Spending time with your top clients to increase revenues is easier than finding new ones. They've got money, remember, and more of it could be yours." –pp. 156-157.

The lesson I hope you learned from that story is that it is very valuable to focus on the 20% of your brides who provide 80% of your business in bridesmaid dress sales and other accessories.

Your consultants should have the courage to ask where your brides are finding or buying any other accessories they've already purchased or are considering purchasing and invite them to come back and do business with you.

The biggest source of hidden money that you are likely sitting on is converting your existing customer base into additional sales by asking them to come back into your store. One way you can do this is by incentivizing them to get their bridesmaids back into your store. For example, you could offer an additional $5 discount off every bridesmaid dress when a bride brings in a copy of her testimonial that she has posted online. Remember, the things that get rewarded get done.

If you are slow and aren't doing anything to convert leads, you are making a big mistake. Test two different offers with a small segment of your list. When you discover which one pulls in the most brides, focus more on that lead generation strategy with the rest of the brides on your list.

5. Market smarter to brides.

Educational offers are the best way to market to brides today. If you can provide information that helps each bride, she will trust you much quicker than by just sending out a specific offer.

Here are eight ways you can market better to brides today:

1) Relate to brides and target what they want most.

The key lesson to remember is simply this: Brides will suspend their disbelief about the experience of buying a dress if they feel like you relate to them AND if you target what they want most. If you don't quickly build trust and relate to her as a new bride, she will be very skeptical about whether you can actually solve her problem of finding her perfect dress. On top of skepticism, brides today are scared with all of the doom and gloom they hear in the news every day. When they aren't confident, they *have* to get their confidence from you.

Brides desperately want to have the wedding of their dreams but they are scared that they can't have it now. They are fearful that it really isn't affordable or possible. You can change all of this by being more certain and expressing that confidence through the helpful information that you share.

Here are some suggestions to create content where you can better relate to brides and express your confidence:

Create educational videos that speak to the bride and her concerns.

Create videos that are designed to answer questions you've been asked by brides and a few that you should be asked by bride. In this way, you can build each bride's confidence that you are simply the best choice to find her wedding gown.

Create several one to two minute videos that answer your most frequently asked questions and several more videos that answer questions you should be asked (that bride's don't think to ask until after they come into the store). These are great ways to help you capture attention, gain new and more pre-sold leads, and set your store apart from the competitors in your area.

Here are some questions for you to carefully consider as you put these videos together:

- What is the problem that brides in your area face?
- How can you better describe that in the advertising and marketing you do?
- How can you tell your story in such a way that brides feel that they are like you?

Enter into a conversation that is already occurring in her mind of your brides. Do your best to talk to her about what's on her mind and what she is worried about. This will help you alleviate fears and trust you more to the point that her resistance will drop and the likelihood that she will get her dress from you will dramatically increase.

Never forget where a bride is in the process of buying. There are three areas where a bride can be in the buying process and she should be marketed to differently depending on where she is. These three areas are:

- **Is she new to looking for a dress?** This is the best place for a bride to be when you are marketing to her.
- **Is she looking at several stores and looking at several options?** You will really have to build contrast when marketing to this bride to succeed in selling a dress here.
- **Has she already decided on a dress and are looking for the best price or value?** You may not be able to convert this bride at all if her mind is set on a dress and she is looking for the cheapest price (and you don't really want this customer either).

Once you've created the videos, you should post them on different areas of your web site. Each video should accessible to brides based on where they are at in the sequence or process of the sale. You want to do this for two reasons:

- You don't want your competition to see everything you're doing, especially on the back end.
- You don't want brides to see the videos out of sequence or to address issues that they might not even be worried about until it matters to them.

As your bridal consultants find out where a bride is in different steps of your marketing sequence, they can send the next link to her with a video or special report explaining what the bride should do next. These videos should be covertly positioned as educational information, but have specific marketing recommendations designed to get the bride back into your store to make an additional purchase.

You don't want to become irrelevant to the bride. In order to avoid this, you've got to provide information that keeps you relevant to her and causes her to feel gratitude for you providing the information that will help her as she plans the next step in her wedding.

2) Your offer has to stand out in comparison with what else the bride is seeing in the marketplace.

To get the best results, you need to have a very appealing offer or brides won't leave the house or their busy lives to come into your store.

Your bridal store doesn't exist in a vacuum. When advertising does cut through and gets noticed by brides, remember also that your ad is only one of the many messages that she is seeing. Brides make decisions about what to do, which store to go to, and when they should go all based on what they see (and your ad isn't the only one she is seeing). The key to cut through the clutter and get noticed is to have a compelling message that stands out so that she sees why she needs to take action now. To build contrast in a hypercompetitive environment, you have to be aware of what your competitors are doing and compete in a way that highlights your differentiating point and value.

Remember, the most successful marketing offers you can use are those that utilize appealing offers or gifts to brides. Since you are in a hypercompetitive market, you have to stand out in unique ways. What does it take to get you out of your house or business to go into a business that is marketing to you? If you are honest with yourself, it likely takes a pretty dramatic offer to incite you to action.

Brides are no different. They are busy living their lives and planning all of the details of a wedding that has become in many respects a Herculean task for even the most excited of brides. It would be so much easier to grab and keep her attention if you didn't have any competitors also trying very hard to get her to also come into their businesses instead of yours. In order to properly plan and execute great marketing campaigns, you have to have them planned out in advance *and* you have to delegate each task to a dedicated team who will work together to make them successful.

One of the reasons why a marketing calendar marked out a year in advance is so helpful and necessary today is that it allows you to have a specific strategy or promotion coming up each week or two to help to get more brides into your store. If you don't, it is easy to stop promoting the store and get into a mindset and behavior of little to no action that is not healthy.

Marketing planning of this type requires tremendous focus and discipline. One of the advantages of being a part of my coaching programs is that I help you create promotions month by month so that you can utilize them in your store. If you would like to apply to be a member of one of these coaching groups, please email me at info@bridaltrainingsystems.com with the subject line "Coaching Programs."

I think that always looking for new ways to improve is so critical and important. Staying on top of what is working is one of the benefits of reading this book as well. You should always ask questions of others to find out what is working and look carefully at what others in unrelated industries are doing to bring customers into their businesses. Never be content with how things are. Constantly seek to be learning and improving your marketing.

3) You have to use urgency and scarcity in covert ways to get brides to pay attention to you and act on your ads. Since all of us procrastinate, scarcity and urgency combined with consistency and sequenced marketing encourage decision.

All of us are busy and consumed in the multi-faceted aspects of our lives. On top of how busy we all are, we all procrastinate. We all should do more than we do on key areas of our businesses.

Brides are no different. Many brides who have been engaged for weeks or months still haven't begun the process of shopping. This isn't because they haven't been invited into a bridal store. They have likely been invited repeatedly by David's, your competitors, and probably even your own marketing offers. The problem is that unless there is a compelling reason to act, brides rarely will. When urgency and scarcity are combined, you can interrupt the daily pattern brides find themselves in and inspire them to visit your store.

On top of this, you have to use a combination of multiple offers to get their attention and encourage them to come into the store. A big marketing lesson is to make sure the brides who have already purchased something at your store come back and buy more from you. You can't take anything for granted today. Every sale matters now more than ever.

As part of your marketing system, you should have a sequence for brides who buy and a sequence for brides who don't buy. These sequences should be set up so you can send sequential communications to ensure that you aren't losing brides that have come into the store once but haven't purchased anything yet. In addition, have specific follow up phone and email sequences to ensure that brides who haven't returned to either buy their dress or buy bridesmaid dresses or other accessories from you get another appointment scheduled so they can do so.

Think carefully about how you promote yourself to the brides who have purchased from you and what you can do to get them back into your store. This can help you tremendously to ensure that you have a constant flow of brides coming into your store.

4) Perception is more important than anything else in marketing in business, period.

If you've ever spent time in David's looking at their merchandise, you've noticed that the quality of their gowns is quite different than the quality of the gowns that you offer to brides. If you haven't been into one of their stores lately, you owe it to yourself to go in and check out what they are doing. You will notice that even though the quality of the gowns is lesser than what you are offering, they are still bringing brides into their stores and selling them this merchandise. This is because David's does a tremendous job advertising and promoting their bridal stores to brides all over the country (and now internationally).

They continue to sell gowns of lesser quality year after year because they are doing a better job of creating a perception in the marketplace that their stores are the best place to shop to buy a wedding gown. This infuriates most bridal store owners because they know that the quality of the gowns they sell is so much higher than that of what is sold in David's. Perceived quality is much more important than actual quality in the mind of the brides in your area. It isn't right, but that is the way it is. You can fight these perceptions or you can go out and create your own perceptions in the minds of the brides.

5) You have to use a mix of marketing mediums to grab and keep the attention of your brides. The best way to ensure your ads get results are to be sure that they appeal to emotion and employ psychological triggers.

The more I study how the human brain reasons, the more convinced I am that the science of neuromarketing should be mastered and studied by every wedding professional who wants to maximize their effectiveness in grabbing attention and persuading brides to buy.

Since 95% of why a bride buys from you is based on a subconscious decision, it is critical to understand how to utilize these psychological triggers to get better results in your marketing and sales efforts. When you study how and why selling works, it is amazing to see how little triggers actually activate the buy switch in the bride's brain. When you understand this and use it in your marketing and selling processes, you will see dramatic results.

A valuable exercise is to watch QVC or infomercials to see if you are motivated to act or buy something. You should particularly observe and notice *why* and *consciously determine* which psychological triggers were used to create that emotional response in you when you do want to buy what is being sold. When you understand how emotion is triggered in you, you'll be better prepared to start using these triggers with the brides you work with on a daily basis.

Joe Sugarman says in his book *Triggers*:

"The real underlying psychological triggers that motivate, inspire and influence a prospect to make a buying decision are often unknown to even the most experienced salesperson. Knowledge of these triggers can be a powerful weapon in the battle for your prospect's business.

Many of the triggers are very subtle, many are exactly the opposite of what you would expect, and still others you are probably using yourself right now but don't even realize it." -- *Triggers*, p. 1.

One powerful trigger you should employ more often is the reason why. Brides know that you want their money, but they *really* want there to be another reason – so address it when you write your marketing copy. You can do this by asking and answering questions like:

- Why are we going to such an extent to make it easy for you to get the perfect dress?
- You may be wondering why we are offering such a great deal on....

It is very important to have a **reason why** to those questions. If you don't have a reason why, the bride will not trust what you have to say. Strive to include this in every promotion that you do. When you employ psychological triggers that increase desire and prompt the decision to buy, you will be more successful.

Barry Callen in his book *Perfect Phrases for Sales and Marketing Copy* says:

"Behavior is the result of fear and desire. When the desire exceeds the fear, people act. Your goal in writing sales and marketing copy is to increase desire and reduce fear." Because this is true, it is important that everything you write as you put together your marketing campaigns uses powerful emotional words that get to the heart of the matter and trigger an emotional response.

6) Stand for something. Too many people are in business, but don't know what their business is about.

As I've mentioned, the future will be bright for the specialists in unique bridal niches. Generalists (or those who carry the same lines as all of their competitors and the Internet vendors) have a big reason to fear continuing commoditization and becoming less and less relevant as time passes. Those who seek to dominate market squares or specialized market niches will be much more successful than those who continue to try to be everything for everybody. Choose to stand for something unique and exclusive instead of appealing to everybody, everywhere. It is nearly impossible to sustain any unique difference over time when you are doing what everyone else is doing.

Some serious reflection on this issue is critical to the future success of your store. Specialization will help you become more successful, more profitable, and better known in your market. Generalization, or being a me-too store, will limit you to mediocre results, miniscule profits and obscurity. Which one do you *really* want?

If you are having difficulty determining which direction your business should go in, consider what segment of the market you currently serve. Then, think about where you want to be.

Are the two compatible? You'll notice that bridal specialists who serve specific niches find themselves in the high profit, high strategic value or position in the marketplace. Bridal generalists who are constantly finding their dress prices commoditized find that they are in the low profit, low strategic value position where they have very little control.

As a generalist, the bride has control and will decide to buy from you based solely on the basis of price which usually means that your profitability will be lower.

Where are you going? What trends are influencing what you are selling?

Do you know what your business is all about?

A big question that I hope this chapter has caused you to think about is this: Are you moving in a direction that you can sustain over time?

Stores who have low profitability and a low strategic position in the marketplace are generalists. If you have been trying to be everything to everybody, I hope you can see the futility of trying to sustain this position over time. It is much better to be in a high strategic value position where brides come to you because of your recognized expertise which has higher profitability as well.

The BIG marketing lesson here is simply that the specialists are the ones who have the most sustainable position in the marketplace over time.

Where are you?

Where do you want to be?

7) Social networking is important, but is it translating into business for you based on the amount of time and effort you are putting into it? It takes time to establish and maintain a solid presence on Facebook and Twitter to remain relevant to the brides in your area.

Here are two questions you should be thinking about for your business:

- Are you using creative contests to get more fans that are cost efficient?
- Are you utilizing Facebook and Google Ad words to generate traffic to your web site and convert newly engaged brides into visitors and buyers in your business?

One bridal retailer recently sent me this email describing a Facebook promotion that netted a large number of fans in an inexpensive way. She says:

"This was a plan that cost a little bit of time in the store and a free giveaway but results were amazing! In January we wanted to increase our fan base on our Facebook page. We planned that we would have girls come into the store and pick out the dress that they would want for prom that year and took a picture of it. We then posted the pictures on our Facebook page and had people like the photo, each like was 1 vote, we ended up taking 24 pictures. To hook the girls we told them that we do sell from stock and register the dress and if that particular dress was not available when they won they would have to pick another dress of equal value. This caused 5 of the girls to put the dress in layaway the day. We put all the pictures up and voting started on March 1. In 2 weeks, we added almost 3,000 fans to our page. We realize that not all of these are girls going to prom or brides getting married soon but at any given point in time everyone of our Facebook fans will know someone close to them that is getting married and if we are name they are already familiar with and know we are experts in our field and have beautiful dresses then they may suggest they come to us.

Voting was super close and exciting and in the end 2 of the girls tied. For the number of fans I got from the experience it cost me 13 cents a fan that I am now able to market my store.

This week it came full circle as one of our brides was a friend of one of the girls in the contest and told us she had found out [about us] from the contest."

Contests are a great way to get others engaged in promoting your brand. You should think about how you could apply this and other social networking contests at your store too.

8) The store with the most social proof wins. Skepticism in the marketplace looms large (and will continue to increase). Those who capture and showcase the most persuasive testimonials will overcome this skepticism to win the battle of perceptions in your market area.

Some bridal store owners seem amazed by stores who get so many testimonials on their web site. The simple truth is this: You get testimonials because you ask for them. If brides are feeling fear and skepticism, the only way they'll get past those feelings to come into your store is if they see massive quantities of testimonials from their peers or brides who have purchased from you and who can reassure them that they can trust you as a wedding professional to help them plan the perfect wedding.

When I talk with bridal stores about this, many of them sense the need to do this, but very few are actually implementing systems in their stores to capture and disseminate these testimonials to the eyes and ears of the public. If you haven't started capturing testimonials, today is the day to begin. You can't afford to let another bride who has purchased from you leave your store without capturing either a written or video testimonial of her experience at your store (and how it compared to the other stores she visited in your area).

It is no secret that people would rather watch a movie than read a book. Brides today would rather watch a short video featuring one of her peers over reading a testimonial any day of the week. Are you providing this easily accessible experience for prospective brides to view on your blog and social networking sites? If not, start now. The bridal stores that grow quickest are those who have the most social proof. These testimonials eliminate skepticism and doubt and provide clear proof of the best place to buy a wedding or prom gown.

Every area of your store should promote how you have helped brides using their words. Have testimonials posted in your dressing rooms, at your front desk (which bridal consultants can use to overcome objections), all over your web site, and constantly look for creative ways to add more testimonials to what you are doing. Don't ignore this critical area of your marketing. The store with the most social proof in your market area *will* win. You can never have too much social proof. Never stop gathering these video and written testimonials and you will be rewarded with brides who are persuaded by their peers to do business with you.

What is weighing you down? What forces, shifts, and changes do you need to make at your store so you can be more competitive and make more sales and more money? I hope this chapter has opened your eyes to the problems bridal retailers face and what you must focus on and do going forward to take more control so you can maximize your results.

CHAPTER 4

USE BRIDAL SMARTCUTS TO ACCELERATE YOUR SUCCESS

*"I believe it's better to be first and wrong than it is to be 100% perfect
but two years too late."—Michael Dell*

In this chapter, I want to talk about ways to accelerate your growth through what author Shane Snow calls "smartcuts." A smartcut is "a way to achieve incredible results in an implausibly short time frame."

Shane Snow was a writer for Fast Company and other companies where he had the chance as a reporter to get a behind the scenes look at fast-growing start-ups like Foursquare (who grew over a period of six months from three guys with laptops to a million users, and Tumblr, whose 26-year old founder cashed out for $1.1 billion after growing it to 100 million users. He says:

"Through that work, I soon found myself inducted into more groups (from Young Entrepreneur Council and Sandbox Nework to Forbe's and Inc's 30 Under 30, TechStars, and NYCVentureFellows— programs that put ambitious innovators together)....I was in a unique spot to observe—from the inside—people who were doing crazy things at implausibly young ages or in surprisingly fast times. So, I wrote about them. And I asked myself, how do they move so fast?

He continues:

"Initially, I set out to discover the common patterns among rapidly successful tech companies, but I soon realized that their habits were simply permutations of principles smart people had been using in a variety of contexts throughout history....The step-by-step advice that made an ancient Greek hero rapidly prosperous will be entirely different from what makes a 21st century businesswoman successful, just as the exact methods an Internet startup uses to grow today will be irrelevant in five years. But the patterns of lateral thinking (smartcuts) behind each of their success stories can be harnessed by anyone who seeks an edge—at work, at the gym, in the arts of education, from social enterprise to personal development, from big companies to small start-ups."—*Smartcuts*, pp. 8-10.

There are nine patterns that he talks about in the book that are categorized into three categories: 1) Shorten, 2) Leverage, and 3) Soar. In this chapter, I'm going to discuss eight of the nine patterns as they apply to the bridal business. First, let's look at the three categories:

Shorten:
"Increasingly in today's culture, 'hacking' is something done not just by criminals and computer scientists, but by anyone who has the capability to approach a problem laterally. (This is the original usage of the term, in fact.)...Use... 'hacker' thinking to shorten paths to success...Lateral thinking doesn't replace hard work; it eliminates unnecessary cycles. Once they've shortened their path, overachievers tend to look for ways to do more with their effort."—p. 11.

Leverage:
Snow says that there are three ways to do something: the hard way, the cheap way, and the smart way. With leverage you're able to do things the smart way. The longer the lever, the less force you need to

exert to get the results you're after. What leverage points could help you get what you want in your business?

Soar:
Snow says this is like crossing the monkey bars where you swing from one handle to the next and use the chain holding the rings as a pendulum to propel you towards the next ring. Even if you have short arms or a small wingspan, you can still cross the monkey bars with enough momentum because of this principle.

So, let's get into eight patterns and how you can use them to accelerate the success of your business.

1. Jump into the game and accelerate your results by trading up. Don't follow the same steps that everyone else does to become successful. Instead, think outside the box about how to get to the result you're after.
One of the best examples of this principle is found in Gene Simmons' business book *Me, Inc.* The first KISS music album was released on February 21, 1974 and the way they got noticed and signed by their record label was ingenious. I never would have thought I would have learned so much about business from a rock and roll superstar, but his new book *Me, Inc.* is a fantastic book on what it takes to succeed in business today. He tells the story in the book about how he got noticed by the record labels, managers, music magazines, and music professionals when they first started. It is a great example of this principle which Shane Snow calls "hacking the ladder." Gene Simmons started his first band in the early 1970s with Paul Stanley. It was called Wicked Lester. The band disbanded in the summer of 1972 and Paul Stanley and he created KISS by Christmas of 1972, 'the band [they] never saw onstage, the band that [*they*] wanted to be." Gene Simmons says:

"So I began reading the music-industry trade publications *Billboard*, *Cashbox*, and *Record World*. Every week, I would see what the charts reported on what was selling and what was not. Every week, I learned

which band was playing at which concert venue and how they did financially. Every week, I would learn about different music industry figures, who they were, what they did, and how they did it."
That self-education paid off and was the foundation of his idea of how to get his new band noticed.

Simmons says:
"By early 1973, it was time to put together a press package to proclaim KISS's birth and to invite the music industry to our coming-out concert at the Diplomat Hotel's Crystal Room. We were second on the bill. The Brats, a popular local band, were the headliners. Third on the bill was a band called Luger. I wrote up a contract for all the bands to sign. I wasn't a lawyer and had no legal training. Why I thought it would be legally binding (it was) or why I thought the other bands would sign (they did) is beyond me. The contract said that each band would go on at a certain time and be off the stage by a certain time. Luger would go on at 8:30p.m. and be off by 9:15. KISS would go on at 9:30p.m. and be off by 10:30. The Brats, who were headlining, wouldn't hit the stage until 11pm. All well and good.

"...When it was time to assemble our press package, I...put together a big mailing to all of the record labels, managers, music magazines, and music professionals whose addresses I could find in the year-end issues of *Billboard*, *Cashbox*, and *Record World*.

"We made sure that none of the other bands' names were on the invites that I sent to music industry people. The press release only mentioned Heavy Metal Masters 'KISS' and our set time, 9:30-10:30. The media and music managers who showed up were undoubtedly impressed when they saw the large room filled with fans. Most of them were probably there to see the Brats, but that fact would never be known to the industry people who attended the show.

"A friend of Peter's (band mate) who worked at a printing shop did us a favor and allowed us to reproduce posters advertising our show, which Paul and I posted on the sides of buildings around Manhattan to help build word of mouth. And Paul and Peter arranged to create black T-shirts with the KISS logo in glitter, and Peter's sisters wore them at the front of the stage, screaming for us.

"Then, KISS hit the stage and tore it up. Afterward we were left with a half hour to meet and greet the music industry people and then get them out of there before the actual headliner hit the stage and our little ruse was exposed. The point: create your own hype. Whether you're in a band, or you're a mere salesman—make them believe in you. Make them believe that they are the last to the party and it's started without them. You don't have to lie, but you do have to craft an image that makes people want what you have.

"I met with Bill Aucoin right after our show at the Diplomat Hotel, and he and I sat down quickly to chat. I arranged for a girl I had been 'seeing' to sit on my lap as we spoke, to give the illusion of rock star grandeur I so admired in my heroes. And the die was cast. It worked like a charm. Bill immediately wanted to be involved. At the time, he was then producing and directing a TV show called *Flipside*, which interviewed John Lennon and other music personalities in the studio. He also produced a TV game show called *Supermarket Sweep*.

"Aucoin agreed to become our manager. Contracts were drawn up....Within six months, in the fall of 1973, we were recording our first album for Casablanca Records...We were young. We were inexperienced. And we simply couldn't believe what was happening to us."—*Me, Inc.* pp. 45-49.

Snow calls this principle "hacking the ladder." This is where you jump ahead of the line by doing things differently. In other words, you don't have to follow every step that others ahead of you have done. You have to look at the result you are looking for and look for creative ways to get the results you are after.

Snow says: "We live in an age of nontraditional ladder climbing. Not just in politics, but in business and personal development and education and entertainment and innovation. Traditional paths are not just slow; they're no longer viable if we want to compete and innovate. That's great news, because throwing out the dues paradigm leads us toward meritocracy. But to be successful, we need to start thinking more like hackers, acting like entrepreneurs. We have to work smarter, not just harder."—p. 30.

One of the principles that Snow talks about in order to get the results you are after is a scavenger hunt game called Bigger or Better that is played by students at Brigham Young University. Snow says:

"Bigger or Better is a scavenger hunt, a sort of trick-or-treating for (young) adults. Players divide into teams and begin with a small object, like a toothpick, then disperse and knock on neighborhood doors, one house after another. At each answered door, the players introduce themselves with something on the order of 'We're playing a game called Bigger or Better. Do you have something in your house that's slightly bigger or better than this...'(display object) '...that you would trade with us?'

"The first few houses are the toughest. People relaxing at night in their homes aren't often *searching* for toothpicks. Even in the friendly Rocky Mountains, a homeowner can be put off by such a request. But before long, a stranger will good-naturedly offer a piece of gum for that toothpick, and the game is on.

"At the next house, the gum becomes a ballpoint pen. At the next: a pack of Post-it notes. Then: a copy of last month's Nylon magazine. The magazine becomes a bouquet of flowers left by an unwanted admirer. The flowers get swapped for an old hat, and the hat is exchanged for a novelty T-shirt. In this phase of the game, the players benefit from a bit of curiosity, a little charity, and the fact that people were planning on getting rid of most of these objects anyway.
"But after enough trades, the players hold objects of significant value in their hands. Now the boy who opens the door sincerely wants the T-shirt. He trades his lava lamp for it. The girls next door like the lava

lamp and decide to part with a vintage mirror. The old woman down the street collects antiques; she accepts the mirror in exchange for an old BMX bike in the garage.

"When time is up, the players return home to compare results. After a dozen or so trades, teams have turned toothpicks into a stereo system, a set of golf clubs, and a television set. One group even drags in a full-size canoe. These are all actual winnings reported to me by Brigham Young University students. There's even a myth that someone once brought back a used car in Bigger or Better. And in 2005, a little farther north, a young Canadian man named Kyle MacDonald famously played an Internet game of Bigger or Better where he started with a red paperclip and eventually traded up to a house after 12 months and 14 trades."—*Smartcuts*, pp. 20-21.

What does all of this have to do with your store?

Here's the lesson. Most people won't trade something of value for something of lesser value unless it feels like a small stretch. You've got to trade something of equal value in the mind of the bride. In other words, the trade is a lateral trade. This is one of the reasons why it is difficult for many to successfully sell. They're trying to make a transaction where one party doesn't feel like they are really getting the value for their money.

Snow says that this game is successful because of "the direction they traded: sideways. The players didn't simply parlay toothpicks for pieces of wood of increasing size; they traded toothpicks for pens and mirrors for old bikes. They didn't wait around for the owners of a vacant house to show up, so they could ask for a trade, and they didn't knock on the same door over and over until a 'no' became a 'yes.' When a door was shut to them, they immediately picked another one. When the ladder became inefficient, they hacked it. And that is what made them successful so quickly. The key to Bigger or Better, in other words, is the 'or.'"—*Smartcuts*, p. 23.

What ladders have you hacked to get where you are in your business?

What ladders should you hack to get where you want to go next?

The key idea here is that following the crowd and doing what they are doing without thinking about how to hack the ladder in order to get the results you are looking for is foolish. The result is what matters.

Snow says:
 "It took the oil tycoon John D. Rockefeller 46 years to make a billion dollars. He clawed his way to the top of the 19th-century business world. Starting with a single oil refinery in 1863, over two decades, he constructed oil pipelines and bought out rival refineries until he'd build an empire. Seventy years later, the 1980s computer baron Michael Dell achieved billionaire status in fourteen years; Bill Gates in 12. In the 1990s, Jerry Yang and David Filo of Yahoo each earned ten figures in just four years. It took Pierre Omidyar, founder of eBay, three years to do it. And in the late 2000s, Groupon's Andrew Mason did it in two.

"Sure, there's been inflation since Rockefeller, but there's no disputing that we've decreased the time it takes innovative people to achieve dreams, get rich, and make an impact on the world—and this has largely been due to technology and communication...At the same time, many industries remain decidedly stuck in the past. Most large businesses stop growing after a few years. Formal education, in many cases, is so slow or out-of-date that venture capitalists pay bright people to skip school and start Internet companies. Conventional wisdom—outside of the technology industry—on innovation and career building has hardly evolved since the 19th century.

"We're multiplying our capabilities as a civilization and yet we still accept the notion that important societal progress, like combating inequality and crime—or even innovating in government and medicine—must take generations. Despite leaps in what we can do, most of us still follow comfortable, pre-prescribed paths. We work hard, but hardly question whether we're working smart.

"On the other hand, some among us manage to build eBay in the time it takes the rest of us to build a house. Pick your era in history and you'll find a handful of people—across industries and continents—who buck the norm and do incredible things in implausibly short amounts of time. The common pattern is that, like computer hackers, certain innovators break convention to find better routes to stunning accomplishments. The question is, can finding these better routes be taught?"-*Smartcuts*, p. 4-5.

"We live in an age of nontraditional ladder climbing. Not just in politics, but in business and personal development and education and entertainment and innovation. Traditional paths are not just slow; they're no longer viable if we want to compete and innovate. That's great news, because throwing out the dues paradigm leads us towards meritocracy. But to be successful, we need to start thinking more like hackers, acting more like entrepreneurs. We have to work smarter, not just harder."—*Smartcuts*, p. 30.

2. Have mentors who can help you avoid unforeseen pitfalls and see things from a different perspective. The most valuable thing mentors can do is provide feedback that focuses on the task that needs to be done and holding you accountable to that task.
Snow says:
"When the Greek adventurer Odysseus embarked for war with Troy, he entrusted his son, Telemachus, to the care of a wise old friend named Mentor. Mentor raised and coached Telemachus in his father's absence. But it was really the goddess Athena disguised as Mentor who counseled the young man through various important situations. Through Athena's training and wisdom, Telemachus soon became a great hero. 'Mentor' helped Telemachus shorten his ladder of success."-p. 37.

Mentors are very helpful in getting valuable feedback about what needs to be done next. To accelerate your growth, you want feedback that helps you focus on the task. If feedback focuses on you, you tend to take things personally and get self-conscious about what you are doing instead of actually doing the work. According to Snow, a great mentor (and this includes what you should be for your team members as well) accomplishes three things to help you successfully grow: "1) gives you rapid feedback, 2) depersonalizes the feedback, and 3) lowers the stakes and pressure so that you'll take risks and try things in new ways that force them to improve." These types of actions will actually allow you to *actually* improve. Those who are afraid to fail or looking foolish in front of others will rarely try new things.

Timothy Gallwey, a noted tennis coach, makes this observation in his book *The Inner Game of Tennis*:
"I too admit to overteaching as a new pro, but one day when I was in a relaxed mood, I began saying less and noticing more. To my surprise, errors that I saw but didn't mention were correcting themselves without the student ever knowing he had made them. How were the changes happening? Though I found this interesting, it was a little hard on my ego, which didn't quite see how it was going to get its due credit for the improvements being made. It was an even greater blow when I realized that sometimes my verbal instructions seemed to decrease the profitability of the desired correction occurring.

"All teaching pros know what I'm talking about. They all have students like one of mine named Dorothy. I would give Dorothy a gentle, low-pressured instruction like, 'Why don't you try lifting the follow-through up from your waist to the level of your shoulder? The topspin will keep the ball in the court.' Sure enough, Dorothy would try hard to follow my instructions. The muscles would tense around her mouth; her eyebrows would tighten, making fluidity impossible; and the follow-through would end only a few inches higher. At this point, the stock response of the patient pro is, 'That's better, Dorothy, but relax, don't try so hard!' The advice is good as far as it goes, but

Dorothy does not understand how to 'relax' while also trying hard to hit the ball correctly.

"Why should Dorothy—or you or I—experience an awkward tightening when performing a desired action which is not physically difficult? What happens inside the head between the time the instruction is given and the swing is complete? The first glimmer of an insight to this key question came to me at a moment of rare insight after a lesson with Dorothy: 'Whatever's going on in her head, it's too d---much! She's trying so hard to swing the racket the way I told her that she can't focus on the ball.' Then and there, I promised myself I would cut down on the quantity of verbal instructions.

"My next lesson that day was with a beginner named Paul who had never held a racket. I was determined to show him how to play using as few instructions as possible; I'd try to keep his mind uncluttered and see if it made a difference. So I started by telling Paul I was trying something new: I was going to skip entirely my usual explanations to beginning players about the proper grip, stroke and footwork for the basic forehand. Instead, I was going to hit ten forehands myself, and I wanted him to watch carefully, not thinking about what I was doing, but simply trying to grasp a visual image of the forehand. He was to repeat the image in his mind several times and then just let his body imitate. After I had hit ten forehands, Paul imagined himself doing the same. Then, as I put the racket into his hand, sliding it into the correct grip, he said to me, 'I noticed that the first thing you did was to move your feet.' I replied with a noncommittal grunt and asked him to let his body imitate the forehand as well as it could. He dropped the ball, took a perfect backswing, swung forward, racket level, and with natural fluidity ended the swing at shoulder height, perfect for his first attempt! But wait, his feet; they hadn't moved an inch from the perfect ready position he had assumed before taking his racket back. They were nailed to the court. I pointed to them, and Paul said, 'Oh, yeah, I forgot about them!' The one element of the stroke Paul had tried to remember was the one thing he didn't do!

Everything else had been absorbed and reproduced without a word being uttered or an instruction being given!

"I was beginning to learn what all good pros and students of tennis must learn: that images are better than words, showing better than telling, too much instruction worse than none, and that trying often produces negative results."—pp. 5-6.

One of the really interesting examples that Shane Snow shares in the book about the power of great feedback is where the audience gives the feedback. I think this is really important for bridal retailers and entrepreneurs because as a general rule, we don't test things enough. The story he tells is about how *Upworthy*, an Internet site designed to repackage videos and other online content into viral content that is shared spends time and effort to test the headlines to figure out what will cause people to actually watch and share a video or content online.

According to Snow:
"According to *Upworthy's* calculations, *My Last Days* (a film about Zach Sobiech – a young man with cancer and the video tribute made about his life prior to his passing) had the potential to reach a lot of people. But so far, few had seen it. The filmmaker had posted the documentary under the headline, 'My Last Days: Meet Zach Sobiech." Though descriptive, it was suboptimal packaging. In the ADD world of Facebook and Twitter, it's no surprise that few people clicked. *Upworthy* reposted the video with a new title: "We Lost This Kid 80 Years Too Early. I'm Glad He Went Out with a Bang," and shared it with a small number of its subscribers, then waited to see who clicked. "Meanwhile, *Upworthy* sent the same video with a handful of other headlines to different subscribers. For example, 'I Cried Through This Entire Video. That's OK Though, Because This Kid's Life Was Wonderful' and 'The Happiest Story about a Kid Dying of Cancer I've Ever Seen.'

"*Upworthy* watched the 'feedback' pour in, monitoring both the percentage of people who clicked each headline and the number who shared it with their friends. It was a perfect, dispassionate science experiment, where the feedback could show *Upworthy* editors exactly which packaging would have the biggest impact—before they released it to the rest of the world. In moments, the results became clear: people clicked on the third headline 20 percent more than the original. But that wasn't the end of the test. *Upworthy* wrote alternate versions of the winning headline and sent it out to several other groups. It repeated the process a ruthless 18 times, for a total of 75 variations in all...In the end, *Upworthy* tweaked the winning headline one more time: This Kid Just Died. What He Left Behind is Wondtacular." In the end, that immediate feedback resulted in more than 10 million people clicking through and watching the video.

What can you learn from that example? Well, I think a big lesson is that we don't take enough time to test out which marketing campaign headlines will have the biggest pull. Test different headlines and study what will actually cause brides to click through so you can prepare content that will yield better results, create more traffic to your site and get shared by brides more frequently, thus expanding your reach.

3. Create opportunities by placing yourself in the right place at the right time. Follow the 80/20 rule in everything you do.
Snow says:
"The difference between catching a wave and getting crushed or passed by [in surfing] is a matter of centimeters, which means the chance of being in the exact right spot in that water to grab a big wave without *any* effort is akin to winning at Powerball. Being in the water when a good wave comes requires maneuvering into precise position. "Surfers make it seem easy. The good ones can recognize the roll of incoming waves, so they can position themselves in the perfect spot to catch them. And at the last minute, a surfer will paddle vigorously to align herself with the wave and match its speed. Luck is often talked about as 'being in the right spot at the right time.' But like a surfer, some people—and companies—are adept at placing themselves at the right place at the right time. They seek out opportunity rather than wait for it."—p. 106.

What are examples of being in the right place at the right time in the bridal business?

- Anticipating trends and actually having the right silhouettes and style of dresses in your store when it becomes hot
- Building and capitalizing on social media buzz
- Spending time developing the 20% of your business that accounts for 80% of your results – actually determining what these areas are and then capitalizing on them in your business

Perry Marshall talks about the 80/20 Power Curve in his excellent book *80/20 Sales and Marketing*:

"The first thing to understand about economics is it's 80/20 all the way up and down. If we line up 100 customers from least able to buy to most able to buy, AND least tempted by your proposition to most tempted, HERE is how they stack up. A lot of people assume their customers are all roughly equal. They are not—not even close! That's the 80/20 Power Curve in action. This example assumes that the average customer spends $100, and you collected a total of $10,000. Here you will see that the least interested person wants to spend $27. The most interested person will spend $1,426 (notice he's way past the top of the chart). So, the most interested person will spend 50 times more money than the least interested one. It's also interesting to notice the people who actually spend the average amount, which is $100, are people near the 'top 20 percent' mark. In other words—only 20 percent of these customers represent a serious opportunity for you. Handy rule of thumb: 80/20 says that 20 percent of the people will spend 4 times the amount of money. It also says that 4 percent of the people will spend 16 times the money. Memorize this—it's one of the most powerful facts that you could ever know about business."— *80/20 Sales and Marketing*, pp. 92-93.

He explains the 80/20 rule as follows:

"A few years ago I held a seminar in Chicago called 'The 80/20 Seminar for Direct Marketing.'...It cost $3,000 to attend and I had about 80 people in the room. All of them ran businesses of one kind or another, most of them online. To illustrate the all-pervasive nature of 80/20, I said, 'Everybody stand up if you have shoes on.' Everyone stood. I said, 'If you own fewer than 4 pairs of shoes, please sit down.' A bunch of people sat down, and about 50 were still standing. 'If you own fewer than 8 pairs of shoes, sit down.' More people sat down, about 30 left. 'If you own fewer than 16 pairs of shoes, sit down.' Thirteen people, 9 of them women, still standing.

"'32 pairs of shoes.' Three women standing. I smiled. 'Don't be embarrassed ladies. Just tell the truth, cuz I'm illustrating a principle here. How many of you have more than 64 pairs of shoes?' Two sit down. One left standing. She cringes with embarrassment. 'How many shoes do you have?' 'Umm, about 80.' 'Thank you so much. You can sit down now. Give this woman a hand!' Everyone clapped. '20 percent of the people own 80 percent of the shoes. Can you see that?' I said. All nodded in agreement.

" 'Everybody stand up again—everyone who owns at least one domain name.' They were all marketers, so it was pretty much everybody. 'Sit down if you own fewer than 10.' Half the room sits down. 'Fifty.' Half sits down again. We've got maybe 20 still standing. 'Two hundred.' A bunch more sit down, 10 standing. 'Five hundred.' Five people left. I keep going—1,000, 2,000, 5,000.

"At 5,000 domain names, I've got two people left. At 10,000, one guy sits down. Mickie Kennedy from Baltimore, one of my best customers, is the only one left standing. 'How many domain names do you own? 'Twelve thousand.'

"Mickie was a 'Domainer,' the domain-name equivalent of flipping real estate. He owned entire portfolios of domain names, some selling for tens of thousands of dollars. 20 percent of the people owned 80 percent of the domain names, and in a room of 80 people, one guy owned nearly half. Almost everything is like that....If you can see 80/20 at work in this list, you can see it in any part of your business. Once you've learned to recognize it, you can't not see it. Look at the tree outside your window: 80% of the sap travels through 20 percent of the branches."—pp. 1-3.

He continues:

"The Power Curve shows you why McDonald's always sells small, medium, and large drinks. It's because people's capacity to consume varies widely. As you'll see in a minute, though $1.00 for small, $1.40 for medium, and $1.85 for large barely scratches the surface of people's true differences. But most important, the Power Curve shows you the almost limitless capacity of the top 1 percent. Which brings us to...The Principle of the $2,700 Espresso Machine.

"Let's say 1,000 people walk into a Starbucks shop today. The least anyone will spend is $1.40 for a 'Tall' Coffee of the Day. Let's plug those numbers into the Power Curve and see what it tells us. One thousand visitors means 1,000 members. The 1,000[th] member (the lowest-spending person in the lineup) spent $1.40. We enter the data like this at www.8020curve.com.

"The tool predicts the customer wants to spend $537 at Starbucks today. How does a person spend $537 at Starbucks? Do they buy 100 lattes? No. They buy three lattes, two blueberry scones, and one espresso machine! As I'm writing this, Starbucks' web site features two espresso machines (the Musica Lux by Nuova Simonelli for $2,699.95 and the Aroma Espresso Machine by Saeco for $275.00).

"Starbucks 10X spread between the ordinary machine and the extraordinary machine is no accident, by the way. Them folks at Starbucks ain't dumb. They understand Power Laws...The Espresso Machine is a paramount strategy of successful business. Yes, you can always find companies that ignore it. But most of them aren't doing well, and the Power Curve virtually guarantees you that they are leaving money on the table.

"Hotels have $1,200-per-night suites on the top floor. Airlines have red carpet clubs for their top 20 percent customers. International flights offer $10,000 first class seats and $20,000 luxury sleeping pods.

For the airlines, that sure is nice compared to getting $385 for a seat in coach.

"The book *Whale Hunt in the Desert* by Deke Castleman describes how Vegas casinos get 20 percent of their income from a super-elite class of gamblers called 'Whales.' Whales fly in on private jets and bet $100,000 on a single round of blackjack. Casinos lavish Whales with dedicated staff, perks, amenities, and high-end luxuries that are virtually invisible to every other guest in the hotel.

"80/20 doesn't just work in Vegas. A tiny $1-million charity will most likely get $100,000 of its donations from one single trust, foundation or individual donor. A $200,000 per man one-man tax practice can and should get $20,000 of business from a single customer.

He then shares this thought:
"This is not merely about selling to the affluent, or conspicuous consumption, though you should never ignore either of those things. That's because the Espresso Machine Principle applies to all aspects of product and service sales:
- How much the unit costs.
- How often they come back and buy more. One espresso machine buyer in 50 will buy another one every week. (Probably not at Starbucks, but they'll buy it somewhere).
- How many units they buy at one time. One espresso machine buyer in 50 is gonna want 100 units all at once.
- People who buy units in quantity, and often. One espresso machine buyer in 2,500 will want 100 units every week."—p. 95-96.

So, what does this mean for you? Well, consider the following about your brides:
- Repeat buyers: of the brides who buy more than once, 20 percent of them are responsible for 80 percent of the repeat purchases.

- Money: 80 percent of your total sales comes from 20 percent of the buyers
- Quantity: 20 percent of the orders represent 80 percent of the quantity (in other words, 20 percent of your brides are also buying bridesmaids, renting tuxedos, and buying everything you offer).

Marshall continues:

"What this means is that if all you sell is scones and cups of coffee ranging from $1 to $5, your business is probably doomed. And if it's not doomed, you're destined to earn a meager living and barely scrape buy.

"The principle of the $2,700 espresso machine applies to almost anything you might choose to sell. That means you can add a $290 product and a $2900 product, and you'll probably double your sales. If you have thousands of customers, the spread will be even wider. Many businesses do not have product offerings spanning a 100:1 range, so they're missing all kinds of opportunities to sell to their existing customers.

"When you take full advantage of this, your sales and profits immediately go up, making it easier for you to go get more customers."—p. 97-98.

Here are some questions for you to think about when you consider this bridal smartcut. How are you going to catch the wave that will carry you farther and give you a sustainable advantage?

- If the average wedding dress is selling for $1,355, do you have a $13,500 offer for one bride who absolutely has to have it?
- What are you doing to ensure that the 20% of the brides who will buy everything you have are actually doing so? Are your follow-up systems in place?
- When you consider all that you sell in your store, do you see the 80/20 rule in effect?
    - 20% of your vendors account for 80% of your sales

- o 20% of your salespeople account for 80% of your sales
- o 20% of your brides buy 80% of your bridesmaid sales
- o 20% of your brides rent 80% of your tuxedo volume
- What kinds of packages could you put together to incentivize brides to take action and do more business with you? Remember, you want your offer to be so compelling that brides can't say no.
- Think about how you utilize your time. If you pay yourself or someone on your team, $20/hour, that means that that person is worth at least $1000 per hour at least one minute of every day. Spend more of your time doing things that will pay you the highest value for your time.

Are you placing yourself in the right place at the right time?

Are you carefully watching market conditions to find the good waves and getting in the water and maneuvering yourself towards the best waves to get the best lift and accelerate your success?

Like the best surfers, the best retailers are those that move to where the best market conditions exist. Don't ignore this critical rule to make one of the most important smartcuts of all.

4. Be a superconnector. Look to align yourself and give to others in a way that helps them give back to you.
Snow says:
"Which is easier—making friends with a thousand people one by one or making friends with someone who already has a thousand friends? Which is faster—going door to door with a message or broadcasting the message to a million homes at once? This is the idea behind what I call superconnecting, the act of making mass connections by tapping into hubs with many spokes..."

"Imagine you're at a party and you don't know any of the other guests. You look around at the dozens of people and, if you're extroverted, you'll probably strike up a conversation with someone nearby. If you're a little more timid in unfamiliar territory like I am, you might wander around in hopes that someone strikes up a conversation with you. Now imagine that a friend of yours shows up. She happens to know everybody at the party and she decides to take you around and meet everyone you should know. You soon meet a dozen people, with very little effort. Your friend is a superconnector."—p. 127.

Who are the superconnectors in the wedding business for you in your area?

You should write their names down and figure out what you can give to them to help them so they'll want to introduce you to their networks.

Consider this example of J.J. Abrams, one of Hollywood's most successful directors:

"Born in New York City, with a Super 8 film camera already in his infant arms, Abrams had spent his entire life wanting to make movies. By his early 40s, he'd become one of the most successful and sought-after directors in the business, and possibly the most powerful man in sci-fi since Steven Spielberg. Abrams had created the hit TV shows *Alias* and *Lost*, directed *Mission Impossible* and *Star Trek* films, and made a movie with Spielberg himself. And now, Abrams had been anointed heir to George Lucas's legacy, meanwhile launching and maintaining a dozen other high-profile directorial projects. But before all that, like most artists, Abrams struggled to get his first break.

"He wrote nine screenplays that went nowhere. 'I think each one was worse than the one before it,' he once told author Steven Priggé. 'I couldn't do it.' Then he ran into a writer friend, Jill Mazursky, whose father was a well-connected movie director. Abrams proposed that Mazursky and he co-write a script and that she work her father's network to get it into some high-profile hands. The plan worked, and Abrams's first screenplay became *Taking Care of Business*, starring Jim Belushi.

"This is the classic Hollywood networking story: make friends with people who have connections and work them to your advantage. Be nice to them when you need them, then move on. When we look at Abrams's subsequent film credits, we can see that the method worked well for him. He collaborated with bigger and better writers and directors and actors, from Harrison Ford to Michael Bay, and used their credibility (Sinatra style) and networks to work his way up the Hollywood chain. But then something curious happened. The self-serving Hollywood networking theory starts to break down when we look at Abrams's credits from after he became wildly successful; it turns out that even once he was on top, he continued to cowrite, codirect, and cocreate almost all his projects. He started lending his own Sinatra-style credibility to less known but talented writers and directors and actors, so they could climb their ladders faster...."

"Abrams is known, acquaintances tell me, for his kindness and lack of ego, in addition to his penchant for mystery. That's how he attracts the best people to his staff. And that's how he's managed to climb so far so fast...Initially, Abrams helped out better-connected people than himself, and doing so helped him superconnect. But once he was the superconnector, he still helped people. That's how to tell if someone is a giver, or a taker in giver's clothing." —*Smartcuts*, pp. 131-133.

What are you giving to brides to build trust with them?

What are you giving (or should you be giving) to other wedding professionals in your area so they want to introduce their brides to you?

Here are several ideas:
- Give your time and expertise once a month and put together a wedding planning seminar to help brides in your area – unite with top vendors in each category – share the cost of the venue and share the leads – get to know one another by helping one another

- Give brides useful and helpful information to help them with the confusing and overwhelming process of planning a wedding. There is no reason why you can't help them better prepare and introduce them to the best wedding professionals. This can be done through a blog, a web site, a newsletter, a podcast, or an event.
- Create a networking event for local wedding professionals. The entrance fee could be five leads per individual. If you have 20 wedding professionals come, you all now have 100 new leads to work to offer your products or services.

Choose to be a superconnector. It is a bridal smartcut that will pay you huge dividends and help you accelerate your success.

5. Build better perceptions and momentum. Understand and leverage the eleven assets you have at your bridal store in ways that help you maximize your potential and power.
To grow your business, you need to better leverage the assets you have. Your own individual assets aren't enough.

To help you better understand how you can leverage your business assets, I've listed the eleven biggest assets any bridal store has (regardless of size) below. I'll also ask you to think about both sides of the leverage spectrum and why one store has more power and leverage than another (with the same asset). I'll also ask you to carefully think about how you can better leverage these assets at your store.

Take the time to carefully think about what I am going to ask you here. You won't ever develop these assets and use them to gain more leverage unless you embrace the new realities of what I'm trying to communicate to you here first.

Then, and only then, will you move past belief to take action and develop these assets into better leverage points to launch your business to a higher level.

1) Your brand identity and all of your intellectual property (business name, brand identity, logo, etc.)
Which has more power and leverage? A store that relies on the manufacturers of the lines they carry to brand them OR the store who builds their own brand and then leverages it in many ways?

Why? How can you better leverage this asset at your store?

2) Your status as an authority figure, celebrity specialist
Who has more power and leverage in the bridal business?
Vera Wang OR any competitor that isn't well known or thought of as an expert or authority? Kleinfeld Bridal OR the me-too bridal store?

Why? How can you better leverage this asset at your store?

3) Your processes and systems
Which has more power and leverage? A store with no processes and systems OR a store with well thought out processes and systems that anyone can run (without the owner having to be there all of the time)

Why? How can you better leverage this asset at your store?

4) Your brand reputation in your market
Which has more power and leverage? A bridal store known for what they carry OR a bridal store known for the experience brides have at there?

Why? How can you better leverage this asset at your store?

5) Your bridal consultants and staff
Which has more power and leverage? A well-trained bridal consultant who sells 3 out of every four brides OR a poorly trained bridal consultant who sells 1 our of every four brides>

Why? How can you better leverage this asset at your store?

6) Your brides (who have already purchased from you)
Which has more power and leverage? A store who is content to just sell the wedding gown to a bride OR a store who consistently invites and sells to brides who buy and asks for referrals after every sale?

Why? How can you better leverage this asset at your store?

7) The territory you hold with certain bridal / prom lines
Which has more power and leverage? A store with no exclusive lines that carries what everyone else and Internet vendors carry OR a store who carries what no one else has and what can't be found online?

Why? How can you better leverage this asset at your store?

8) Your connections (people brides in your area should know but don't)
Which has more power and leverage? A store who introduces brides who buy from their store to the top wedding vendors in their area (and charges these vendors for this opportunity) OR a store who knows top wedding vendors, but doesn't take the time to introduce brides to them (because they are too busy or because brides will meet these vendors on their own)?

Why? How can you better leverage this asset at your store?

9) Investments (Inventory)
Which has more power and leverage? A store with limited inventory that doesn't have a lot of depth of selection or sizes for brides to try on OR a store with depth of inventory so brides can try on dresses in their own size?

Why? How can you better leverage this asset at your store?

10) Your relationships with key vendors and suppliers.
Which has more power and leverage? A store who barely knows their key vendors OR a store who really gets to know their key vendors and spends their time and money (through purchases) to build better

relationship?

Who do you think gets more attention when challenges come up? How can you better leverage this asset at your store?

1) Toll positions – Will others pay you to be in front of your brides (who they want to sell to as well)?

Which has more power and leverage? A store who gives access to their brides for free (handing out business cards and flyers to brides just because business owners dropped by) OR a store who helps build bridge between their brides and the other wedding businesses that want to be in touch with those brides (and charge for the opportunity)?

Why? How can you better leverage this asset at your store?

When you leverage the assets you have in your store, you can create better perceptions and accelerate the speed at which you build momentum.

6. Build a better and more compelling offer. Make sure you create vivid pictures that act as a smartcut to help brides visualize themselves using what you are selling.
"Arizona State psychologist (and best-selling author) Robert Cialdini once attended a training program for insurance salesmen as part of a research project on social influence. The attendees were given an article titled, 'Add a Picture—Make a Sale' that laid out some of the most successful selling strategies in the industry. The instructor explained this technique to his new recruits as follows:

'If you are selling life insurance, start by getting 'em alone in a quiet place and making 'em imagine that they just totaled the car. If you are selling health insurance, first make 'em suppose that they're laid up in the hospital too sick to work. If you're selling theft, get 'em to think how it would be to come home from vacation and find everything gone. And take 'em through every picture, every step along the way."
–*The Art of Woo*, pp. 188-189.

What vivid pictures can you help paint in the bride's mind to escalate the value of what you are selling her?

"People tend to think that things they can easily visualize are more likely to happen. If an airplane crashes or a hurricane blows ashore, the sale of flight and flood insurance goes up because people have recent, vivid images in mind that planes sometimes go down and big storms sometimes cause severe damage. Moreover, the more 'available' an idea is, the more people believe it to be true....To see is to remember, and to remember is to believe." – *The Art of Woo*, p. 189.

Here are several ways you can create more vivid pictures for brides as you sell to them:
- *Posters* - Put posters all over your store of happy brides in dresses. These vivid pictures help brides to imagine themselves on their wedding day. The posters should also depict your best selling gowns. This 'availability' will helps you put ideas of potential dresses that brides could wear into her mind. This is value that you can create since most other stores don't have any posters or images of brides in their store. This works even better when the images are your own that you created so you can brand your store.
- *Ask more direct questions that help brides picture their wedding day in their mind.* Ask: "Can you imagine...?" or "What will it be like when...?" questions help you to do this.
- *Capture video testimonials of brides talking in visual pictures.* Ask brides who have purchased their dress from you to talk about what their wedding day will be like in the dress they've chosen that day. When future brides watch these videos on your web site or in your store, they will see an 'available' picture that will help themselves begin picturing their perfect day.

Here are two questions you can ask to help brides talk in more visual pictures:
- Where will you be getting married? or How did you choose to get married at _____? (the place they've already told you)

- How will the dress you've chosen today help you create the wedding you've always imagined?

In the example I just mentioned of the insurance agents, what could you do to help the bride better imagine herself wearing one of your dresses in a vivid way for her wedding? Carefully consider this question and how you are painting pictures in the minds of the brides you are working with.

This is just part of creating a compelling offer. You've got to show why your offer is better than anyone else. It's got to be simple and compelling.

Snow says:
"Sometimes bigger is not better. Sometimes more of a good thing is too much. Sometimes the smartest step is a step back....Simplification often makes the difference between good and amazing."—pp. 160-161.

At a recent Quantum Leap Day meeting (a twice yearly meeting I conduct with those in my coaching groups), we talked about experimenting with offers that are more simple. For example, you could have a sale, where you have fewer price points and a simple, yet compelling offer. For example, when a bride buys one of your sale dresses (priced at one of three price points), she can also get a free in-stock veil or tiara with the purchase of the gown. The three price points are: $499, $749 and $999. Look at your offers. Could you make them more simple?

In his book *Niche Selling: How to Find Your Customer in a Crowded Market*, author Bill Brooks makes the following observation: "**People who are confused and outnumbered rarely make buying decisions.**"

Is your offer compelling and easy to understand? Building a better offer will help you refine and strengthen this smartcut for you and your business.

7. Ask for the sale. Master the process of selling and be sure to ask.
To master something implies that you are working at it all of the time.
You aren't content with what you knew before. You keep learning
and figuring out what works, and what doesn't.

When I speak with bridal retailers, I often ask those bridal store
owners in attendance how many of them are asking for the sale more
than once when selling. My informal survey revealed that many store
owners and their bridal consultants aren't even asking once for the
sale. Teach your bridal consultants to ask for every sale at least five
times with each bride. When you require this, you'll make more sales
since most sales today are happening on the third request. If you are
only asking once or not at all, you will not make the sale. There is
more resistance in selling today, and if you aren't asking more, you are
losing a lot of sales. You are getting the bride ¾ to almost all of the
way sold and then letting her leave so that she is nearly over her
resistance to buy. Then, she ends up buying at the next bridal store
she goes to. Your competitors are thankful because you have worn
down the bride's resistance for them so it is easier for them to make
the sale because of your efforts.

Don't make this mistake. Train your consultants to ask for the sale at
least five times with every sale they make. Without fail, the brides who
aren't buying are only being asked once or twice. This helps the bridal
consultants to see the importance of persisting and overcoming the
bride's objections until she buys. Train your bridal consultants to
implement the sales training they have been taught. Give them the
tools to persistently ask for the sale at least five times. When you do,
you'll see your sales and closing percentages go up and you'll be
ecstatic about the result.

A great example of this principle is that of pitchman Arnold Morris as
recounted by Malcolm Gladwell in *The New Yorker*:

"The last of the Morrises to be active in the pitching business is
Arnold (the Knife) Morris, so named because of his extraordinary

skill with the Sharpcut, the forerunner of the Ginsu. He is in his early seventies, a cheerful, impish man with a round face and a few wisps of white hair, and a trademark move whereby, after cutting a tomato into neat, regular slices, he deftly lines the pieces up in an even row against the flat edge of the blade.... Arnold wasn't merely entertaining; he was selling. "You can take a pitchman and make a great actor out of him, but you cannot take an actor and always make a great pitchman out of him," he says. The pitchman must make you applaud and take out your money. He must be able to execute what in pitchman's parlance is called "the turn"--the perilous, crucial moment where he goes from entertainer to businessman. If, out of a crowd of fifty, twenty-five people come forward to buy, the true pitchman sells to only twenty of them. To the remaining five, he says, "Wait! There's something else I want to show you!" Then he starts his pitch again, with slight variations, and the remaining four or five become the inner core of the next crowd, hemmed in by the people around them, and so eager to pay their money and be on their way that they start the selling frenzy all over again. The turn requires the management of expectation. That's why Arnold always kept a pineapple tantalizingly perched on his stand. "For forty years, I've been promising to show people how to cut the pineapple, and I've never cut it once," he says.

"It got to the point where a pitchman friend of mine went out and bought himself a plastic pineapple. Why would you cut the pineapple? It cost a couple bucks. And if you cut it they'd leave."

One story that is particularly interesting about the importance of sales mastery:
"Arnold says that he once hired some guys to pitch a vegetable slicer for him at a fair in Danbury, Connecticut, and became so annoyed at their lackadaisical attitude that he took over the demonstration himself. They were, he says, waiting for him to fail: he had never worked that particular slicer before and, sure enough, he was massacring the vegetables. Still, in a single pitch he took in two hundred dollars. "Their eyes popped out of their heads," Arnold recalls. "They said, `We don't understand it. You don't even know

how to work the damn machine.' I said, `But I know how to do one thing better than you.' They said, `What's that?' I said, `I know how to ask for the money.' And that's the secret to the whole damn business." --http://gladwell.com/2000/2000_10_30_a_pitchman.htm

A question for you to consider: How much time have you spent or do you spend on getting better at selling and training your bridal consultants to utilize the sales scripts that will help you succeed?

What difference in results is there between a staff of trained bridal consultants over those with little to no training who wing it when the phone rings or when working with brides?

8. Don't give into fatigue. To accelerate success, you've got to keep working and keep at it. Strive to 10X your efforts in the right areas to get better results.
Sterling W. Sill makes this observation in an essay he wrote on The Law of Idleness. He said:
"It's a natural law that out of idleness comes weakness. Nature hates idleness in all its forms. She gives continuous life only to those elements which are in use. Tie up an arm or any other part of the body in uselessness and the idle part will soon become lifeless. Reverse the order and give an arm more than normal use, such as the activity engaged in by the blacksmith who wields a heavy hammer all day long, and the arm grows strong. This law governs physical, mental, spiritual, social, and personality development. It says that the way to growth is activity, whereas the way to death is idleness. Running water purifies itself, but the stagnant water of an inactive pond becomes impure and unhealthy, and so do the cells of a sluggish body or an inactive brain. Laziness is the influence of an inactive mind upon the cells of the body.

"Nothing is more common than mental inertia. For every ten people who are physically lazy there are ten thousand with stagnant minds, and stagnant minds are breeding places of fear, ignorance, sin, and crime. The person who is active generates power and breeds courage.

The one who has power in his righteousness has little to fear, while the unprofitable servant allows his fear to destroy his faith. We can build up our faith and our industry to where it will eliminate our fear.

He continues:
"Don't worry about getting tired, for weariness usually does not come from overwork, but from lack of interest in what you are doing. The muscles never grow fast until we give them so heavy usage. The possession of potential power and the use of it are two different things. The use of our strength makes us powerful, while the pursuit of easy things makes us weak. It is seldom the work we do that makes us tired. Most likely are we tired because of the work we have left undone. "When things are really clicking for us, we seldom get tired, and we can then accomplish many times the work we previously did. Fatigue is caused not by work but by worry, frustration, and resentment. The kite always rises against the wind, not with it. The strongest oak tree of the forest is not the one that is protected from the storm and hidden from the sun, but the one that stands in the open where it is compelled to struggle for its existence against the winds and rains and scorching sun. A great oak struggling in the wind sends down a stronger root upon the windward side...When we are struggling we grow. When we retire so that we can take things easy, we are usually on our way out. The law of success says that idleness always leads to deterioration and death, and these should be avoided by those who would be strong."—*How to Personally Profit from the Laws of Success*, pp. 81-84.

Remember what Grant Cardone said in his book *The 10 X Rule*: "Big thinking, massive actions, expansion, and risk taking are necessary for your survival and future growth. Staying small and quiet are just ways to continue being small and quiet. Keep thinking this way, and sometime in the very near future, no one will be able to see you, hear you—or be aware that you ever existed. Commit to 10X thinking and 10X action. This is the major difference between success and the alternative. It is not about intelligence, economics, or even who you know—because without massive action, none of those things matter."—pp. 202-203.

Everyone has bad days in the wedding business. You may have just experienced a day like this when nothing seemed to click and you weren't selling like you wanted. Everyday isn't perfect. It takes perseverance to get back up and go into the store when you've left the previous day absolutely frustrated with what happened. But, having the faith to go on and the resolve to succeed no matter what is at the heart of what will help you grow your business and get it to where you want it to be. But, when you persist through your failure and learn what works and what doesn't in selling, you can come out victorious in the end. You can learn how to approach brides, how to present gowns in a way that emotionally involves them and trigger decision by the questions you ask and the things you say. You can persist through any last minute objections and continually ask for the sale until it happens.

I think my favorite quote on the importance of persisting is by boxing champion Mohammad Ali who said: "Inside a ring or out, ain't nothing wrong with going down. It's staying down that counts."

We all get discouraged by bad days from a mistake we've made or from a bad day at the store. How we bounce back from those adversities to persist on is a lot of what the greatest selling secret is all about. Jay Chiat, who helped found the legendary Chiat/Day advertising agency said: "Everybody's got to have failures. The point is how long are you going to remained depressed? If it's a week, you really have a problem. With me, it's about an hour-and-a-half max, and then I get on with it. The ability to handle your failure and continue on, without getting depressed or diverted, is important." -- Richard St. John, *8 To Be Great*, p. 201.

Don't let failure or discouragement stop you from getting back up and going at it again. Your ability to persevere will have more of an impact on your ability to sell and to utilize the smartcuts I've discussed in this chapter than any other single thing. When you make the determination to persevere, you will rise above your difficulties and you will experience the thrill of success.

Use these bridal smartcuts to accelerate your success. You can think and act smarter in your business. You can accelerate your growth and hack the ladder by choosing smart actions that can get you to where you want to be faster. You can do it and these principles I've discussed in this chapter will help you get there.

Chapter 5

Be More Persuasive and Push for the Sale Without Being Pushy

"It's not what you've got, it's what you use that makes a difference."—Zig Ziglar

Persuasion, and your ability to use it effectively, is a big key to succeeding as a bridal retailer. You have undoubtedly used persuasion skills every time you have negotiated a lease, a territory with a manufacturer, or dealt with any bride who wanted to purchase something from you. The principles of persuasion are the same whether you are dealing with a bride, her mother, or any other customer you interact with. If you are going to get better at marketing your bridal store and selling to the customers who come through your doors, you must master the skills of persuasion. My goal in this chapter is to help you be more persuasive so you can sell more and get what you want more of the time.

I want to carefully explore each of these ten principles so you and each of your bridal consultants can become better persuaders. The ideas and principles are from a wide variety of books and people I've studied and learned from over the years. Three of the most important books

I'll quote from extensively here are *Perusasion IQ* by Kurt Mortensen, *27 Powers of Persuasion* by Chris St. Hilaire and *Split-Second Persuasion* by Kevin Dutton. Here are the most important principles of persuasion you must master if you want to build a more prosperous and successful bridal store.

1. Understand the motivation of the bride you are trying to persuade _before_ you begin persuading her.
Chris St. Hilaire makes this point in his book, *27 Powers of Persuasion*: "In order to persuade, you have to understand the people you're persuading. At the most basic level, that means understanding how the ego works and learning to recognize when someone is feeling threatened. A threatened person is not going to be open to your ideas, which is why many of the powers [of persuasion] are geared toward making people feel safe and included. So you must learn to identify who is feeling safe and who is not. You are part of the dynamic, so you have to pay attention to your own ego too." --p. 5.

He continues:
"To evaluate other people's egos, you can start by realizing that when they walk into the room, their biggest concern will be how you will make them feel. Will you ask their opinion or ignore them? Lighten their load or ruin their week?...No one is immune to feeling insecure. Throughout the conversation, whether they are conscious of it or not, your listeners will be shifting between feeling threatened and feeling safe." –pp. 7-8.

The key point is this: when a bride feels safe, she will open up to being persuaded. When she feels threatened that you are trying to sell to her, she will close herself off to any attempt at persuasion you attempt. A lot of what you do in your initial approach when she comes into the store (and particularly in your pre-sales efforts *before* she comes into the store) will help her relax and open up to the experience you will create at your store.

What causes a bride to close herself off to any attempt at persuasion?

It is usually an emotional reason. If you don't address it and help her to feel safe again, you will never be successful in persuading her to buy from you. I once talked with a bride who loved a dress but just couldn't commit to buy the dress on her first visit. I stepped back and said, "I know you love this dress. What is it that is holding you back from going ahead and getting the dress you love?" She finally opened up and told me the reason that was holding her back. She told me that she had just been offered a package deal at another bridal salon that she had just been to. When she finally opened up and shared this detail with me, then we were able to have an honest conversation about how our total offer compared with what she would get from the other store. It was amazing to see her face and her shoulders physically relax when she finally told me what the real concern was. It was an emotional fear of losing out (because of the total package of what she would get including flower girl dresses that we don't offer). When I told her of a place in town where she could get flower girl dresses with the money she was saving on her dress (the $100 by buying on her first visit), I could see that she was open to be persuaded. If I wouldn't have known what her concern was and I kept pushing for the sale, I would have lost it (and probably never known why). As it turns out, we had a great discussion about her wedding and how the dress she loved at our store would help her create the experience she wanted. She ended up buying that dress. The BIG lesson is this: When you feel that a bride is closing herself off, stop selling, and start asking questions to find out what her concern *really* is. When you know what is really going on, you can be helpful and persuasive. Without that information, you'll be dead in the water.

One motivation or de-motivation of brides that causes them to wait to buy is because of resistance. It is so important to understand the two types of resistance that your brides have and how to overcome these in order to become persuasive.

Kevin Hogan explains: "Broadly speaking, there are two kinds of resistance. The first is because of reactance (a knee-jerk deflection of anything that infringes on our personal choice or freedom), and the second is because of anticipated regret of complying or failing to comply with a request." – *The Science of Influence*, p. 91.

In other words, brides don't buy on their first visit usually because they don't want the purchase to limit them from other dress options they could see if they waited. In order to overcome this, you must understand this motivation and sell against it (so they see that waiting will cause them to regret that decision later on). You can do this by offering an incentive for buying on the first visit. This incentive can be combined with additional bonuses a bride will get from other wedding vendors and your referral program on top of the dress so that the total savings and benefits *far outweighs* waiting. This eliminates the resistance of reactance. If you don't have something like this in place at your store, you should put together your own incentive that will help you cut through resistance.

Most brides aren't very good at predicting what emotions they will feel when they make a choice that doesn't work out the best for them. Many of these brides choose to leave without buying the dress they loved even though their bridal consultant attempts to overcome their desire to look elsewhere. A bridal consultant can be effective by sharing specific examples of what has happened to brides who have already made this choice and who chose to wait. This causes brides to actually experience the emotion of what it might feel like to lose the dress they love and is very persuasive. You have to be careful here, because you don't want to come across as manipulative. They key is that you want to help a bride in this situation truly understand what will happen if she waits. Remember, as a professional persuader, your job is to help her overcome her initial resistance by experiencing what the emotion of regret will *feel* like. The better you can do this, the more successful you will be at the art of persuasion.

A lot could be written about this, but I'll sum this up by saying you absolutely, positively MUST know the bride you are selling to (and she must know and trust you). In other words, any sale is more about the bride who is buying than it is the dress you are selling. When you truly understand her and what motivates her about her wedding, you will be much more successful than a bridal consultant who ignores this and just goes about selling "beautiful" wedding dresses.

2. Believe in who you are selling to. Believe you can help her find a dress she'll love and you will.
This seems like such a simple persuasion tactic, but it is one that we often forget. I can't tell you how many times I've talked with bridal consultants about this who have been struggling with their sales.

They start complaining about the types of brides they're working with and how they won't buy or they can't make up their minds or something like that. I've reminded them that the brides they work with will mirror what they think about them. When you say and believe to yourself, "I like this bride. I can help her find a dress she'll love today. We're going to be great friends," you go about the appointment much differently than if you have the attitude: "This bride will never buy today. She brought all of these negative friends who don't like anything and it will just be a waste of my time." By projecting these thoughts, you can act in a way that will prevent you from being persuasive.

With every bride you work with, you must believe that you can make a difference and act as if she already likes you. When you approach a bride and her bridal party, say in your mind, "I like these people." It will change your view about them. You will act differently because you have chosen to smile and be their friend. When you have this attitude, it is amazing how all of a sudden everyone in the bridal party tends to like you as well. If you've been struggling with this, it is likely because you've been feeling down or feeling some insecurity about yourself. Make the choice to flip your attitude to the positive, even if you have been having a down day (or the last bride you worked with didn't buy). Let that bride see and meet the most excited bridal consultant she's ever met and you will open the doors of trust so you can be persuasive as you sell.

Ignore this, and you'll stumble and fall more often than not. Lighten up and learn to love something about every bride you work with. It may be her smile, her demeanor, her ring, or something about her wedding. Remember, brides have insecurities and fears too. When they feel they are around an ally and a friend, they'll open up and you'll be able to help her break down the wall of resistance she had when she first walked in the door.

The best way you can do this is to use the first 30 seconds to a minute that you have with a bride to help her feel safe and that you are there to help her find the perfect dress that she'll love (and thank you for helping her to find). Brides are always on high alert when they first come into a bridal store. If you can help them relax and see how their experience of dealing with you as a true professional will be different than anything else she has ever experienced, you'll be much more successful in opening the doors to persuasion and the sale. The goal of that first few minutes is not just to get her to fill out a bridal registry form. It is really to help the bride feel valued, to educate her in a non-threatening way and to help her see that you are her friend and are there to help her specifically. Let her know how much you value her by thanking her for coming in. Say, "I'm ____. I'm so glad that you've come in today. What's your name? What special occasion brings you into our store today?"

That sequence of questions will help you start the process of getting to know the bride. Ask questions that allow her to talk about herself and her excitement of being engaged such as: "What a beautiful ring! Did you pick it out or did he pick it out for you?"

Never forget that your ability to persuade is dependent upon the base of trust that you have built with a bride. Trying to persuade without having a foundation of trust won't get you many sales. Your belief in the bride you are selling to is critical to your ability to persuade her. Your belief in her and your confidence in yourself that you can help her find the dress she'll wear on her wedding day are the most important bricks in the foundation of your ability to persuade the bride.

3. Get over what you know and focus on what matters most to brides. You'll be much more persuasive when you focus on what she wants as opposed to what you sell.

When I talk with bridal store owners about what they are doing to market their bridal stores, this is one of the pieces of advice that I most often give. Sometimes, it is easy to get so caught up in what you know (because you've worked hard for that knowledge and you're excited) that you lose track of what brides are really looking for because you're in the process of sharing everything you know with them.

A great analogy to why this doesn't work is found in fishing. If you go fishing and throw **all** of your expensive lures and bait into the water at the same time, what happens? You end up scaring the fish. You don't catch anything. If you want to persuade brides to do business with you, you must persuade them by talking about what matters most to them, not what matters to you.

Since brides are so skeptical today you must project confidence as you do this (but not arrogance) and you must ask great questions to get the bride talking about exactly what it is she is looking for. Once she starts answering questions and senses that you really care about her, then she will open up and start letting down her guard.

Being non-committal is what brides think is their best self-defense against an aggressive bridal consultant who they perceive just wants to sell them something. If you can come across different and be genuinely interested in the answers to the questions you ask, you'll be so much farther ahead than a bridal consultant who only seems interested in going through a pre-set list of questions.

When you get good at asking better questions, you'll be able to peel through the superficial layers. But, as with an onion, the deeper you go, the strength and size of the resistance can increase. Very few brides will reveal all of the personal factors that go into why she wants to buy a certain wedding dress. It isn't until after trust is really built that you have earned the right to go deeper and find out the reasons behind her choices and decisions.

The very best bridal consultants have mastered the ability to peel through the surface issues a bride may present and get to the core of what really matters and why it is such an important issue. In order to get to this level of selling, it is critical that you ask great questions to collect information at deeper levels so the bride really feels that you care and that you can help her.

Here is the point: *A bride will form her opinions about you and your store (and your ability to help her) not by what you say, but by the questions you ask.*

To prove this is true, consider the following two scenarios:
Bride: I'm looking for a wedding dress.
Bridal Consultant #1: Great. We have lots of dresses. Let's see if we can help you find one.

Bride: I'm looking for a wedding dress.
Bridal Consultant #2: Congratulations! Tell me, have you already started looking for dresses? What has been your experience so far?
Bride: I've been to one other store.
Bridal Consultant #2: When you were there, did they explain the four silhouettes of wedding dresses?
Bride: No, they didn't.
Bridal Consultant #2: No problem. Let me show those to you really quickly as it will be really helpful to you in finding your dress.
[Explains 4 silhouettes of dresses]
Bridal Consultant #2: Have you had a chance to try all four of the silhouettes on yet?
Bride: No.

Bridal Consultant #2: What silhouettes were you drawn to? What did you find out from trying on that silhouette?

Bride: I like how I look in sheath gowns.

Bridal Consultant #2: Great. We have lots of sheath gowns here at our store. What type of fabric are you drawn to?

Bride: I don't know.

Bridal Consultant #2: Well, there are five main types of fabrics that most wedding gowns are constructed from. They are satin, tulle, chiffon, organza, taffeta, and silk. Would you like to feel these five different fabrics and get a sense for which one you like best?

Bride: Sure.

Bridal Consultant #2: Is there a particular fabric you're drawn to?

Bride: Chiffon.

Bridal Consultant #2: Ask you know, fabric is just one of four things that makes up the overall cost of the dress...

Which bridal consultant do you think the bride has more of a connection with?

Which bridal consultant sounds more like she knows what she is doing? Obviously, it is the second.

Why? There are three main reasons:
1) The bridal consultant is teaching the bride something she didn't know.
2) The bridal consultant talks to the bride on her level – she doesn't assume anything and she offers help *in the direction that the bride wants to go*.
3) The bridal consultant teaches, then asks questions to get more clarity and dig a little deeper once there is a solid foundation of trust.

Be sure that you have earned trust by asking great questions and helping brides feel comfortable around you and what you are helping her to find. The majority of brides aren't familiar with the details of wedding gowns and this approach helps you build your expertise and helps lower her defenses as she senses that you know what you are talking about and how you can help her specifically.

To be more persuasive, you've got to get into the mind of the bride you are selling to. This is not an easy thing to do. But, it is the secret behind building trust and setting up an environment where you can be persuasive and help a bride feel that you are an ally to her finding the dress she loves. Be sure your persuasive message is in sync with what the bride wants. When you tie this with psychological triggers that help her make the decision to book an appointment with you or come into your store, you'll be so much more successful at persuading brides to buy from you now.

4. Focus on the bride in front of you as though she is the only person in the world at that moment.

Great politicians who are master communicators possess this ability to persuade. Chris St. Hilaire makes this observation about a friend who met the late Margaret Thatcher, the former prime minister of Great Britain. He said:

"Mrs. Thatcher is not someone you would normally think of as warm and fuzzy, but she was a tremendously successful politician. My friend was in a greeting line at an event she was attending, and he couldn't stop talking about how charismatic she was. Naturally I asked for details. He said, 'She took my hand with both of hers, made eye contact, and asked me how I was. We had about a fifteen second conversation, but I'll remember it the rest of my life because she was completely engaged in what I was saying.'

St. Hilaire continues:
"It's not hard to learn the moves: eye contact, press some flesh, ask a question about the other person. What's difficult is not paying attention to the dozens of distractions all around you, and treating every one of the hundreds of people you meet to that same level of attention and interest." –27 *Powers of Persuasion*, p. 50.

Are you so focused on the bride in front of you that you aren't bothered by the numerous distractions around you? Can she sense that attention to detail?

Research has shown that touch (beginning with but not limited to a handshake) can be a valuable tool in persuasion. If you study what great persuaders do, you'll notice this commonality among them.

Chris St. Hillaire says this of the power of touch:
"Your own use of touch has to be something that you are comfortable with and that is socially appropriate. Be careful not to cross any lines that the opposite sex might find either offensive or distracting. That said, there are many studies showing that the human touch eases anxiety, slows the heart rate, and drops blood pressure in the person being touched. The healing power of touch is a real phenomenon, and you can use it to put your colleagues at ease. It's usually acceptable to touch a colleague on the hand, forearm, shoulder or upper back. In one-on-one conversations, touching the other person's arm or hand will instantly make that person stop talking. You can do it to subtly get the other person to be quiet if he or she is talking too much, or to get the other person to stay quiet while you're making a point. In general, the person who initiates the touching is asserting power....You don't need to touch someone a lot in order to establish that you're open to friendship. One light touch on the arm while you're making a point is all it takes." –27 Powers of Persuasion, p. 154-158.

A bridal consultant who often sold $350 to $500 an hour on Saturdays once told me that one of her secrets to selling was that she touched her brides on the arm when she would talk to them when they were in the dress and that it made a big difference. I thought that was a weird statement, but I noticed and watched her do it and I was amazed at how she used that skill to persuade. The studies in the book 27 Powers of Persuasion have solidified my opinion that there is a reason why this works. You should make a habit now to pay attention to how great persuaders use touch and physical presence to persuade and then utilize what you learn to help you be a more effective persuader as well.

5. Credibility is the pivot point in influence and the basis behind all persuasion. To be more persuasive, you have to increase your credibility and perception of competence with the brides you serve.

Kevin Hogan makes this statement in his book, *The Science of Influence*: "Credibility matters. Credibility is the pivot point in influence. Unfortunately, it doesn't matter whether you have credibility (or are credible); it matters whether you are perceived that way. The perception of your credibility is critical to your being recognized as a person of influence. Credibility is an emergency of six component factors of which the first is the most crucial to success in persuasion. What factors make up credibility? 1) Competence; 2) Trustworthiness; 3) Expertise; 4) Likability; 5) Composure; and 6) Sociability.

"Competence is the first major component in the credibility puzzle....Building your true competence level and building the perception of your competence are two separate projects: You must be the expert and you must be perceived to be the expert." –p. 58.

As you work with brides, you have four ways to show them that you are credible. The first one is what the bride sees you doing (or how you behave in their presence). Think about this for a minute—in the presence of a bride what behaviors does she see? Are you bold or timid? Verbal or quiet? Aggressive or meek? Each one of these behaviors says something about your credibility to the brides you work with. Typically, most people see those who are bold, verbal and aggressive as being more credible than someone who is shy, quiet and reserved.

The second way you show brides that you are credible is by your composure. In other words, are you poised or nervous in the presence of a bride? Does she feel like she knows more than you or does she look to you for expertise and advice? Are you relaxed in her presence or tense? Are you calm as you approach the close of the sale or are you anxious? Again, brides perceive that those who are relaxed, calm, and poised are more credible than those who behave in the opposite way. Remember, it is the perception that counts. You may be nervous, scared, and anxious, but you can't let the bride perceive that you feel this way. Instead, you need to show that you are a competent and credible source for her to find her dress. When she feels this about you, she will have confidence in you and be much more likely to be persuaded by you. This is an important consideration (especially when you are just starting out in the bridal business). You may be nervous, but you can't let your fears hold you back from coming across in a way that is projects your poise and confidence.

The third way you show brides that you are credible is your likability and how you react in social settings. Brides respond better to bridal consultants who are good-natured than those who are irritable. They would much rather be around someone that is cheerful and friendly than someone who is gloomy and unfriendly. You can come across as being likable by how you act in their presence and more importantly by how strong of a desire you have to truly help her find the right dress.

The last way you show brides that you are credible is by being inspiring to them about their wedding. This can be projected in many ways, but if she feels like you approve of her ideas and give her additional resources and ideas that will help her wedding plans come together, she will see you as a credible source for the purchase of her dress. You can't be inspiring if you aren't excited about her and her wedding. If you are tired, you can come across as uncaring and unfocused and this can shoot down your credibility in her eyes.

I remember when I was in high school and I met with a banker in our small local town in Northwest Missouri. I was trying to sell him some fundraising tickets for a dinner that our scout troop was hosting. He was a little annoyed that I was meeting with him and completely brushed me off. I never forgot how he made me feel and I never went by that bank without thinking about that experience. He wasn't inspired by our cause and didn't see me as credible. However, a good friend's father knew that banker and took his son in to see him and sell him the exact same fundraising tickets. The same banker bought ten tickets from him. That experience is a good reminder to me of why credibility is so important. My friend Robert got the sale because he had a referral and the credibility of his father to get the sale.

You may find that you aren't as persuasive as you would like for this same reason. The more consultative and inspiring the experience of finding the perfect dress is, the more likely it is that you will make the sale. When you have credibility because of these four indicators, you will come across as a credible person and you will have properly set up the foundation so that you can successfully sell. Without that foundation, you will spin your wheels in the sales process. This is the real reason why your pre-sale marketing approach is so important. It allows you to build credibility with the bride in ways that are meaningful to her before she even arrives at your store.

Here are some questions for you to ask to determine how well you are projecting your credibility to your brides in your pre-sales marketing efforts:

- Are you stressing your knowledge by educating brides about what they most need to know about buying a wedding dress?
- Are you promoting your experience and what it will mean for them (that they can't get anywhere else)?
- When you communicate with brides do you do so in a fluid manner (without using 'um' and mispronouncing words that they know)? Do you come across as being knowledgeable about what it is that you are selling or does it seem that they know more than you?
- Are you communicating clearly with her? It has been proven that seven out of ten marketing communications are misunderstood today.
- Do brides sense that you are an expert?

- Are you likable?
- Are you inspiring? Do you borrow the credibility of others to enhance your own?

These are great questions to carefully consider as you promote your credibility. Remember, credibility is the pivot point in influence. It is what will help you build the foundation to be more persuasive.

6. Master words that persuade and use them in your sales conversations. The key is to give specific instructions or steps when directing or attempting to influence behavior.
Chris St. Hilaire makes this observation in *27 Powers of Perusasion*: "Choice, fairness, and accountability are three of the most popular words in the English language. Politicians learned this a long time ago, which is why the words pop up so often in political campaigns....The typical response to the words choice, fairness, or accountability is almost Pavlovian. It doesn't matter what the topic is, I can say, 'I just want to make sure you have choices, and that in the end someone is held accountable so that we ensure the fairest result,' and I'll get the whole room nodding in agreement. What does it mean? Something different to everyone. But the fact that they are all nodding is what's important, because from that point of agreement you can lead the discussion where you want it to go." –pp. 62-63.

This is a great point. Part of being persuasive is gaining agreement on something before you attempt any effort at persuasion. Allowing brides the option of choice is an excellent way to begin an appointment. However, this option of choice should be limited to one of their favorites of each cut of the dress to begin with. You don't want to overwhelm them with too many options because it will end up being frustrating for them and for you. Then, from these choices, you can allow them to feel like they are in control because they are telling you what they like or don't like about the dresses they are trying on. When a bride comes into the dressing room with the dresses she has chosen, always ask, "Which of the dresses you've chosen do you like the most?" Then, when she answers, say, "Let's try that one on first." This persuasive way of setting up the sale can help you start off the sales process with a dress that she loves so you have a comparison to come back to as you try on the other dresses.

You'll notice in that example, that I asked for her choice, but then followed it with the specific instruction to try that dress on first. I didn't say, "Which dress do you like most? Would you like to try it on first?" Why? Because more often than not, the bride will say, "No, I'll try that one on last" and you won't be able to persuade her.

Kevin Hogan says this about the importance of giving specific instructions or steps when persuading: "Decades of research reveal that specific instructions are necessary to influence and induce compliance. What does this mean to you? It means that you need to walk people step-by-step through a process that leads them to the door you ultimately want them to open. Anything short of doing this is unlikely to succeed in the short or long-term. I want to direct your attention (did you catch that?) to another technique that can be remarkably influential or explode in your face. Fear. Fear is something we are all wired to fight or flee from. Our irrational fears are those that we attempt to conquer and overcome. No one likes to experience fear. Fear literally can motivate people in ways few other things can....If you are going to use fear in a communication in order to foster change or alter behavior—or encourage someone to buy your product, idea, or service—you must also include a step-by-step set of instructions in your message in order for it to be successful.

"This formula, therefore, is:
"Negative Emotions + Behavioral Plan = Behavioral Change

"To help you see how powerful this combination is when used correctly, consider this experiment that was conducted with 164 UCLA students. Here was the scenario as it was presented to them: "You've parked your car in the lot and you are rushing to class for an important quiz you don't want to be late for. You realize on the way that you may have left your car unlocked!

"A number of the students were then told to imagine how they would feel if they went back to the car, found it was locked all along, and now had missed the quiz. Others were told to imagine how they would feel if they didn't go back to the car and instead took the quiz, only to discover afterward that the car had been vandalized. How would they feel then?

"All students were asked whether they would go back to the car or go to take the quiz. Of those told to imagine the car vandalized, 69 percent said they would return to the car and see if the doors were locked. Of those who were told they would miss the quiz, 34.5 percent said they'd go back and check on the car. The control group showed 46 percent returning to check on the car.

Kevin Hogan continues with this lesson:
"In general when the students experienced anticipated regret, they said they would take he action appropriate to prevent the regret from happening. We all know that what people say they will do and what they actually do in real life are very different things. Later research has in fact validated this fact. When people experience anticipated regret, they tend to take action to prevent the regret. As people of influence, that's a mighty important thing to remember." – *The Science of Influence*, pp. 104-106.

Now that you know this principle, you can set up the sale properly so she buys on the first visit and prevent what happens when a bride returns to find that the dress she fell in love with has been sold to someone else. You are much more persuasive when you help her experience anticipated regret by getting her to think about what *could* or *might* happen. Here is how you should phrase that situation when talking with a mom and daughter now and they express the desire to keep looking at other stores:

"I know you want to make the best choice and see if there is anything else out there that you like better. Can I share with you a quick story about a mother and a bride who made that choice this past week?

They, like you, found a dress they loved, and thought that continuing to look around would ensure that they didn't find anything they would like better. They went to several other stores and found the same four silhouettes and cuts you've tried on here, but couldn't find anything they liked better. Meanwhile, another decisive bride came in and bought the dress she loved. When they returned two days later, the mother broke down in tears because she realized she had let another mother and daughter choose which dress she would wear for her wedding. She realized she no longer had the choice, because the dress was gone.

"I want you to think about this scenario carefully before you make your choice. What happens if you go out and don't find a dress you like better than this one (that you've already said you love)? Two things will happen: 1) you'll lose the first visit advantage savings, which is only available on your first visit, and 2) you could lose the dress you love most. My question for you is this: Do you really want to let another bride decide for you which dress you'll wear at your wedding?"

That is a great example of using anticipated regret to be persuasive. You should look at ways you can use this principle to be more persuasive in your selling efforts.

Be more persuasive by detailing the specific instructions that you want a bride to take after you overcome an objection and as you close every sale. If you don't give specific instructions about what a bride should do next, you shouldn't be surprised when she chooses to leave your store without buying anything.

My encouragement to you is to use these persuasive strategies to help you better sell to the brides you work with on a daily basis. The first few seconds of interaction you have with every bride are so critically important. The better you get at learning how the principles of persuasion, the more successful you'll be at selling and the happier all of you will be (the bride will get what she wants—a beautiful dress and you'll make the sale!) When you master these skills, you'll be able to change the behaviors and attitudes of brides and persuade them to buy from you.

7. Use your own charm and emotions to spread enthusiasm and excitement.

Erik Calonius points out this interesting research in his book *Ten Steps Ahead*: "Visionaries are particularly good at persuasion, and they certainly know how to charm....The enthusiasm of visionaries is understandable. But what makes us go along with them? Brain studies have identified 'mirror neurons,' which apparently link observation to imitation. Mirror neurons play a part in learning—for instance, we watch a teacher play the guitar. Every movement of another, it seems, is tracked. In one experiment, a group of subjects watched someone move his finger. That was enough to illuminate the same part of the brain (seen via fMRI) as if the observers were moving their own fingers. Some scientists now believe that mirror neurons play a similar role in emotions, in which we mimic and even empathize with the emotions of others."

He continues:
"Neuroscientists have also identified what they call emotional contagion. When we empathize with someone's emotion, it lights up the brain as though we'd felt the emotion ourselves. It's the reason that when one baby cries in the nursery, they all cry. It's not that the one baby has awakened the others (although that may be true). It's that the other babies quite literally feel his pain. Other studies have shown how an emotional contagion spreads through communities of people, so that happy people can spawn an epidemic of happy people around them. The magnetism of a single leader, of course, can infect an entire group, for good and for bad. In a remarkable description of Apple in the mid-1980s, John Sculley recalls the force of personality that Steve Jobs radiated throughout the firm: 'I couldn't explain what was going on when I arrived,' Sculley recalled in Odyssey. 'It was almost as if there were magnetic fields, some spiritual force, mesmerizing people; their

eyes were just dazed. Excitement showed on everyone's face." –pp. 112-113.

It isn't enough today to just be persuasive about why you are the best choice. You also have to be persuasive with your own charm and enthusiasm to persuade brides NOT to do something that may be a bad idea for them (such as buying a dress from a competitor who doesn't offer all of the value added options that you do and that will save her money in the long-run). You may be persuasive when you are excited about the dress and when she is too, but how persuasive are you when she is excited, but you know it isn't the best idea for her? A good example of this would be a bride who chooses to buy a dress online as opposed to buying it from a full service bridal retailer like your store. Are you persuasive in a way that allows your charm and emotions to come through so the bride can sense your true empathy and desire to help her?

Chris St. Hillaire makes this statement in his book *27 Powers of Persuasion*: "Not every persuasion campaign is about urging people to do something. Occasionally you need to persuade them *not* to do something you think is a bad idea. The most effective method is to agree with the larger concept, then challenge the details. You're already familiar with this concept if you pay any attention to political ads. The formula is to have either an expert or an average citizen saying, 'We all want X. But the Z Act isn't the way to do it. Z will....' Fill in the blank: 'limit our choices'... 'take away our rights'... 'fail to hold people accountable'... 'raise our taxes'... 'provide no oversight', and so forth. These ads are either incredibly irritating or outstanding, depending on your feelings about the issue. But they work. That's why you keep seeing them." –pp. 171-172.

When you know a bride is going to buy a dress online, you should say: "I know you want to get the best possible price on your gown. But buying a dress online isn't the way to do it. Buying a dress online will cause you to get a dress that will:

- Have wrinkles all over it which you will have to pay extra to have pressed out.
- Have loose beading or missing beads on your dress caused during shipping which you will have to pay to have fixed (most shipping companies aren't as kind to your box as you would like to think they are).
- Possibly have stains on your dress that you likely won't be able to properly remove without damaging the delicate fabric and beadwork on the dress.
- Likely arrive in the wrong size (and you may not be able to alter it to fit your figure).
- Will very likely look completely different than the picture you saw online. Many brides have experienced this much to their shock and horror and then come to us in tears hoping that we can fix the problem. Many times repairs can be made, but often at a great expense."

Then, you can explain with passion about why you offer the best choice and can prevent her from dealing with all of the heartache when purchasing a dress from your store. The same charm that can be used to spread enthusiasm and excitement can also be used to help brides avoid a mistake that may cost them big stress, worries and ultimately cost them more than the savings she thought she might be getting.

If you are drawn into a conversation with a bride over a specific objection, be sure that you don't get drawn into the disagreement. Strive to objectively help the bride see where her decision may lead and then use your charm and enthusiasm and the powerful words of third party brides to draw her to make a decision that will best benefit her.

Here are three tips to help you use your charm and emotions to spread enthusiasm and excitement:
1) *If you need to think about an answer before answering the bride, look down, not up.* Looking down appears thoughtful to the bride. Looking up seems like you don't know and you're searching for the

answer. Being thoughtful allows you to come across with more charm with the bride.

2) Be inclusive and reassuring as you talk with each bride. Let her know how much you care by your attention to detail. Those who have great charm are those who take away fear through reassuring statements and eye contact.

3) Study those who are masters of the principle of charm. Study those who have great charisma. They have the ability to draw in their listeners by how they say things and how inclusive they can be. Chris St. Hillaire says: "If you know what the objections are likely to be and have already developed answers for them, the strategy is simple. Listen to the objection, wait a few beats, ponder it, and then say, 'So you're saying that if we do X, Y could be the result. Good point.' Wait another beat or two. 'What if we handled it like this?' You have recognized the person's reality, boosted his or her ego, and dealt with the objection." –pp. 150-151.

8. There is a power in numbers. Use them to provide persuasive statistical facts to emphasize your point as you persuade.
Chris St. Hillaire says: "Advertisers have long recognized the near-magical selling power of numbers, especially weird ones. In 1879, Ivory Soap was boasting about being '99 and 44/100% pure,' whatever that means, and the current ad campaign for Miller Genuine Draft Beer is based on its having 64 calories....You'll usually see numbers presented in one of the following ways: as a single impressive amount (over 10 million sold!), as a comparison (3 out of 4 dentists prefer Colgate), or as a percentage (the president has a 63 percent approval rating). As a businessperson, the best way to present numbers often depends on what's available to you." *–27 Powers of Persuasion*, pp. 112-113.

Numbers are a powerful way to persuade. It is another way to provide third-party credibility to what you are promoting. For example, when you say that nearly 2/3 of your bridal business comes from referrals, it is a powerful statement because it implies to brides that the majority of your business comes from the referrals of those who have already had a great experience at your store.

Since numbers are so powerful, do you know the numbers of your business that you can promote to the brides in your marketing? You only really need one or two great numbers or statistics that can be very persuasive in your marketing. What will these be for you?

Here are a few examples of numbers you could discover and use in your marketing:
- What is your return rate of brides who come back and buy something else from you?
- How many testimonial letters do you receive from brides each and every month?
- Has your bridal store been featured in five or more news stories over the past year?
- What percentage of your business comes from referrals?
- In your pre-sales collateral, can you identify how many of your brides are decisive and buy their dress on their first visit (and save money)?

Numbers can be very powerful and unfortunately, many marketers use numbers to promote their own cause or their own point (which may not be entirely accurate). Consider this example of a story from September 2009's NBC's *Today Show*:

"Every year, when there is a slow news cycle or a particularly alarming child kidnapping case, parents are treated to scare stories about child abduction that are inevitably 'supported' by misleading numbers. In September 2009, as children were returning to school, NBC's *Today Show* played into parents' fears by citing the National Center for Missing and Exploited Children's statistic that '39% of all abductions occur walking to and from school.' After the piece and during the discussion with his guests, Al Roker, to his credit, stated that 'a lot of these fears are irrational, because of the 60 million kids in the U.S. under the age of fifteen, only 115 children were taken, and when we hear a statistic that almost 40% of kids have been abducted, that's an alarming, maybe misleading statement.' So we're talking 39 percent of 115 children, which is about 45 children out of 60 million. Meaning there is less than a one in a million chance your child will be abducted while walking to school." –p. 115.

Part of the reason why numbers are so powerful is because they directly tie into the psychological trigger of specificity. The more specific you can be in your marketing, the more credible it is. That's why, if you can identify the numbers to the above questions, you can put together a very compelling case for why brides should buy from you. For example, you could say:

- ____% of all of the brides who buy their wedding gown from us also buy their bridesmaids dresses from us.
- More than ____% of the brides who buy from us write a note or letter explaining how much they love our store. We love this positive feedback and look forward to receiving your testimonial letter about how we've helped you get the wedding dress of your dreams very soon as well.
- Our critically acclaimed bridal store has been featured in different media publications more than 12 times this past year.
- Nearly 2/3 of all of the brides who buy at our store do so at the recommendation of a close friend.
- 3 out of 4 brides who visit our store buy their dress from us on their first visit and save $100. We look forward to helping you find and save money on your wedding dress on your first visit as well.

As you can see, you can use numbers in a variety of ways to share positive aspects of how your store is promoted to the brides in your area. What numbers can you start using to be more persuasive in your marketing approach?

One word of caution. While numbers are very persuasive and provide evidence that your argument is correct, you've got to use good numbers. Nothing will hurt your credibility more than using bad numbers that someone disproves. However, good numbers that promote your cause can be very powerful ammunition for brides to share with their friends and to boost your overall persuasiveness. Explaining the reasons why a bride should buy from you with your differences and advantages will help you build contrast so you can be persuasive in your pre-sales marketing materials.

9. Give your brides information that will help them persuade other members of the decision making process.
If you have brides who have to bring their mother back with them before they can buy their dress, you've seen the power of this persuasive strategy. Listen closely to what brides say to their mothers or their friends as they are deliberating whether they should go ahead and buy their dress at your store. Without fail, you will usually hear them make comments that you or your bridal consultants originally shared with them about how they'll save money if they buy their dress now and other points of contrast that help the bride and other members of the party choose to buy from you. If you have brides who have to talk with their mothers or other members of their family before they can make their decision to buy, are you arming each bride with information that can help her make a compelling case for your store and why she should buy from you?

There are four main areas of information that you should share in your marketing communications to enhance your powers of persuasion according to Chris St. Hillaire. He says:

"Arming your advocates means making sure that those who agree with you have the information they need to influene other people, either when you're not around or when you're in a meeting and need a show of support. You can give different advocates different talking points, but don't give any one person more than three. Talking points can be about:
- Statistics, trends, or other numbers: 'The number of people buying this type of software goes up ten percent each year.'

- Third-party validation: 'The legal department said this deal is bulletproof.'
- Track record: 'This division met or beat every deadline over the past six months.'
- Experience: 'Marissa has more knowledge about this field than anyone else in the company.'" –pp. 120-121.

I think these are four excellent areas where you can build contrast. What statements can you make in these four areas about your store? Are you pointing these out to your brides in your marketing collateral (especially on your web site)?

Specificity is so important in being persuasive. Joe Sugarman makes this interesting comment on p. 143 of his book *Triggers*: "Being specific and precise in your explanations and statements is very important, in part because it can affect your credibility. Let me give you an example. If I say, 'New dentists everywhere use and recommend CapSnap toothpaste," it sounds like typical advertising lingo—puffery designed to sell a product. It is so general that it will probably cause a prospect to discount the statement you have just made and maybe everything else you say. But if I say, '92% of dentists use and recommend CapSnap toothpaste,' it sounds much more believable. The consumer is likely to think that we did a scientific survey and that 92% of the dentists actually use the toothpaste." -- *Triggers*, p. 143.

Here is the important point: statements with specific facts can generate strong believability. Consider the impact of these statements:

- 71% of the brides who buy at __*the name of your store*__ do so because one of their friends recommended us
- There are only 3 of this gown in the entire state and you are wearing the only one in your size.
- There are over 10,000 individual beads that are sewn onto this dress all by hand. It takes 38 days for one highly skilled seamstress just to sew on all of the beadwork.

- There are 72,000 nerve endings at the bottom of your feet. Our customers tell us that these shoes are amongst the most comfortable they have ever worn and that they feel like they are still walking on air when they take them off.
- Over 1,000,000 sold!

Here are 3 benefits of being more specific in what you sell:
- You are more believable and credible.
- You sound like an expert on the subject. Expertise builds trust and confidence.
- Specificity helps you eliminate skepticism and makes your message more credible and trusted.

Look at what you are saying when you sell. Add specifics to your claims. Research the facts and use the details. At market, you will notice that some manufacturers use this principle very well when selling their gowns. The best ones detail with specificity exactly how a fabric was picked out, what type of beadwork was used, or how long it takes for beadwork to be sewn onto a gown. This is a powerful trigger when you honestly research the facts and share them with those to whom you sell.

The best time to be persuasive and overcome an objection is before it comes up. Joe Sugarman makes this point in his book *Triggers* about why it is so key to bring up an objection before it comes up and how doing this really helps you close the sale later, especially if it is one that will be a major obstacle to making the sale.

He says:
"Why does this work? First, realize that you can't fool your prospect. If indeed something isn't right with what you are selling, the prospect will either know, sense, or feel it. You might think you can pull the wool over the eyes of the prospect, but in reality your prospect is a lot sharper than you think. So if you feel that there is something negative in what you are selling that the prospect might notice or respond to, bring up that negative feature first. Don't wait until later in the sales presentation—bring it up right away. By presenting a negative feature up front, you melt away that initial resistance and come across as

honest rather than deceptive. The trust and respect you get from prospects will lower their defense mechanisms, and so they'll be prepared to receive the real advantages of your product or service."-- *Triggers*, p. 25.

One of the most common objections that bridal stores face is the bride who says she can't make a decision without seeing several other bridal stores first. The best way to overcome this objection is to bring it up first and within the first few minutes that the bride comes into the store.

Why? Because, then when you get to the end of the process of trying on gowns and finding the perfect gown for a bride, it has already been discussed and she feels comfortable with going ahead with her purchase. If you avoid doing this simple thing at the beginning, it will be brought up anyway and the bride will go shop around more and may never be back to your store.

Another powerful way to arm your brides is through a principle called "flagging." Kevin Hogan explains what this principle means and how you can use it to be more persuasive in his book *The Science of Influence*. He says: "Flagging is one specific technique that you can use to dramatically increase compliance in almost all aspects of influence....The point of placing a flag in someone's memory is that, once it is there, it becomes part of their permanent memory and gives you a point from which to establish a key piece of the persuasion process. Here's a real life example:

"Remember, when you bought your first house? Did you want something that would be big enough for your family to live in comfortably?"

"Now, the real estate agent has no clue if this is true, but by flagging the memory of the decision to buy the house you add this specific recollection into their memory as if it has always been there. If you were to ask, 'What caused you to buy this house?' people will generate numerous possibilities internally before giving you a reason. That reason could be helpful in the persuasion process, but one thing is certain: The reason that they state probably had little to do with their decision in the first place!

"Therefore, they will be more likely to doubt the generation of their own recollection, and even though you now have a piece of information that is useful, it also has drawbacks.

"What for example? Specifically, the person may have generated a number of internal responses of their reason before saying what it was. This cause question marks to pop up in the mind and makes a further conversation more interesting but less likely to persuade.

"If you flag a memory you will get one of two responses. Either the people will accept the flag (most typical) and think in terms of *comfortable*, in this case, or they will rapidly tell you just why they did buy a house.

"'No, it wasn't space or comfort at all. I needed a home that was near the school.'"

"At this point you have a client with a dramatic recall (still as unlikely to be accurate). This allows you to utilize their flag in the persuasion process that has begun. Once people have a flag anchored in place, it primes mental processes to think in terms of the flag. Yes, you can bet that the nearness to school factor will be a determining factor at this point."

He continues with this key point:
"You can flag another person's memory through their own generation of the flag or by planting the flag yourself. The flag should always be something that was considered by the other person at some time. If the flag is self-generated by the other person, they are more likely to internally argue or struggle with the flag because, although they originally came up with the flag, they generated other options that

they considered and they might recall these other points and begin to oscillate internally.

"Imagine I were to say: 'Pick a number. I'm thinking of 61,000.' What is your number?

"Now, imagine that I say to someone else, 'Pick a number. I'm thinking of 14.'

"The responses from the two individuals are going to be dramatically different. Very few people will pick a number higher than 100 in the latter case. In the former case where I said I was thinking of 61,000, people will pick numbers in the thousands, tens of thousands, and even hundreds of thousands.

"In both cases, I primed the response by stating an anchor or flag—in the first case a big number and in the second a small number.
"The faster I ask for a response, the closer to the anchor the response will be. These numbers mean nothing but have direct impact on suggestions given to the person." –pp. 203-204.

Then, he shares this fascinating strategy:
"Let's move this interesting phenomenon into the persuasion and marketing arena. Research participants were shown apartments to rent. They were given rental fees for the apartments that varied from very high to very low. When the individuals were given high numbers, the individuals focused on the positive aspects of the apartment. When they were given low numbers they were much more likely to focus on the negative aspects. In further research, participants who are asked to accept one proposal or another are more likely to focus on the positive aspects of the proposal. Participants asked to reject one of two options are likely to focus on negative aspects of the two.

"And there are more, but it all comes down to one key concept. Anchoring is priming and it is an associative error. Whatever you mention to prime their thinking is going to cause error in the thinking toward the anchor—even when you tell someone that this is what you are doing! What does this mean in the real world?

"...Clearly, if you are selling a service for $1,000 and want to sell the most of them possible, then you should probably should set a high anchor. "What you will gain from this experience is easily worth $9,000. I could ask for half of that fee but I'm not going to. Instead I'm only going to ask only $1,000 for this experience."—p. 205.

Now, how can you use the principle of flagging and anchoring to build value and sell more dresses? A great way to do this is to position your store against what brides are all familiar with (the dresses at Kleinfeld on *Say Yes to the Dress*). When brides come into your store, you can position the experience against the price they might have thought they would pay at Kleinfeld (approximately $10,000) to the highest price dress you sell in your store. Then, you can help them try on gowns at your store that are under both prices (and more within the bride's budget). It also raises your value in her mind when you can give her an amazing experience and throw in a few surprises that she wasn't expecting as well.

Are you using the flags of statistics, trends, or other numbers to prove why you are the best in a persuasive way with the brides you serve?

Are you offering third party validation through numerous and persuasive testimonials?

Are you highlighting the experience the bride will have at your store in a way that helps her to see that your track record makes you a much more reliable choice for her to get her dress?

If a bride isn't able to make up her mind on her first visit because she doesn't have her mother or other influential members of her party with her, are you empowering her with the information she'll need to make it back to your store quickly with the right decision makers?

You are responsible for imparting this information to her. You can't rely on someone else to do it for you.

10. Use stimuli that grab attention and trigger decision.
I've always been fascinated by what triggers the brain to buy. When you understand triggers, you can incorporate the language patterns into the things you say to brides as they come into your business. Every advantage matters today and a book entitled *The Buying Brain* reveals many great ideas for how you can tap into and trigger decision in the brain. The book is essentially a treatise on how and why brains buy and is a fascinating look into the newest research over the past five years and how you can utilize these findings as a bridal retailer to successfully persuade brides to buy now.

One of the most fascinating parts of the book is the section that explains what the brain likes and what it rejects and how to use that knowledge to market correctly. According to Pradeep, the brain is frustrated by:
- "Tasks that take too long to resolve
- Clutter
- Messages that distract or don't apply" –*The Buying Brain*, p. 29.

The best kind of stimuli you can use to persuade are the kind that the brain can't ignore. The book points out three things you can use. They are:

1) Novelty. Novelty is very powerful because we are all drawn to something new. Everyone has experienced the phenomenon where a brand new gown comes in and is immediately sold by a bridal consultant who loves it and purchased by a bride who has never seen anything like it. This happens because of this principle. According to Pradeep, "Novelty is the single most effective factor in effectively capturing all [the brain's] precious attention. Novelty recognition is a hard-wired survival tool all primates share. Whether looking for prey or berries or suitable mates, our brains are trained to look for something brilliant and new, something that stands out from the landscape, something that looks delicious. A novel message, product, package, and/or layout is the key to penetrating their busy and selective subconscious minds. Breaking through the clutter in this way helps products stand out on the shelf and elevates a great logo from a sea of competing symbols and letters. To be embraced, a consumer touch point must first be noticed." – *The Buying Brain*, pp. 29-30.

2) *Eye contact.* Do you look a bride in the eye when you talk with her and seek to overcome her objections? According to extensive research that has been done on this, "Eye contact is particularly important to a social species such as ours." –p. 30.

Eye contact helps a bride sense our empathy and our desire to help her find the perfect dress for her wedding. When you evaluate how well you did in making a sale, be sure to include this as an item that you look for and analyze. Lack of eye contact also shows the bride your insecurity. This may be due to your lack of confidence in your ability to handle a particular objection. When you are confident, you look into someone else's eyes. A lot could be said about this, but be sure to look into a bride's eyes to grab attention and to connect with her on a deeper level.

3) *Pleasure/reward images.* Studies have been done where brain waves have been measured and recorded to be higher when a certain product, picture or logo is flashed in front of someone's eyes. This means that if you know what triggers the pleasure/reward circuits of the brain, you can celebrate the happiness and deep pleasure a bride will have from wearing the dress she has found at your store. The best pleasure/reward images you can use are the ones triggered in the bride's imagination by the questions you ask and the word pictures you use.

Utilize these stimuli to be more persuasive as you sell. President Dwight D. Eisenhower made this great observation about leading soldiers which I think has great application to how well we persuade those we work with. He said: "I would rather try to persuade a man to go along, because once I have persuaded him he will stick. If I scare him, he will stay just as long as he is scared, and then he is gone."

Choose to be persuasive in a way that builds you credibility and gets to the heart of what the bride really wants. Then, you can persuade her to go along with your desire to help her find the perfect dress and you will be much more successful in your efforts to do so.

Chapter 6

Market on Message to the Right Market with the Right Media

"The aim of marketing is to know and understand the customer so well the product or service fits [her] and sells itself." –Peter Drucker

I'm often asked what it takes to roll out a successful advertising and marketing campaign. There are a lot of books that have been written on this subject and a lot of advice that has been shared about what works, what doesn't and why. It is easy to point out what not to do when dealing with advertising because the wisdom has usually been gained the hard way: we spent money on something we thought would work, but didn't.

I recently talked with a store owner who had just spent money on newspaper advertising because she got such a great deal on it. When I asked her if her target audience of brides read that newspaper, she didn't know. She ended up spending money on something that didn't give her *any* results. She was confident that because she got a great deal and listened to the newspaper touting how many readers there were that she couldn't go wrong. BIG Mistake. She ended up losing money she couldn't afford to lose and vowed that she wouldn't spend money on advertising anymore because it didn't work.

In this chapter, I'd like to share with you the advice I would give her based on my own experience and based on the feedback I've gotten from hundreds of bridal store owners who have listened to my advertising recommendations over the years.

To do this, I would like to discuss the points that I believe at the heart of all successful marketing and sales campaigns.

1. To be successful in marketing or selling, you must evoke an emotional response. Without this, your message will fall on deaf ears.

One of the greatest examples of this principle in action that you and I can learn a tremendous amount from was P.T. Barnum. He had a terrifying experience when he was twenty-six years old that completely changed the way he marketed and sold the circus events he promoted. Barnum had helped to operate a circus for six months in 1836 (many years before he was involved in the Barnum and Bailey circus). Here's what happened:

"One day he had just bought a new suit of clothes that he wore with pride. He left his hotel in Annapolis, Maryland and noticed a dozen men following him and quickly gaining on him. At first Barnum thought the men were admiring his suit. However, he quickly learned the men wanted his life. They roughed him up, ruined his new suit, and led him to a rail where they prepared to hang the young showman. Barnum protested, finally realizing that the men about to hang him thought he was a minister who had killed a local woman. Barnum spoke as quickly as he could but could not get the men to listen. They had been informed by Barnum's partner—by his partner, mind you— that he was indeed the minister who committed the murder."

"Barnum couldn't believe it. He begged for a chance to talk to his partner and clear up the error. The men finally agreed. They pushed and shoved him all the way back into town. By the time the mob reached the hotel, there were now fifty men ready to hang Barnum. They walked right to the hotel where his partner was waiting, laughing so hard he had to hold his belly. Barnum's partner explained that the whole thing was a joke on Barnum. The mob laughed and dispersed. However, Barnum was fuming. Finally his partner explained:

'My dear Barnum, it was all for our good. Remember, all we need to insure success is notoriety. You will see that this will be noised all about town as a trick played by one of the circus managers upon the other, and our pavilion will be crammed tomorrow night.'

"Barnum's partner was right. The cruel joke made the circus the talk of the town, and business boomed. Barnum had learned...the power of getting attention." –Joe Vitale, *There's a Customer Born Every Minute*, pp. 43-44.

Now, obviously if that had happened to you or I we would probably strangle our partner, but the lesson Barnum learned is an important one in marketing and selling as well. Because an emotional response was created, Barnum was able to get attention that increased his business.

Bridal stores who master the ability to get attention and emotionally involve brides in their marketing and sales efforts will be drastically more successful and sell more dresses than those who simply rely on the advertising of a manufacturer they are carrying to create that excitement for them, especially when there are a lot of other retailers that also offer the same thing.

P.T. Barnum once wrote: "The great secret of success in anything is to get a hearing. Half the object is gained when the audience is assembled."

What are you doing to create excitement and build drama for the brides in your area through your pre-sales efforts?

Are you persuading them that you are worth the time and effort to come see (and to come see first) so you can position your competitors in a way that highlights the differentiating point that is most favorable to you?

If not, you are missing the entire essence of the magic of marketing. Let me give you another example of a French entrepreneur / showman named Monsieur Mangin that Barnum learned this principle from who sold pencils. Now, you would probably agree that pencils don't seem like something that would be very easy to market. They could be perceived as boring and as a commodity. Listen to how this marketer created an experience that got attention and got people emotionally involved.

"Mangin would appear on a street corner dressed in unusual royal garb, riding a team of large horses. He would park, open his wagon with a great deal of pomp and circumstance, and slowly begin to put on a theatrical performance. A crowd would always form, wondering what was happening. The French entrepreneur would then demonstrate his pencils, involve members of the audience, and end by selling his product to nearly everyone present.

"Years later, Barnum met Mangin and complimented him on '...your manner of attracting the public. Your costume is elegant, your chariot is superb, and your valet and music are sure to draw.'

'Aha! You never saw better pencils,' Mangin replied. 'You know I could never maintain my reputation if I sold poor pencils. But, my miserable would-be imitators do not know our grand secret. First, attract the public by din and tinsel, by brilliant sky rockets and Bengola lights, then give them as much as possible for their money.'"—*There's a Customer Born Every Minute*, p. 45.

That's a great observation about what it takes to successfully market anything. What are you doing to stand out and be unique to grab attention?

Here are some suggestions for how you can do this in your store:

- At your next bridal show, have something that grabs the attention of the brides who go by your booth (the chance to win a free dress, win prizes with a spinning wheel, etc.) What makes this idea work so well is that other brides see their peers interacting with you and having a great time and leaving your booth excited with the chance to win something when they come into the store or knowing they won something they can redeem when they come into your store.

- Put banners and signs in your windows that create interest and excitement. If you can create curiosity to find out what is going on inside, brides will stop to check it out.
- Have a referral program that gets brides talking about you. When you sell a dress, take a picture of the bride in your store that she can broadcast to all of her friends via Facebook and that will result in additional sales. You can't ignore the power of creating excitement through social networking.
- Create displays or information on the home page of your web site that create curiosity and interest for brides who are coming online to check you out. A countdown clock is one great way you can do this.
- Create displays in the front of your store when brides first come in that they have to ask about. You can do this by putting a sign on the display that says, "Ask me how you can save $100 off your wedding dress purchase today." This can help the walk-ins who haven't been properly prepared with the pre-sale sequence to decide to buy from you before they even try on any dresses.

One of Barnum's best strategies for gaining attention was one he utilized when an unemployed man came to Barnum looking for work in New York City in the 1860s.

"Barnum gave the man several bricks and said: 'Now go and lay a brick on the sidewalk at the corner of Broadway and Ann street; another close by the Museum [that he was trying to get people to come buy tickets to and come visit]; a third diagonally across the way at the corner of Broadway and Vesey street, by the Astor House; put down the fourth on the sidewalk in front of St. Paul's Church, opposite; then, with the fifth brick in hand, take up a rapid march from one point to the other, making the circuit, exchanging your brick and every point, and say nothing to no one.' The unemployed man asked why in the world Barnum wanted him to carry out this bizarre routine. Barnum said, 'No matter. All you need to know is that it brings you fifteen cents wages per hour. It is a bit of my fun. And to assist me properly you must seem to be as deaf as a post; wear a serious countenance; answer no questions; pay no attention to any one; but attend faithfully to the work and at the end of every hour by St. Paul's clock show this ticket at the Museum door; enter, walking solemnly through every hall in the building; pass out, and resume your work.'

"The confused but now employed man did as he was told. Within 30 minutes over 500 people were gathered in front of Barnum's museum watching the mysterious silent man move the bricks. Then, when the man went into the museum, people bought tickets and went in after him. This unusual stunt was so successful that the police had to stop it. The crowds in front of the museum were blocking traffic." – *There's a Customer Born Every Minute*, p. 49.

If P.T. Barnum could attract that kind of attention in the 1860s with an involvement device that grabbed people's attention and brought them to the doors of his business, what could you do if you just thought about how to attract brides to your doors and get them excited about the experience they will have?

Take the ideas I've given you above and brainstorm how you can expand on these to create excitement and an emotional response that will get brides thinking about and coming to your bridal store. Then, you can focus on finding what they're looking for and help them find it.

2. The best marketing or selling activities create memorable experiences that brides want to be a part of. If you aren't marketing an experience (even if you create one) at your store, you are making a mistake.

I talk in great depth about the importance of selling experiences, not dresses in my book: *Bridal Boosters and Breakthroughs*. If you don't have a copy yet, you can get one on Amazon.com through the link on my web site www.BridalBusinessSuccess.com.

Pairing your marketing and selling activities into great and memorable experiences that brides and their friends want to be a part of is a great way to grab attention and create excitement about your store. Here are five ways you can create excitement that involves brides and creates a memorable experience.

1) Have a contest where brides have to come into your store to participate.

You should consider fashion contests (for best dressed bride, best dressed bridesmaids) and could consider cooking contests, look alike contests in conjunction with recent brides who have just gotten married, or the number of rice kernels in a jar that brides have to guess in order to win a free dress or to have the amount of the dress they purchased donated to the bride's favorite charity.

The key is that you always want to tie the reward you're offering to something you want to sell. For example, the best-dressed bridesmaids need to buy bridesmaids dresses at your store to compete in the contest. Then, the winners of a drawing from those who have purchased will receive a limo ride and night out on the town with bride and other members of the bridal party. You could join with other local wedding vendors to create a lot of excitement about this kind of event which would also include publicity for you and your store.

2) Offer and show collectible wedding dresses or formal gowns.

This is something you could do that could draw widespread attention to your store. You could contact celebrities or mini-celebrities in your local market who have gotten married and donate money to their favorite charity in exchange for letting brides in your local market see their wedding dresses displayed. You might even be able charge admission to brides to see them, but give them a credit towards their dress if they buy a dress from your store. People love to see collectible items that others have worn in their wedding. This could be a great way for you to interact with celebrities in your area and promote them. You could even promote an upcoming event that they will be at so that it is a true win/win event for everyone.

This would be an especially great way to promote pageants at your store. If you had pageant winners showcase the dresses they bought from you or other dresses they wore in the pageants they won in your store, you could donate something to their organization (which is always looking for money for scholarships for future participants).

3) Hold psychic readings for brides and their bridesmaids.

It is amazing how much appeal psychics and fortunetellers have today. A funny way in which you could create an experience would be to hire a psychic who would come into your business once a month and do a reading for a bride and her bridesmaids about what the future held for each of them. This would be a fun thing you could do that would get brides and bridesmaids talking about you and could take place in your store so they would have to be there (where you could conveniently talk to them or encourage them to buy bridesmaid dresses after the fun event). You would obviously want to offer these kinds of events in a fun, lighthearted way. A quick search on Craigslist.org under services will probably give you a long list of individuals you could contact about doing something like this. As an example, here is an example of one for someone offering free psychic readings: No catches, just want to sharpen my ability...we'll be helping each other! In addition to my psychic ability, I have a psychology degree and counseling background. Psychic readings can bring clarity to your situation and help you to evaluate your options while managing life's challenges in a healthy manner. Sessions are by phone and last about 15 minutes. Call ____ at ....

You could even talk with the psychic about telling the bride and her bridesmaids that their future includes beautiful bridesmaid dresses from your store. Think about how you could use this idea to create an experience that would get brides talking about you and create a unique experience for the bride and her bridesmaids to come visit you, especially since they all want fun things to do together (and there aren't that many options to them that are truly fun and unique besides shopping for dresses together).

4) Hire a band or local musical group to come and perform for brides and their bridesmaids at a Girls Night Out Event.

If you aren't already holding these types of events monthly or at least quarterly, you really should. Brides love live music and this is a great way for you to promote other musicians in your area. They will probably do it for free if the timing is right (they don't have any other paid gigs during the time of your event) and if they are allowed to promote themselves to the brides and bridesmaids who will be there. If you draw large enough crowds, you could even bid out the opportunity to play at the events to the top bidder which would generate additional advertising revenue for you.

5) Sponsor a local service event that will give you publicity or do something dramatic that gets you attention.

I have seen many bridal retailers do these types of things to great success. You can walk or run in certain events such as a walk-a-thon or fun run. You could even do something that people want to see or would be curious to see.

There are many things you could do that would create excitement for you and your brand if you would just sit down and think about them. You could also use the participation in these contests as a way to motivate your sales staff.

The ultimate showcase of this would be dressing a local celebrity in a wedding dress or formal dress that you could then promote to other brides. You could also attempt to break a record or have all of your previous brides who purchased a wedding dress from you show up at your place of business at a certain time to get a group picture that promotes "All of these brides trusted ---the name of your store---with their wedding dress...Shouldn't you too?" or a variation on that idea.

You could also leverage your relationship with past brides and have them show up at a local service event that would get the community talking about what a great thing you and your store helped put together. This can get great publicity, especially if you are the one who is documenting and promoting it and putting the information on your blog or web site.

All of these are great examples of ways that you can create fun experiences by connecting the experience of shopping at your store to something that will get brides and their friends talking about you. The better you do this, the more successful you'll be at marketing and selling at your store.

3. It pays more to entertain than to educate.

Walt Disney once said: "I would rather entertain and hope that people learned something than educate people and hope they were entertained." Why did Disney have this belief? The reason is simply this: it pays more to entertain than to educate. With the explosion of information and its accessibility online, more and more people today expect to get information for free. Yet, those same individuals will gladly pay money to be entertained or to create memories through shared experiences.

You must educate brides that you are the best store to come to, yet you must also sell them on the idea through cleverly disguised entertainment. Most people don't want to read or sit down to learn something unless it has an obvious benefit to them personally.

If you can create an experience and a connection to you through the videos they watch, you can create a powerful way to promote your business in a way that grabs attention.

In a way what you are really after is creating and giving good feelings to brides and those who are shopping with them to the point that they trust you enough to go ahead and buy from you.

Joe Vitale makes this point:

"An unspoken truth in marketing is that the only reason people do anything is for the feelings they expect to get. Without those feelings dangling before them, they will not spend money with you. Although people sometimes spend money to feel frightened (such as when they rent a horror movie), they typically spend money to feel better. In short, make your business more fun and you'll start getting more business." – *There's a Customer Born Every Minute*, p. 64.

Why is this so important? A lot of it goes back to how the brain works and associates feelings and products. Robin Lewis and Michael Dart explain this phenomenon in their book, *The New Rules of Retail*:

"...The most successful companies [are] those creating superior experiences, and constantly striving for better. And it was not just confined solely to a superior product, brand, or service, or just the shopping experience. We realized, for example, that when consumers simply *hear* the names of companies such as Trader Joe's, Whole Foods, Disney, Apple, Abercrombie & Fitch and others, they get excited in anticipation of both the shopping and consumption experience. In fact, we probed deeper and studied some of the new work in neurology depicting the biochemical effects in the human brain that can affect behavior, particularly consumption. We found that brands like those listed above actually trigger a chemical high in the brain. So when consumers hear the brand name, they're likely to scoot to the store or brand ahead of all competitors. For instance,...Starbucks creates a neurological experience, indelibly connecting with all five senses and the most important 'sixth' sense: the mind, and the emotions it triggers. As proof of the Starbucks connection, one need only to observe the long waiting line at a Starbucks in an airport right next to a McDonald's (or any other coffee vendor), with no line at all. Simply providing a great product with a deep understanding of the target consumer is merely the price of entry today. The superior competitors will be providing what we are calling neurological connectivity." –p. 12.

How are you connecting the experience brides have at your store with the emotions of feeling good about their weddings? Most brides have been planning this day for years in their minds and the better you can tap into all of that pent-up emotion in a way that helps you educate and entertain will ensure that she walks away from your store with her dress.

When brides sense that you are a real person and are sincere about what you are offering them, it makes any type of marketing or promotion that you may be offering much more persuasive. If you can, use a picture of you in the ad or personally sign the letters or postcards that you send out. This adds an element of entertainment that they aren't getting from their competitors. They are drawn in because of their connection to you. Another big secret to educating brides in an entertaining way is to write the marketing copy in such a way that it is better matched to your target audience. The better the match, the more successful the promotion.

One of my favorite viral advertising campaigns of the past several years has been "The Man Your Man Could Smell Like" promotions done by Old Spice and actor Isaiah Mustafa. These were done by ad agency Widen + Kennedy. Ad expert Stefan Mumaw makes this statement about what made this ad so successful:

"Old Spice had an obvious stigma to overcome. They're old. They smell like spice. They're old and spicy. They make us all think of our grandpa. But brands like Gillette and Axe were kicking Old Spice's spice, so something had to be done. Old Spice desired to appeal to a younger demographic, that 20-something crowd of guys...."

The promotion succeeded because not only was the ad entertaining with Isaiah Mustafa promoting how their man couldn't look like him, but they could smell like him with Old Spice bodywash. The original ads were very well written, funny and entertaining. But, what made the ads go viral, was the way in which Mustafa answered questions live.

Mumaw says:

"As [Mustafa] answered questions, the team quickly processed and uploaded the responses to the YouTube channel they had created for the spots, to the tune of 181 video responses in a 24-hour period. Clad in his traditional towel and rippled pecs, the Old Spice guy answered questions about his love live, what he does for fun, how President Obama could be more manly, and he even proposed for a Twitter follower. He answered questions from Internet celebrities like Digg founder Kevin Rose, blogger Perez Hilton, and even groundswell chat board behemoth 4chan, whose followers number in the hundreds of thousands and has the power to shape the digital opinion of a vast number of the target audience. The results were astounding. In a single day, the YouTube channel pulled 6.5 million viewers, Twitter followers went from 8,000 to 70,000 in a two-day period, and Facebook fans jumped on to the tune of almost 32,000. The total brand reach in the first six months of the campaign has topped 110 million views." –*Chasing the Monster Idea*, pp. 92-94.

Every bride thinks her life is different and that her wedding experience will be different. When you are selling to someone, remember that brides likely have the opinion that their wedding and their situation is different – and that you could never understand. Brides are not reading a monologue, they are conversing with it. The bride might be reading your ad and thinking, " Yeah, yeah, yeah, but you don't understand me. My life or my wedding is different."

Here is an example of how an educational article can be used to explain why brides should schedule an appointment at a bridal store instead of just walking in unannounced. Notice how the copy draws the bride in with language that helps her feel and know that you really care about her and her experience. The wording says:

"Many brides have heard that they shouldn't buy a dress at the first store they go to. While it is a good idea to look to ensure that you make the best choice (it is your wedding after all), it is a myth to believe that you can't buy a dress you love at the first store you've been to. After all, you have great taste and are going to pick beautiful dresses from any store that you go to. A large percentage of brides end up buying the first dress they try on for this reason. Their eye is drawn to a dress they really love and they end up getting that first dress they tried on. Those brides who are indecisive usually come back and end up buying that dress after they've spent time and money on gasoline by driving all over that they could have easily saved by trusting their instincts and getting the dress they loved when they first tried it on.

At ___*name of your bridal store*___, we even have a special incentive for decisive brides who buy on their first visit. I've attached a coupon that you can use when you schedule your appointment at our store. We are able to offer this special savings since we have the price of two visits built into every dress. When brides choose to buy the dress they love most on their first visit, we pass those savings along to them. Trust your instincts. You may not find your dress at the first store you go to, but if you do, don't hesitate to begin enjoying the euphoric feeling you'll have knowing that you have that part of your wedding all taken care of. Remember, when you choose to bring lots of friends to help you shop, you also bring lots of opinions. Be careful that you don't let the opinions of your friends influence what **you** really want to wear (because, after all, it is *your* wedding)."

This is a very persuasive way to not only educate brides, but also help them see the advantage to buying on their first visit. The big mistake you can make when writing educational advertising promotions is to think that entertainment only means humor. Brides can be entertained in many ways by engaging their minds and helping them plan the fun and exciting event that they are preparing for.

Here are three places where you should be striving to entertain and educate your brides:

- *Your web site* – Are you writing articles or sharing information that is helpful to brides? If not, you should start...now.

- *Any promotion you do* – People respond to ads because they feel they have a chance to win something or get something they might not otherwise get. Are you promoting any contests you do in such a way that brides can have fun by (imagining themselves winning)? Are you pointing to those emotions in the ads that you create and put together?

- *Videos* – people love to watch videos that explain information. You can tie explanations or demonstrations of hair updos or other things that brides need with information about why they should buy a dress from you and your store. Contact other wedding professionals in your area and ask them to come to your store where you can shoot videos introducing them and their service to brides in your area. You can charge these advertisers for their participation in this kind of promotional video as well, but the key is to create something entertaining that brides will want to watch that also educates them not only on the service or product you're promoting, but that also promotes you as a celebrity and an authority and as the best place to buy a wedding dress.

Remember, the price for personal empathy is great disclosure. The more you are willing to tell and show brides about you and what you do, the more they will empathize with you, especially if you get into the world and tell them about how you can help them solve their challenges in preparing for their weddings. Brides are looking for authentic human beings with whom they can do business. The more you reveal about yourself, the more likely you will connect with the brides in your area.

The more you pay attention to how brides respond to what you do, the more successfully you'll be able to elicit emotion and excitement that will draw and attract brides to your store who are ready to buy what you have to sell.

4. Does your marketing get you and your store brand out of your comfort zone? Does it challenge you? Does it scare you a little bit?

To be effective, marketing should point out what is different about you in a way that wows your brides and prom customers. You can't be like everyone else and stand out. The most successful businesses are those who have come up with disruptive hypothesis in their marketing approach to point out why their message and their brand stand out and are different.

Remember, getting out of your comfort zone keeps you on the edge of your fear which can help you channel that energy into growth and excitement that can set you apart from those around you who are content to just remain with the status quo.

5. Brides are tired of trickery. They want an authentic voice behind the message. Even though consumers are skeptical today,

they want to believe and will do so in mass if they can get behind you as an authentic voice that speaks to their wants and needs and will help the bride and groom get what they want (an amazing wedding).

What makes up an authentic voice? It has to be one that the bride relates to, values, and trusts. This is so important since the rising generation of brides is sick and tired of hypocrisy and hype. They want to know what you really know and feel and how it will help them.

When you have a unique edge and an authentic story, you can differentiate yourself from your competitors. A good reason to do this is so that you don't get lumped into the commodity classification.

Author Seth Godin makes this observation in his book, *Purple Cow*: "Remarkable marketing is the art of building things worth noticing right into your product or service. Not just slapping on the marketing function as a last minute add-on, but also understanding from the outset that if your offering isn't remarkable, then it's invisible."

You don't want your store to be invisible, so it is critical that you make your brand authentic and that you have a definable edge that is truly unique. This will give you an edge. It is enhanced when you can be an authentic voice that brides trust and look to for advice and help as they plan their wedding.

Rohit Bhargava in his book *Personality Not Included* recommends becoming authentic by: 1) Defining a credible heritage, 2) Demonstrating your passion and belief, 3) Fostering individuals instead of people so that you are developing leaders around you, and 4) By having motives beyond profit.

Young entrepreneur Ryan Blair has this to say about the importance of connecting and dropping the hype to today's younger generation. He says:

"Why do I have to listen to my parents' music? Why isn't Jay-Z up there? Where are the authentic people who will lead the next generation through the worst economic time since the Great Depression? Where's the rock and roll of this generation?

"Our generation doesn't believe anyone has a perfect life. We think inspirational speakers are a joke. We want authenticity. Where are the leaders of our generation with the real stories to inspire us to greatness?...whatever is left standing will be authentic and what isn't will be gone, because our generation recognizes the smell of BS like no other." –*Nothing to Lose, Everything to Gain*, p. 28.

One of the best ways to be and stay authentic is to be in the mud of the marketplace. When you work with brides on a daily basis and help them find what they are looking for, you know what they are looking for, what you don't have, what you need and what is selling better in your area better than anyone else. When you're in the mud of the marketplace, you understand what the bride is dealing with and you can come up with better solutions to help her get what she wants quicker and with less stress. You also understand the attitudes and preferences of the brides in your area.

Speak up and let brides know that you understand where they are coming from. Too often, bridal retailers don't allow brides to know how authentic they really are because they don't put out videos, special reports or other information that allow the brides in their areas to get to know and feel the hearts of the store owners and bridal consultants. Brides come to know that you have their best interests at heart when they hear you talk in ways that helps them see what you do for them. One way you can do this is to talk about what you do when you go to markets and how you select the dresses you bring into your store. When you share this information with them, brides better understand the sacrifices you make in their behalf and they are able to see your authentic self shine through.

6. There is power in a great story. Are you telling stories or letting brides tell them for you?

If you want to have massive success in your marketing campaigns, you must take control of the story you are telling to brides. It should be a consistent message and one that you and each member of your team shares in the same way with a little bit of theater and excitement mixed in.

One of my favorite examples of the power of story is that of William Wrigley, Jr. He was the eldest of eight children born to a Philadelphia soapmaker in 1861. He went to Chicago in the spring of 1891. He was 29 years old, had $32 in his pocket and unlimited enthusiasm and energy. He also had great talent as a salesman.

His father was a soap manufacturer, and at the start of his new business in Chicago, Mr. Wrigley sold Wrigley's Scouring Soap. As an extra incentive to merchants, Mr. Wrigley offered premiums. He knew his customers would be more likely to carry Wrigley's soap if they received a little "something for nothing." One of these premiums was baking powder. When baking powder proved to be more popular than soap, he switched to the baking powder business.

Then one day in 1892, Mr. Wrigley got the idea of offering two packages of chewing gum with each can of baking powder. The offer was a big success. Once again the premium - chewing gum - seemed more promising than the product it was supposed to promote.

At that time, there were at least a dozen chewing gum companies in the United States, but the industry was relatively undeveloped. Mr. Wrigley decided that chewing gum was the product with the potential he had been looking for, so he began marketing it under his own name. His first two brands were Lotta and Vassar. Juicy Fruit gum came next in 1893, and Wrigley's Spearmint was introduced later that same year.

Wrigley legitimized chewing gum by advertising. He became the largest advertiser of any single product. He once observed:

"Advertising is like running a train. You've got to keep on shoveling coal into the engine. Once you stop stoking the fire goes out and the train will gradually slow down and come to a dead stop." By the time of his death at age seventy in 1932, Wrigley had spent $100,000,000 in advertising. The growth of his company never slowed down.

Getting a foothold in the chewing gum business was not easy. Several times the young company was on the verge of going under, but hard work overcame the difficulties, and the business forged ahead.

The gum was mixed like dough, rolled, cut into sticks, and packed by hand. He began advertising with trademark arrows and elves, and gradually his gum gained acceptance. On two occasions he collected the names of every telephone subscriber in Chicago and sent each a package of chewing gum.

In the very early days, William Wrigley Jr. personally did much of the selling to the trade. He had a gift for seeing his customers' point of view and accommodating himself to their needs.

As the company grew, Mr. Wrigley showed an unusual knack for inspiring enthusiasm in the people who worked with him.

Mr. Wrigley was also one of the pioneers in the use of advertising to promote the sale of branded merchandise. He saw that consumer acceptance of Wrigley's gum could be built faster by telling people about the benefits of the product through newspaper and magazine ads, outdoor posters and other forms of advertising. Then, as more and more consumers began to ask for and buy Wrigley's chewing gum in the stores, the storekeeper would naturally want to keep a sufficient stock of Wrigley brands on hand.

In the early 1900s, production reached 40,000,000 sticks a day (all selling for 5 cents a pack) and his packaging quickly grew to include wording in 37 languages.

Wrigley's death came in the depths of the Depression, which he combated by providing shelter in his Chicago buildings and feeding five hundred jobless men daily through the Salvation Army. The hard times had little effect on his business, however. Just prior to his death he wrote, "People chew harder when they are sad."

As the company continued to grow, it steadfastly applied this basic principle: "Even in a little thing like a stick of gum, quality is important."

--Information from "The Story of Wrigley" on *Wrigley.com* and *So Who the Heck Was Oscar Meyer, The Real People Behind Those Brand Names*, pp. 92-94.

As is evident from this story, a big key to telling your story is to start right and then be consistent. You've got to take responsibility for how you promote yourself and your story. You can't wait for others to do this for you. It is the biggest mistake you can make as a retailer in marketing.

What will you do at your store to put back what is missing from your store?

How can you incorporate more theater and experience into how you sell and educate brides coming into your store?

You can only do these things if you are committed to self-renewal and reinvention and you specifically work to innovate around the core of what makes your bridal store work.

7. To be mega-successful, you must promote what you do as being a new idea or concept. Something that is boring or common will never have the power to move brides to take action and come into your store and make a purchase.

Too many bridal retailers try to do the same things as their competitors. They make it difficult for brides to see how they are different and so as a result, brides differentiate based on the price of what you sell.

One of the most fascinating things I enjoy studying is how buying decisions are made. In the previous chapter, I mentioned lessons about persuasion from the book *The Buying Brain*. The book also has some fascinating research about why new ideas or concepts are sorted and remembered better than those that are all lumped together. The author Dr. A.K. Pradeep says:

"The 'ease of processing' of your message is therefore very important to the brain. A complicated ad that requires cognitive resources will likely be ignored by the brain. So as you balance the complexity of an ad with ease of processing, lean towards ease....While it is true that 'simple puzzles' intrigue and attract the brain, if the puzzle requires more than a few seconds to resolve, the brain gives up, and often rejects the message, with prejudice against your brand." –p. 18.

By positioning yourself as something different than what a bride is used to seeing, your story and your marketing campaigns rise in importance and significance to the brain. What is new and unique grabs the attention of the brain, especially when what you are offering to brides speaks to her and helps her solve a specific challenge or problem she is facing.

Apple is a great example of this. According to Dr. Pradeep: "Apple made an innately strategic decision a long time ago to help the brain do what it loves to do: identify and categorize. Apple focused on consumer ease of use, inherent fear/distrust of complicated and, therefore, intimidating technology, and designed beautiful products and packaging, which in turn gave the Apple brand enhanced meaning and an even stronger consistent, and lasting identity. Apple also strictly controlled distribution, giving their product an identity that was separate from other computer brands. And they adhered to price points above the category norms, imbuing the brand and the products under that umbrella with the aura of desirability." –p. 130.

In other words, Apple positions their products into a category of one with unique packaging, price, and new technology. If you watch any of their product launches, you'll see how they masterfully present their new product releases in this format and most importantly into a category of one (so there is no need to compare) because their product is perceived to be the very best.

Dr. Pradeep continues:

"Context has a huge impact on how the brain processes an experience. Apple understands this, especially in their retail operations. If you shop a store aisle, where everything is piled up or kept in bins, your takeaway is a perception that all is cheap. Implicitly, if it's of value it won't be piled up in the corner. On the other hand, this can also work to some brands' advantage; a bargain retailer deliberately stacks things up to give you the view that you are getting a deal. For luxury brands, of course, the opposite is the case. When you go to a Rolex store, your watch is displayed in a locked case. And when they bring it to you, they polish it and present it on an elegant padded case. The unspoken but clearly communicated message is that this brand is inherently precious, highly valued, and valuable, and therefore, worth the price. The feeling of desire is actually heightened by this air of exclusivity, reinforcing the individual elements of Rolex's Brand Essence Framework." –pp. 130-131.

Is the way that you are presenting the gowns you sell in your store allowing you to present yourself in the context of being truly unique and in a category of one as a new idea? If not, you should carefully think about what it is that you are actually selling.

You must be the one who controls the message about your store. Perception is the reality for brides. If you don't believe this is true, go to YouTube.com and type in the name: Joshua Bell and violin experiment. What you will see is a short video that shows nearly 1,000 people walking by Bell in the corner of a Washington DC Metro station where he played for about 45 minutes. Every few minutes, someone might stop by and listen or toss a dollar into his open case. In that short performance, he made $32, yet he is one of the world's most famous musicians. He was playing on his $3.5 million Stradivarius violin (one of the most rare and expensive violins in existence). Yet, very few of those who walked by had any idea who he was or paid attention to the amazing music he played. The previous night, he played to a sold out concert in Boston where the average seat was $100. In other words, because of context and perception, Joshua Bell's performance at the Metro station made him $32 where his performance at Boston's Symphony Hall was worth approximately $220,000.

Create the perceptions you want brides to have about you and your store. There is no excuse for letting someone else brand you or being like Bell in the Metro station where brides are walking by your store and have no idea who you are. When you build your own brand, you'll truly stand out and the financial rewards will be much greater to you and your business as well.

8. Use game-based marketing to grab attention and generate interest.

It is harder than ever to grab attention of today's bride. There are so many competing influences for everyone's time that standing out and drawing brides into your place of business is becoming increasingly more difficult and challenging. In their book, *Game-Based Marketing*, video game innovator and entrepreneur Gabe Zichermann and writer Joselin Linder explore the power of game-based marketing and a concept they call 'funware' which is a model designed to incorporate and use games and game mechanics to reach today's customers.

Zichermann and Linder believe that today's customers are what they call "Generation G, the greatest game-playing demographic in history." The brides and prom girls that you are trying to attract at your store respond well to game-based marketing because it essentially makes shopping more fun. It reverts them back to fun experiences of their childhood and involves them in tension relieving activities like the games they are used to playing.

The authors make this great point about why traditional marketing isn't working as well as it used to. They say:

"In this socially networked, choice-driven world, the old methods of reaching consumers with advertising messages have simply stopped working as well as they need to. Game mechanics, on the other hand, are steadily rising to the surface. In everything from the airline you fly to the ATM card you use, savvy marketers are turning to the power of games to increase their return on investment, provide essential predictability, and—above all else—engender the kind of customer loyalty that wasn't before possible."

They continue:

"Whereas marketers have used 'traditional' loyalty programs and advergames for years to create engagement and buzz, this book—and the movement it represents—is focused on integrating the power of games into every aspect of product marketing and promotions. Understanding this opportunity will empower you to create breakthrough strategies that leverage the power of social networks and human behavior in ways designed to cut your marketing costs and bolster your bottom line." –*Game Based Marketing*, p. 6.

I've been a proponent of game-based marketing for quite some time. Here are the most important lessons I've learned from this book and my own experiences:

1) Have a loyalty program that rewards multiple purchases.

Zichermann and Linder report: "On the Web, the stickiest sites are social networking and multiplayer games....In the offline world, the most successful loyalty programs are those run by airlines and other hospitality companies. Online, hundreds of millions of game-players spend billions of minutes each month chasing points, levels, badges, and rewards—both real and psychological."

They then, make this claim, which I find absolutely fascinating:

"Many innovative companies and organizations already understand the power of games and are well on their way to reshaping industries from financial services to space exploration. Undoubtedly, the rise of generations weaned on games and the promise of Funware will reshape your industry, too."—p. 14.

What is "Funware"?

According to the authors, "funware is a term that summarizes the ubiquitous presence of games or game mechanics in our lives—also serves as the buzzword for game-based marketing. By becoming more aware of the Funware in which we are already engaging, either as a marketer or as a consumer, we are increasing our ability to produce a desired outcome. In other words, if one remains a passive participant in these games—either as a brand or a player—encouraging specific behaviors that lead to desired outcomes is more difficult. The core premise of Funware for marketers is its ability to drive user behavior in a predictable, overt, and focused way. Put another way: Funware is the art and science of turning of turning your customers' everyday interactions into 'games' that serve your business purposes." *–Game-Based Marketing*, p. 20.

One way you could encourage brides to participate in special programs is to email or text them when you are having a specific promotion. When brides buy something on a specific day or during a specific time period, they can be entered in a drawing to win a prize. I've seen this done this very successfully on numerous occasions. Successful prizes include offering the winner of the contest their money back on the dress they've purchased, a one night stay at a five star hotel, electronics gadgets and other great prizes. Each time, this type of promotion has been conducted, there is a measurable increase in the excitement brides have about buying something from someone else. The question you must consider is: How will you capitalize on this trend in the future?

Will games shape the way you market to and influence brides to buy from you?

There is no question that many industries are already heavily utilizing simple to complex loyalty programs. Nearly 80% of all Americans have one or two credit cards that accumulate points and multiple frequent traveler accounts with airlines, hotels, or car rental agencies. Any rewards program of this type is really a game designed to give you status, rewards, special access, and special treatment. When you accumulate points, you are doing your best to win in a way that rewards you.

Loyalty programs succeed largely because of two very powerful and interconnected psychological triggers: hope and the desire to collect. When you believe that you should be loyal to a company in order to get a future reward later, you are acting and being influenced by the psychological trigger of hope.

Joe Sugarman says in his book *Triggers* that hope is powerful because it motivates you based on a future benefit that is neither assured, nor guaranteed. He says:

"Hope can be a great motivator in the buying process. A woman buys new face cream in the hope that it will make a difference in her wrinkles. An intense golfer buys a new golf ball in the hope that it may take a few strokes off a golf game. In short, there is an implied possibility that a product or service will provide a future benefit. The future benefit is neither assured, nor guaranteed; it is a dream, a fantasy, or, at the most, a possibility."--, p. 159.

Zichermann and Linden point out:

"But what is a loyalty program if not a complex, multilayered, gamelike exercise in achieving status, rewards, and special treatment? Whether you seek free upgrades, a Gold Card, or entrance into the Red Carpet lounge while waiting at the airport, what you are invariably seeking is a win. The underlying drive to keep playing based on a belief that you will someday win those rewards is exactly what gives loyalty programs their power."—p. 15.

I really believe this will be a game changer for many bridal stores in the future. Those who successfully implement loyalty programs that are tied to additional purchases and leverage those sales into continuity-based income will be the ones who rise above the other retailers to prosper and succeed.

How can you combine and utilize the trigger of hope in the marketing promotions that you employ at your store?

Some serious thought into this and the development of your own game-based marketing strategies can help you draw and successfully sell to brides who are looking for what you sell.

2) Incorporate games that make the experience of shopping at your store even more fun.

Like other consumers, brides really respond well to games. The best games incorporate some type of 'beat the clock' component to them and we've found that this works really well for us. We've done this by marketing the fast approaching deadline to a contest or promotion we're doing on our web site. As the clock approaches zero, brides know how much longer they have until they must come into the store to take advantage of the savings and the promotions they want to get. It is also a visually interesting aspect of our web site. When you arrive and you see a clock that is counting down, it grabs your attention and invokes curiosity since you want to find out what is happening or what will happen when the clock timer hits zero. Once they click through to find out about the promotion, you can invite them to call and schedule an appointment and print out a copy of the offer, which they can bring in to save money off the dress or accessories or be a part of a game that you've created.

You can use all types of games of chance at your store to create excitement and have brides excited about making the decision to buy from you. Most brides or prom girls have played one of these before at some time in their lives and are familiar with the concept that makes it easier to explain and have them play.

Here are three examples of how you could use games of chance:
1) Roll the dice and get a discount on a primary or secondary purchase.
In the case of a homecoming or back to school prom promotion, have the girl roll a single die to see how much of a discount she will get off the dress (a one gets 10 percent off, a six gets 60 percent). I don't really recommend giving discounts on a primary sale item like this, but this may be a good way to help you move some of last year's prom merchandise so that you can buy new merchandise

for next season. It is better to have a promotion like this linked to a secondary purchase. We once conducted a Tour De Chance Event, which allowed brides who purchased their wedding dress to roll a pair of dice to find out how much they would save on their veil or tiara – the secondary item (a 2 = 20% off; 10, 11 or 12 = FREE veil or tiara). You could do something similar with some thought and planning.

2) Have a Bingo Card to encourage brides to return to your store.
Have a bingo card featuring 16 items at your store (4 in a row). Each time a bride tries on one of the featured items, you can have one of your bridal consultants stamp it out on a card. Every 'bingo' that the bride gets (horizontally, vertically, or diagonally) can have a pre-determined gift certificate. The bingo card should have an expiration date of 30 days from the time she purchased the dress or came into the store.

3) **Enter brides into a contest.** One way you can use games of chance this way is to enter everyone who buys something into a contest to win a FREE iPad, iPod or get the money back for the item they just bought at your store. These types of games reward certain behaviors you want or that the majority of people are already doing and then equating those into the opportunity to get something else for what you just got.

Ideally, the reward should be something the bride wants, but that also encourages her to make additional purchases. Here are some examples of things you could do:

- *Now That You've Voted, It's Time to Start Your Own Party (Wedding Party, that is)* – the promotion run during an election season could include the following text: "Since you're probably frustrated enough to start your own political party, we've decided to help you start your wedding party instead and save big on your wedding dress. Simply come to our store November 1-6 and you'll have your chance to vote for $50, $100 or $150 OFF any wedding gown over $599 plus be entered into a drawing to get your dress for FREE. With these kinds of savings, you'll be happy to vote AND be pleased with the outcome." The idea behind this promotion is to take something that is on the mind of a lot of people and link that idea into the activity or behavior that you want brides to actually engage in.

- *Any type of referral program*

- *Special offers for brides who schedule their bridesmaid appointment at the same time they purchase a dress* (when this happens, you could give an additional $5 off every bridesmaid dress with a scheduled appointment that you're setting up while they're buying their wedding dress)

- *Reward written testimonials on specific sites with $5 off a future purchase* (such as a bridesmaid dress)

Two powerful ways you can utilize this principle in games are during the months of October and December. October is breast cancer awareness month so you can create a promotion to help brides feel good about their purchase with you by donating a certain amount to Brides Against Breast Cancer or the Susan G. Komen Breast Cancer Foundation when they purchase their wedding dress during the promotion. You could also do a Runaway Bride event and donate the proceeds of the entries from the race to a charity of your choice.

Specifically, this type of promotion could say: "Buy any wedding gown at our store in the month of October (National Breast Cancer Awareness Month), and we'll give you $50, $75, or $100 off your dress and we'll donate the same amount of savings $50, $75, or $100 to Brides Against Breast Cancer." Then, the specifics of the offer are:

- You Save $50, We Give $50 when you buy any wedding gown $299 to $499.

- You Save $75, We Give $75 when you buy any wedding gown $500 to $899.

- You Save $100, We Give $100 when you buy any wedding

gown $900 and up.

When you do this type of promotion, brides will not only happily buy their dress, they will also likely comment on how happy they are that the savings are going to such a great cause. In fact, when we did this promotion on one occasion, one bride told us to donate *her* savings to the cause and she would pay full price for the dress. She had lost a family member to breast cancer and so she was committed to help us support this cause.

The other game around a cause that you can use is an annual "Give and Save" event during Christmas. This game involves allowing brides to save a certain amount of money off of her wedding dress when she donates a toy to Toys for Tots or a food item to the local food bank. This type of event can create a lot of excitement and enthusiasm from brides. They will be excited about saving money on their dress or accessories, but more importantly they will be excited about supporting the cause. I have seen this promotion successfully done at many bridal retailers. Those brides who received the savings brought back some great toys which bridal retailers been able to donate to Toys for Tots. Your specific promotion could say the following:

"This Holiday Season, Give and Save: Bring in a gift from the list below and you can save $50, $100 or $150 on your wedding dress. All food will be donated to the local food bank and all toys will be donated to the local Toys For Tots Foundation

- Save $50 off the purchase of any wedding gown **when you bring in a food item.**

- Save $100 off the purchase of any wedding gown **when you bring in a new unwrapped toy.**

- Save $150 off the purchase of any wedding gown **when you bring in a food item and an unwrapped toy.**

People will give much more generously when you equate the cause you are supporting with something they really believe in. You can also use your local media to help promote what you are doing and convert this into some excellent PR for your store.

Using this tactic for a referral program, you can show brides when they buy a dress from you how they can get a 100 percent refund on the purchase of their wedding gown by simply referring 8 other people to you who also buy their dress from you. This game works because brides think, "Hey, I can get all of my money back" if I just refer 8 brides to the store." If you have a tiered approach to smaller gifts they can get if they refer people to you, it will just accelerate the process. The biggest benefit is that there is a viral component to this type of referral process since brides who get a 100% refund will talk about it and they will tell their friends about it so they can get their money back. The other benefit is that brides who come into the store to buy from you (who were referred by their friends) will already know about the referral program and will be excited to play your referral game as soon as they buy their dress and this will add up over time.

To make this successful, you can create a special offer at certain times of your day or on slower days of your week to help boost your business. Sonic has done this very well by offering one item on their menu (drinks at 50% off during off peak afternoon hours). This has turned a slow time at their restaurant into a time that is busier for their staff and employees.

How could you use this idea to generate traffic during slower times in your store?

Can you promote greater discounts on certain accessories during slower periods?

One thing you can do is put together a monthly calendar where you can have scratch off things on each day that they can bring in to find out what they might get. These would only be valid during certain times or on certain days. You could also do drawings or have events at your store to promote this.

Another way to do this would be to put a calendar on the wall and have little envelopes inside each day that are only valid between certain times of the day. Then, when the bride comes in, she can pull one of the envelopes out of the day's calendar and see what she has received.

I know many restaurants that do themed promotions based on the day of the week. This way they are able to bring in different demographics of their customer base and encourage them to dine more frequently there. You could do the same by having different days of the week where you promote accessories. Here are a couple of ideas:

- Unbelievable offers only on discontinued merchandise (all gowns that have been discontinued are sold at $399 from 12-3pm).
- Receive a free tiara up to $149 with the purchase of a wedding gown.
- Receive $100 off the purchase price of any gown in the store over $199.
- $10 off bridesmaids, $10 off individual accessories, $10 off tuxedo rentals at a certain time of day or one day a week.

You probably don't need these types of events on Fridays or Saturdays since you are typically busiest on those days anyway. Give this some thought and figure out how you could incorporate a game-based philosophy into how you sell on slower days.

Whatever you do for your game, keep these principles in mind:

- What do you want to achieve as a result of having the game? Do you want to move slow moving dresses, discontinued dresses, or just bring in new customers? Whatever your goal is, make sure it is realistic and attainable. If a contest doesn't seem realistic and attainable, your bridal consultants won't promote it and your brides won't feel like they can win anyway.

- Have a time limit. If the game goes on too long, the brides and your bridal consultants will likely lose interest in it. Games that last a day, especially for incentivizing your sales team are great. A week is fine, but don't extend your game longer than a month or you'll lose interest and focus.
- Make sure that everyone who buys from you has a chance to win.
- Don't forget that the entire purpose of any contest is to create excitement to bring brides into your store. If it doesn't achieve that objective, it probably isn't a very good idea.
- Have clear rules. One of the biggest mistakes you can make in marketing a game is not writing down the rules, so that they are clearly understood by everyone who is involved. The rules for any contest or game should include the following:
  - What specifically must be done in order to win
  - How the contest will be tracked
  - What will happen in the case of a tie.
  - When will the prize be awarded (date and time) – important so you can have media coverage and get brides to come down for the event.
  - Who is eligible to win
  - The time frame of the game (beginning and completion dates)

3) Have a black card and red carpet mentality.

The basic premise of a black card and red carpet mentality is that there are certain things that customers are trained to do by how you set up the selling environment. Frequent customers can get special preferential red carpet treatment by qualifying for the elite black card that a business offers to its best customers. *Game Based Marketing* details how Starbucks customers can get preferential treatment by showing up at the same time each day and tipping their baristas and earn their equivalent of a black card. You can do this by offering a gold or platinum membership card to brides who buy their dress, bridesmaid dresses and rent their tuxedos from you (if you offer them). Once brides qualify for a "black card", they then receive preferential red carpet treatment. This is a very common business practice for the top customer tier in the very best customer experience.

Zichermann and Linder say: "After 20 years, Starbucks has begun to acknowledge its most frequent and loyal customers. By increasing the status and visibility of its most loyal group of patrons through their Black Card offering, Starbucks has come close to evolving a frequent flyer mentality. However, the company still hasn't developed a clear vision for the opportunity at their feet.

"Where airlines have understood the value of the red carpet and priority boarding for years, Starbucks and other coffee houses, have only recently discovered the power of the expedited coffee order. Consumers playing at a lower level subsequently become interested in how they might achieve this preferred treatment. Wondering what they have to do to get there opens a dialogue in which a marketer might suggest, 'All you have to do is buy 10 consecutive cups of coffee.'

"From an operations standpoint, a business's win is even greater: the marginal cost of providing the red carpet experience is almost nothing. In fact, if the program is designed exactly like those offered by the airlines...over time, more and more players will actively seek the red carpet treatment while voluntarily opting into your marketing programs and sharing personal information with you." –*Game Based Marketing*, pp. 36-37.

In fact, you could use the promise of an even better experience and better preferential treatment when brides arrive at your store as a way to entice them to share their personal contact information and wedding date info with you. Then, once they have registered and scheduled their appointment with you, they could be ushered into an even more amazing experience at your bridal store than typical brides usually have. Give some thought to this and you'll discover ways in which you can heighten both the experience and overall value a bride has at your store and the size of your lead list.

4) Use the concept of badging to recognize and reward those who play the games you create at your store well.

Zichermann and Linder say: "The term [badges] may conjure up images of the Boy Scouts of America. Merit badges, for example, are embedded in popular lore; scouts are awarded badges for completing any one of hundreds of challenges laid out by the organization. In the real world of the Boy Scouts, badges are patches bearing images of the completed task, which are displayed as being sewn onto the uniform.

"In a more contemporary sense, it has been repeatedly shown that people will compete for visible badges on social networking sites. Employing Facebook apps that offer ways for users to display their accomplishments is an example of an easy and cost-efficient way to 'badge' your players. Given the advances of Facebook and other social networking platforms, virtual badges may already be more valuable to most users than the physical equivalent....A bumper sticker, for example, that serves as a real-world badge does not lack value. 'Parent of a Fifth Grade Honor Student' is an easy and cost-effective form of badging, however the lack of clarity about who will see the bumper sticker (and whether or not the driver of the car matters to those that do) reduces its value. When a badge is placed on a Facebook profile, it is almost guaranteed that the people who see the badge are socially relevant to the user." –p. 74-75.

Since there is tremendous power in the concept of badging, how could you use this at your store?

Here are a few ideas:

• Loyalty rewards program – reward brides for multiple purchases (could you have a badge for the bride who buys everything she will wear from you and your store?) A tiered referral program helps brides earn 'badges' or benefits more quickly and rewards the behavior you want.

- Offer badges for interacting with certain wedding vendors
- Have t-shirts that prom fashion team members wear
- Print business cards or pass-along cards for fashion team members or bridal ambassadors
- Have a physical gold membership or insider's club membership card (which they can carry and show others)
- Offer special badges or rewards for those who drive farther than 100 miles to come to your store (you might have a 100 miler award, a 250 miler award and a 1000 miler award) that signify their great accomplishment and encourages other brides to do the same

The key component of the way you integrate games and rewards into what you do at your store is simply this: you want a game that has a series of levels that will encourage brides or prom customers to purchase from you multiple times and to spread those purchases out over time and amongst other members of their peer group (friends and family).

Zichermann and Linder make this observation: "In the Boy Scouts, collecting badges helps boys achieve new levels. The Eagle Scouts, for example, require the acquisition of 21 merit badges as well as the completion of an extensive service project. By establishing a relationship between challenges, badges, and levels, the Boy Scouts have built one of the most successful leveling systems to date." –p. 78.

As an Eagle Scout myself, I can attest to the persuasive power of earning these badges and moving up within ranks. It is a combination of positive peer pressure (when you seen your friends ascending, you want to as well) and earning respect and recognition for your hard work. I really like the comparison that the authors of *Game-Based Marketing* insinuate between the experience boy and girl scouts have and what customers at your business should experience as well. There is a real power in games that incorporate badges and levels and allow those participating and watching to see who is winning. If you don't already utilize recognition in some way, you really should figure out a way to incorporate this into your sales and marketing processes.

Another great example of badges and levels is that of the U.S. military. Zichermann and Linder explain: "The U.S. military has one of the most recognizable systems of levels and badges. Although cryptic to the average civilian, every aspect of military dress and communication style is thoughtfully connected to a status marker. So, it probably comes as no surprise that the military has developed one of the most popular and interesting games of all time."

A final example of what the authors suggest for Safeway is a very interesting look at how badges and games could be used when shopping for food. Zichermann and Linder detail three examples in chapter four of their book:

"Despite being the fourth-largest grocer in the United States and a purveyor of a club card program with 1.2 million members, Safeway is missing great opportunities to build game mechanics into a product that everyone loves: food. Some ideas for how Safeway could capitalize on the power of the company's database through Funware include the following:

"**The Healthy Safeway Club**: Designed to encourage healthy and organic eating, leaders in this club could receive badges that label them as 'Green,' 'Greener,' and 'Greenest.' A leaderboard could indicate Safeway's healthiest shoppers and reward players with special recipes, discounts, and even a 'healthy dinner on the house.'

"**The Foodie Safeway Club**: This club would focus on people who love food and who are interested in taste, texture, and style. These players' goal would be to socialize with other foodies while also maintaining an interest in sharing their knowledge of food with others. Badges should allow players access to better eaters with more knowledge, and the resulting leaderboard should be highly visible.

"**The Savings Safeway Club**: Players in this game would be most concerned with buying and preparing inexpensive meals and should be categorized by family size. Rewards could include tips for savings and social interactions with people with small budgets who are interested in eating well. The community options for sharing savings strategies are almost limitless.

"In each case, the different motivations of the various players could be exploited to accomplish the core objective: increased loyalty that's targeted to different styles of 'play.'" –, pp. 86-87.

These examples should give you some ideas for how you could incorporate a game-based marketing approach at your store. Here are five of my own ideas:

- *Have different levels of savings packages for brides at your store (Silver, Gold, Platinum)* – then post the top brides in each of these categories who have given you the best ideas of how they are going to get married. You could even create fun categories (most extravagant, most creative, best do-it-yourself) and then post pictures of what the brides have done. The top bride in each category could compete for a big honeymoon give-a-way package that you could put together.
- *Create badges for brides based on their preferences (geographic, cultural, etc.) so that like-minded brides could interact with one another.* You might even be able to put together quarterly events at your store with these like-minded brides who could interact together in a social or party setting. You could even create Facebook groups or a forum where these individuals could interact. You could widely promote these events on your web site, your newsletter, or even post them on the walls of your store.
- *Create a game for the best creative use of their gown after the wedding or prom.* Trash the dress photo shoots are becoming more popular all of the time. You could invite brides to share creative things they've done with their wedding gown following their wedding or their prom dress following prom. This could be

a great way to re-engage with brides who have purchased a wedding gown from you in past years. These brides could 'like' your Facebook page in order to participate and then you could do something to incentivize them to refer more of their friends back into your store.

- *Prom fashion club* – here you could interact with your previous prom customers and give them opportunities to refer their friends and give you input on prom fashions they'd like to see in the future; you might even have fashion club meetings at your store and have contests where the participants can submit their own ideas for their favorite dress. Girls who have submitted sketches could earn badges and the winners could also earn special designations as well.

- *Rewards cards for brides who utilize your preferred vendor list* – the bride who books her wedding business with the majority of the wedding vendors who pay you to promote themselves at your store could get some kind of special gift or offer. The vendors may even pay for part of the item because it will come back to benefit them as well.

I hope you'll take the time to either implement these ideas or come up with your own unique spins on them at your store. I'd love to hear what game-based marketing strategies you're using at your stores and how they're working for you.

If you need more persuasion that you should put games into the mix of your bridal store marketing, consider that in the next few years, your prom customer base will be made up entirely of Generation G. Generation G is made up of the approximately twenty million Americans who were born between the years 1998 and 2000. They are the first large demographic group whose principal form of entertainment is games. In other words, going forward, the girls and boys who will be coming into your store to rent tuxedos and buy prom dresses will be a part of this group. Since their primary form of entertainment has been games, they will respond to those businesses who integrate what I've been talking about in this chapter.

According to the authors of *Game-Based Marketing*, this group is more "technologically savvy, socially networked, and competitively oriented than any other in history."

They continue:

"Generation G has grown up thoroughly wired to the Internet; as of 2003, nearly 50 percent of Americans were on broadband. Members of Generation G are also leading the social networking charge; more than 7 million of them regularly play on the hybrid game/social-networking site Webkinz. Once you add the rest of the tween-oriented social sites, it's not a stretch to predict 100 percent penetration for social networking in this demographic. Just as e-mail accounts went from being nearly nonexistent in the early 1990s to the principal method of communication on college campuses within 10 years, social networking will likely achieve a similar importance in much less time.

"It also goes without saying that G'ers are also expected to become mobile savvy. With the increasing penetration of iPod Touch, OLPC/Netbook PCs, and network-attached handheld devices like the Nintendo DS, this group is set as well to be the first truly *mobile, social* generation."-p. 163.

This should open your eyes to how important games are and will become in marketing in the future. The question you must ask yourself is: Will you be ready? Will you attract these customers into your stores with game-based marketing methods that grab their attention and get results?

The future will be bright for those who employ and utilize games at their bridal stores. Don't ignore the potential for the game mentality that customers currently have and will have in the future. I hope you'll use the ideas you've learned here to grow your business using the power of games and that you'll share your best ideas of what's worked with me at info@bridaltrainingsystems.com. I look forward to hearing from you!

CHAPTER 7

COMPETE AND WIN AGAINST THE BIG BOX RETAILERS

"Giants have a culture of process. You have a culture of speed....They can't hit what they can't catch. Win on speed."—Stephen Denny

David has become Goliath. In the bridal industry, big box retailers such as David's Bridal and Alfred Angelo are dominant forces. Many bridal retailers have watched as these big retailers have come into their towns and watched their own market dominance shrink and disappear. In order to successfully compete with these giants, independent bridal retailers must learn how to be giant killers. In this chapter, I want to cover ten big lessons and strategies that I think each bridal retailer should employ today if they are to defeat these giants in the bridal industry on a local level. My hope is that you'll carefully consider what I share here and implement these strategies so you can grow your store from where it is now and put yourself on a path to beat the giants who seek to take all of the brides from your market area.

In this chapter, I'll discuss a book entitled *Killing Giants: 10 Strategies to Topple the Giant in Your Industry* by Stephen Denny. I'll share with you some of the insights I got from this book, some of its lessons, and my own thoughts about what it will take for you to compete with and win against the giants of the bridal industry.

1. Fight giants and big box stores on thin ice and away from the relative safety of familiar ground.

The basic premise of this principle is that if you lure a giant onto an area of thin ice, you'll be much more successful battling him there, since his weight will cause him to fall through the ice. Instead of risking losing, the giant will usually retreat and choose not to fight.

In his book *Killing Giants*, Stephen Denny calls this principle "Thin Ice." In his words, "thin ice" is "dangerous to companies who are too big to venture far from the relative safety of familiar ground. The giant's weight shifts and the ice cracks and groans underneath its feet. It's dangerous out here. Better to retreat than to risk everything. But you know the ice can support your weight. You made this patch of ice in the first place. So taunt the giant all you want. When we create our own 'thin ice', we change the environment to suit our needs. We move the public dialogue to a place where the giant is unprepared to go. Rather than risk the loss of face that will come from such a fight, the giant will likely choose to simply not fight at all." –*Killing Giants*, p. 17.

A great example in the book is the online search engine Baidu. Baidu is a Chinese web search engine that competes with the giant Google, but does so by pointing out why they are superior in their mastery over the Chinese language (an area that Google doesn't have dominance in). Here is what they say on their web site, which is a great illustration of the principle of "thin ice."

"As a native speaker of the Chinese language and a talented engineer, Baidu focuses on what it knows best - Chinese language search. Applying avant-garde technology to the world's most ancient and complex language is as challenging as it is exciting. At least people here at Baidu think so. As having diligently disclosed in the Prospectus of our recent Initial Public Offering, we believe there are at least 38 ways of saying "I" in Chinese. It is important that we master all the ways of addressing oneself in Chinese because our users depend on us to address every one of their daily queries. And trust us, pin pointing queries in the Chinese language is an art rather than a science." - http://ir.baidu.com/phoenix.zhtml?c=188488&p=irol-homeprofile

Denny says:

"Baidu gives us a vivid example of forcing a global giant to compete on ground where it can't easily win—the politics of cultural and national identity. Baidu did what the giant never thought to do, producing products that worked locally without worrying about whether it worked globally, and driving home the message in an unmistakable manner, with direct outreach to consumers that pitted Chinese stereotypes against American ones—with Baidu as the winner. As of this writing, Google's future in China is unclear, with the company redirecting search traffic to its uncensored Hong Kong site..." –p. 29.

There are four points that Denny makes in the book that I think bear some thought about how you compete against David's and the big box bridal retailers.

1) Act like a local. In the case of Baidu, they focused on something (language) that the giant Google (who is based in the U.S.) can never really command like the natives who run the Chinese site Baidu.

What things can you highlight at your bridal store that showcase your unique differences and contribution to the community?

2) Promote your local ties. How can you share how long you've been in the community, how you contribute back to the community, and share your own self-generated PR the explains why you are different in your community? One thing we did when we first opened our store was to have the newspaper come and do a story on a specific niche that we served that David's didn't. We were able to highlight our difference and use language that showed to our target niche that we really understood their needs. I also called up a target publication that was sent directly to that niche and did advertising there (which the big box retailers weren't even aware existed) and then I wrote an article about our store and submitted it to the editor and told her she could attach her name to it and even take credit for the writing of the article. When the article came out, the editor only changed 2 or 3 sentences of the article I wrote (which promoted us in a 3rd person endorsement). We then framed the article and hung it in our store where all of our customers could see it and promoted it to brides in that market niche who came in. It helped us to stand out and get recognition from that market niche very quickly. In most cases, big box retailers aren't familiar with the local community and operate outside of it. If you can tap into the local community with your own clever marketing strategies, you can stand out in ways that the larger competitor can't.

The key question is to ask: What argument can David's or Alfred Angelo never win?

In my opinion, there are three main areas:

1) Attention to niche market areas that they don't see as important or meaningful

2) Attention to follow up detail (David's is primarily interested in getting brides into their business first – their follow up if the bride doesn't buy is good, but you can be different and better here)

3) Customer service and overall experience (Big box retailers will never care about a bride's wedding as much as you will) – if you can develop and promote this difference in a clever way, you can really stand out One way you could do this is to communicate: "We care as much about your wedding as you do. When you purchase your dress here, you will always be a friend, not just a number or a sale."

3) Point out how you are like the brides you serve and can identify with the challenges they are facing. It never ceases to amaze me how asking questions and listening can build trust and help brides really feel like you are on their side. Many times, bridal consultants at big box retailers only view what they do as a job and the difference shows (there is a lot of turnover – it is hard to build momentum when everyone is constantly new and learning how to talk with brides).

Again, this is about perception. David's has gotten better at this over the years. Recent marketing and advertising efforts focus on how they are the leaders in what they do. In a recent *Brides* magazine issue, David's promoted the following four specific areas. I've listed them below followed by comments on how you can position yourself against these areas.

1) *Their design team* - In some of their advertising, they have pictured members of their design team (the picture doesn't really allow you to feel like you get to know them) – that is a weakness that you can exploit by promoting you. You can do this by allowing brides get to know you before they come into the store with a welcome video on your web site and a What to Expect pre-sales sequence.

2) *Their exclusivity* – "Every design is exclusive to David's Bridal so you won't find your gown anywhere else" (except at any of the other more than 300 + locations) – you can position this as a weakness by pointing out that even though they may have exclusive gowns, brides who wear their dresses aren't truly unique since brides all across the world are all wearing the same few gowns. By pointing out how you offer limited edition exclusive gowns that brides can have confidence they are truly unique in (since you are the only one in your area who offers those dresses) – you can showcase your unique difference with limited edition gowns since you choose how many to buy and sell in your store.

3) *Doing everything for everyone* - David's positions their stores as being all things for all people – "A Fit for Every Bride. Plus. Petites. Extra length. We've got it all!" Then, they positioned the "White by Vera Wang" collection as something that all brides can afford and wear. This was a very smart strategy on their part because brides have a *perception* and a sense of what wearing a Vera Wang gown *means* to them. How are you standing out in contrast to this? Are you building your brand so that it means something to buy a dress from you? Kleinfeld's has done a brilliant job of doing this. You can too by building your brand around you and the overall experience that the bride will get at your store that they can't get anywhere else. Again, promoting yourself and your individual brand and your ties to the

local community can be a great way to re-position David's as a place that may have a top designer like Vera Wang, but doesn't have the top notch experience and treatment they'll get at your store.

4) *Their leadership expertise* - For example, in their ads promoting their bridesmaid colors, they say: "Lots of places have lots of colors, but when it comes to the latest in fashion, David's leads the way. Only the hottest colors make it to our showrooms." A question for you to ask: What are you the leader of in your market? A second question: What are you doing to pick the colors that make it into your store? I think David's really misses the mark in their advertising here by not romancing the story about how the colors and the dresses actually made it into their store. You could say: "Last year, my staff and I traveled 3,421 miles to bring you 14 brand new colors in addition to the 49 stunning colors we already offer to the most fashionable brides in _____*your region or state*_____. Specificity, especially with numbers is a very powerful way to position your expertise. In this case, pointing out exactly how many miles you have traveled to bring those colors in makes a more compelling case than any generic advertising. You could even make the story more meaningful if you talked about how you helped a specific bridal party and give a testimonial of how they praised you for going the extra mile to get what they were looking for.

4) *Aim at the underserved.* David's has so many different product lines and offerings (and brands) that it can be easy to confuse the bride to what she is really looking for. How can you position yourself as speaking directly to a bride who may feel overwhelmed and confused by all of the options? How can you reassure her that you are there for her and will take care of her throughout every step of her wedding dress experience in ways that David's can't or won't?

When you can point out these differences, you force the big box retailers to come onto the thin ice where independent bridal retailers have the advantage. David's will never be able to offer the personal touch as well as independently owned bridal salons. It is critically important that you exploit this difference in your marketing. They may have more marketing muscle in terms of dollars and cents, but they will never have as much personal heart and intense focus on the needs of brides you serve. If you aren't promoting those differences, brides will be swayed by the persuasive and slick marketing of these big box retailers and you will miss out on a lot of sales that you could otherwise have.

A big point to remember about this is that giants in any industry (and the bridal industry is no different) have different problems than you do. Their focus is more on supply and logistics than it is on truly creating a unique experience for brides who come into their stores. This is a big opportunity for the independent retailer if you will recognize it and capitalize on it.

2. Giants are often slow to move and can't hit what they can't catch. Be more nimble and win on speed.

Denny says: "Giants have a culture of process. You have a culture of speed. They enter a first-phase evaluation. You launch a product. They form a steering committee. You launch a second generation product. They form a 'tiger team' to study your first-generation product while you ship your third-generation product. They can't hit what they can't catch. Win on speed." –p. 39.

Apple is a great example of a company that became a giant by focusing on speed. They are constantly coming out with new versions of their products (iPad 2, then 3 (then iPad Air), iPhone 4, 4S, 5, 5S, then 6 and up. They are constantly innovating so it is nearly impossible for big competitors to overtake them. Apple beat Sony (who was the market giant) to a digital media player (iPod first) through flanking warfare. They re-invented the category instead of focusing on continuing to sell Walkman and Discman products when the market shifted to digital music.

Here are a couple of principles to remember about flanking warfare, which is basically what you have to do as a smaller competitor. You could never survive by attacking them head on. Instead, you want to do four things (as I outlined on pages 38-40 in my book *Bridal Boosters & Breakthroughs*). Here they are as a reminder:

Go into an uncontested area. Flanking is different than offensive marketing into an occupied space because there is no established market for the new product or service. Carrying a new line that no one else has in your area is an example of a flanking move (especially if it meets the needs of brides that no one else is servicing and if no one else can really have access to the line).

Use the element of surprise. The most successful flanking attacks are ones that are totally unexpected. The more surprise that there is, the harder it is for the leader to react and recover. Surprise in today's marketplace is difficult to achieve because many marketers expose their strategy to their competitors too early. Apple uses the element of surprise very well. They always keep new announcements under wrap until they are ready to launch them. They are also masters of using buzz and excitement to get people talking about the products once they are already available in the store. This is a skill that you must focus on improving.

Synchronize what you are doing across a wide variety of platforms so that is all brides can talk about. This makes it very difficult for any of your competitors to respond. The question to ask yourself: What are you doing to promote you and your brand each and every week? If you aren't doing something, you won't be able to stand up to those who do.

Keep at it. Don't just make a claim and move on. As Jack Trout says: *"The pursuit is just as critical as the attack itself."* Karl von Clausewitz says in his book *On War* that "Without pursuit no victory can have a great effect." Continue until you win the argument or the battle. Don't slack off when a competitor begins a retreat. That is the time to pour it on and win decisively.

The old saying "The bigger they are, the harder they fall" is one that lots of bridal store owners would like to believe about David's and Alfred Angelo, yet both of these companies are doing very smart things with their social media and advertising / promotion that you must pay attention to. These big box retailers are doing a lot of things right and they are focusing on a lot of the right things. However, this doesn't mean that they are perfect. The key is for you to look at weaknesses that you can exploit while simultaneously promoting your strengths.

3. Win in the last three feet. The big box retailers are winning the advertising and marketing battle, but all battles are really decided in the last few feet. Are you winning there?

Denny says: "In every transaction, there's a moment just after the giant thinks he's got the sale and just before the customer hands over their money. This gap is an opportunity for a smart, agile competitor to snatch victory from the jaws of defeat. Winning in the Last Three Feet is an old retail expression, but it speaks universally to the idea of understanding that it's never over until it's over. You can have a brilliant campaign—or a brilliant product—but you can't assume the rest will take care of itself. It never does." –p. 65.

If you are going to compete and win against the big box retailers that dominate the bridal industry, you have to fight to win in the last three feet. You have to fight to win by having a better sales approach and incentive that will tip brides over the edge to buy from you instead of continuing to look at other places. You also want brides to come visit you *first* so they have a point of comparison if they do go look at the other stores later on. I know many smart retailers who encourage brides to change their appointments at big box retailers like David's from the morning until the afternoon so they can get in and experience what their store is like first. That way, if a bride does *go* to another store, she will *come back* to you because of the dramatically different experience she had at your store.

The challenge with taking on any giant in the bridal industry is that they have more resources (money and people, specifically) than you do. They are very good at starting lots of things. They spend a lot of money to build awareness. A great example of this was with the Vera Wang White collection at David's. A great push was made for these dresses, yet there are only a limited number. How David's continues to promote this line and expand it remains to be seen. To be successful in competing against this well-known brand, you must create your own buzz worthy events that promote *you* and *your* brand.

Denny makes this observation about giants (which I think is a great point). He says: "[Giants] may have more money and people than you do, but they also have the bureaucracy that you don't. They have mandatory meetings, layers of management, and, most important, deeply instilled corporate cultures. In fairness, the giant's culture may be its greatest strength—but it may also be your greatest blessing...This is a perfect situation for the giant-killer, because you don't want to have to spend the kind of money needed to drive all this demand. You just want to spend enough to switch the customer when they're ready to spend." –pp. 67-68.

Do you stay on top of David's sales and promotions?

Do you know what they are starting and aren't following through with?

When you see gaps, are you pouncing on these opportunities or are you so caught up in your own day-to-day drama that you forget to look for opportunities?

I think Denny says it best: "You don't have to win everywhere. Concentrate on winning at the point of influence. Concentrate on finishing well. Close and strike. Time to win in the last three feet." –p. 69.

Here are five other ways you can win in the last three feet.

1) Win where the big box retailers <u>don't think</u> to compete.

Ask: Where doesn't David's think to compete?

I think this is a great question that would give you some great insights if you would think about it. The thing I've noticed about David's and Alfred Angelo is that they are trying to be all things to all people. They are focusing on so many different specialties that they really aren't taking the time to be great at any of them. As I mentioned, they begin things well, but don't continue with them well. This is obvious with some of their other lines. They're still promoting Oleg Cassini's amazing dresses when he has been dead since March of 2006 and isn't a fashion icon to brides today in the same way that Vera Wang is. Their focus is so broad that I don't think their staying power is really there with some of their older, established lines.

Several years ago, many bridal retailers specialized in higher end wedding dresses instead of trying to cater to the lower price points that David's was offering. Now, David's is offering dresses in every imaginable price point. They are also promoting their exclusivity which is another area where many stores put their marketing focus. The real opportunity to beat David's and other big box retailers who will come is to focus on areas where they don't think to compete and specialize in those areas better than they can or will.

The key point is this: David's will always be good at product launches and designer launches. They have the marketing budget to run TV advertising and create big posters in the windows of each of their stores along with numerous steps along the way. But, they don't sustain those ideas for a long period of time. Look for their weaknesses in these areas and then strike.

Big box retailers are usually so busy putting periods after each market segment and moving on to a new category that they won't really notice if you are putting question marks behind those statements and point out why you are different and why what they are promoting really isn't what the bride wants or needs.

2) Leverage your expertise and build trust around the experience of dealing with you. Even though David's promotes Vera Wang dresses, brides who shop at David's will never have the experience of working with her personally. This is a weakness that you can exploit by promoting how *they do get to work personally with you* (as long as you are building your own celebrity and authority and are doing a good job and promoting why your experience is so meaningful and different).

3) Don't treat the wedding day as a check in the box format. David's web site does a good job of marketing them, but it also has a little bit of a check in the box feel to it of what needs to be done next. Very little emphasis is put on the overall experience the bride will have at the store and the transforming power of one of their appointments. If you can help brides see that their wedding is not about a standardized check in the box, but about a customized personalized experience, you'll have a big advantage over big box retailers who ignore this.

4) Be simple, be memorable. David's $99 sale or $100 to $300 off every dress in the store promotion works well because it is simple and memorable. It is also a bait and switch marketing mechanism in many cases. The thing you must ask yourself if you are going to successfully compete and win against the big box retailers is how you will be simple AND memorable (especially when they arrive at the store and find out that what you have is even better than what you said). Most brides who shop the $99 sale, quickly realize that what has been advertised is not exactly what it appears to be (since there may only be one or two dresses in their size that fit the $99 sale criteria). This disappointment can turn into frustration and anger quickly.

5) Know thy brides. When you know at least three things more about a bride and her wedding day (and the experience she is trying to create), you'll be more successful than your competitors. Knowing more details means the bride trusts you more which also means that you are on track to make the sale. Never get so far away from your brides that you aren't aware of what is going on in their lives and wedding plans. A quick glance at a lot of the comments on Alfred Angelo's Facebook page indicates that they aren't really in touch with what brides want or what they are experiencing at their stores. There is a lot of anger and frustration voiced in these forums. There is a point in every sale when brides are open to persuasive suggestions. Are you in front of brides when they are open to suggestion? If not, what can you do to be there and win?

4. Fight back. Don't be content with the big box retailers taking half of the brides in your market area. Many competitors win by

fighting dirty. Are you willing to fight back to maintain your competitive edge?

Stephen Denny calls this "fighting dirty." He says: "Just because they're bigger than you are doesn't mean you can't pick on them. Is this crazy? No. Just remember that an honest, toe-to-toe fight is the last thing you want. Now is no time for rules. When you choose to fight dirty, you create match-up problems, launch suicide missions, and embrace misdirection. Fighting dirty is dangerous. Tread carefully." –*Killing Giants*, p. 83.

I'm not one who endorses fighting dirty. I just don't think you can fight this way without becoming a little bit of what you were fighting in the first place. But, I do believe you should fight back. There is no excuse for letting another competitor define you and saying nothing about it. Sometimes, you may have to use guerrilla tactics to win the fight, but you should do so tactically so that you end up where you want. Sometimes you can fight the wrong fight and win, yet you end up someplace that you didn't think you would.

The best way to fight and win is to narrow the niche and become the best in the world in that area. It is difficult to defend something that is too big. What small area or market niche can you best defend in the minds of brides in your area? Remember, there are riches in niches. You can specialize in certain niches or carry certain lines that big stores in your area may not think are very important or private lines that they don't have access to. Your specialization in this area can help you build a powerful brand and may even become your core business.

Another key thing to remember is to never let your own pride get in the way. This is where you make mistakes. As Jack Trout says: *"No matter how successful you become, never think like the leader."* In other words, think like the guerrilla soldier. Never lose your focus. Everyone at every level at your store must be focused on selling. This is what makes the wheels move in your store. Never lose touch of what is going through the bride's mind and what is happening in the marketplace (and respond quickly to market shifts and changes).

A great example of this is Southwest Airlines. They have consistently focused on their flying with no frills strategy and today are worth more than the five largest U.S. airlines combined on the stock market. They continually post profits when most airlines are really struggling.

Think carefully about your long-term strategy with regard to how you will fight with your entrenched competitors in certain market segments.

Look for openings where you can come in and dominate the marketplace for brides. Being a 'me-too' bridal store that has what everyone else has severely limits your ability to stand out in the marketplace.

When you look at other businesses in other competitive industries through the paradigm of war (and where individual competitors are at), you'll see why some companies are gaining ground in their marketing and why some are losing the battle.

Hershey dominated Nestle in the candy wars with their Krackel bar over the Crunch bar by focusing on winning in the vending machine niche. They gave better incentives to the owners of the vending machines that Nestle wasn't willing to (and so they got better placement) and as a result more sales. Internet vendors are really fighting dirty against independent bridal stores who carry the same lines they do by offering dresses without sales tax, free shipping, and other incentives (free veil, tiara, or shoes with purchase).

What are you doing to shift the battlefield so the odds are stacked in your favor?

Carrying lines that everyone else has stacks the odds in favor of Internet vendors and you will be used as a try on store.

Building your own brand over the manufacturer's brand stacks the odds in your favor. It is a way to fight dirty without getting dirty. If you are losing sales to local competitors and big box retailers (and you are), think about what you can do to get the upper hand in the battles you are fighting.

5. Do the unthinkable. Do what the big box retailers can't or won't do well.

Stephen Denny makes this point in *Killing Giants*:

"Some parts of the giant's culture and worldview are so essential to their self-image that they can't bring themselves to even question them. Often, these aren't even things the company can articulate. They are just givens. We do things like this and would never do things like that. This dark corner is where opportunity resides. Learn to love what the giant considers taboo. Be willing to do what they aren't and build a business out of it, every day. Go ahead. Do the unthinkable. Eat the bug." –p. 99.

What is the unthinkable that David's can't or won't do?

One thing is that they have gotten so caught up in promoting their celebrity designers that they won't promote their own design staff as approachable individuals and work at building the foundation of trust. They are hanging their star on celebrities (and one dead one). If something happens to that celebrity or that celebrity loses their star power, where will their star be hitched? To their brand or to the celebrity brand?

This is the dark corner where opportunity lies. No matter how big your store is, you can build your brand. No one can compete with that. There is only one you. David's is becoming so tied to its celebrity brands that it may not be able to function without them. Vera Wang is using David's via licensing, but where will her commitment be to them if the dresses don't continue to sell or if the lower price point weakens her own brand so she can't command the high premium prices like she used to? In that case, Vera Wang would likely cease her relationship with David's and then where would they be?

Tying yourself to a celebrity is a great marketing strategy, but the best marketing strategy of all is to turn yourself into a celebrity and promoting yourself, thus building trust and creating a unique experience that will be completely different from the experience

David's is promoting. I talked about this in detail in Chapter 5 of *Bridal Boosters & Breakthroughs*. What brides who buy at David's really get is this: They buy a non-unique dress that brides all across the country will wear from a bridal consultant who has never met the celebrity whose dresses she is selling. If you can position their experience in that way while simultaneously positioning yourself as an approachable celebrity they can truly get to know and work with, you will have a huge advantage.

Celebrities like Vera Wang also have certain requirements about what can or can't be done when using her brand. This is an advantage for you as well. Why? Vera Wang has a very specific taste and that may not be what brides are really looking for. David's *has* gotten much better with styling in recent years. While their styling is improving, they still won't take risks with some dress trends because they have to produce each dress for 300+ stores. Making mistakes with inventory are much more costly for them than they are for independent bridal retailers, especially if they are under contract to put so many dresses from Vera Wang or other celebrity designers in their stores. If the styles aren't very good or don't sell, they have a lot of money out there that may not come back very quickly. This is where you can compete and win since you can respond much quicker to trends that are happening in the marketplace than they can. You can bring in a few pieces and afford to make small mistakes to find out what is really selling, whereas a mistake on their end can be very costly and slow to recover from.

Here are five things you could do that big box retailers may not be willing to do:

1) Share your knowledge in a way that builds a relationship with the bride. Any information that is shared by big box retailers is done in a sterile, non-relationship building way. You can share special reports that build your authority and celebrity and most importantly that build a one-on-one relationship with them. Always look for ways you can share information with brides that will be meaningful to them and that will help them get answers to questions and challenges they are facing.

2) Address the fears a bride may be facing head on in a personalized way that opens a relationship with the bride. This can be done through education and is best done through written and video testimonials. Incentivize brides to share their experiences with you by offering them an incentive for sharing their thoughts on paper or in a video format that you can use to answer the bride's most common questions. Do this in a way that allows brides to overcome their fears of buying a wedding dress. Make a list of questions that brides have and create a series of videos where you answer each of those questions in a way that allows brides to get to know you personally. Even if big box retailers were to do this (which they likely won't), brides won't have the added benefit of meeting the person in the video like they can if you are to do these for your store.

3) Offer an outrageous incentive if the bride refers her friends. You can do this in tiered levels or even offer the bride her money back if she refers 8 of her friends. Big box retailers would likely never attempt such a program because the red tape of something like that with 300+ stores would be very challenging to track on a corporate level. This is an advantage you can tap into.

4) Think hard about where big box retailers can't go and put together your own road map of how you could go there and prosper in that uncontested area. Also think about what you can do that they can't. This is where your true opportunities lie. What contracts or supply arrangements are they locked into that may be a disadvantage to them? Look at David's web site and think about this question in comparison with your own strengths and specialties. What opportunities do you see? What are they taking for granted that you could exploit? Bureaucracy really limits how much creative thinking big box retailers can do. Don't limit yourself by thinking small in these areas.

5) Look at what really brings in the money for the big box bridal store. Since the big box retailer's business model depends on volume, what could you do that would disrupt that volume and bring it into your store instead? Ask yourself: How do they really make money? What problems arise as a result of focusing more on volume than on an individualized, personalized experience?

Choose to do more unthinkable things that a big box store would never conceive or dream of doing. There may be big opportunities for you in those areas.

6. Make the inconvenient argument about why buying from you is better.

Most bridal retailers really don't promote their differences very well. If you can articulate why you are better and make the inconvenient argument that positions your store as a better buy than David's or Alfred Angelo, you will win the sale. If they do this better than you, they win the sale. Your goal should always be in the words of Stephen Denning to make brides "think for a moment, realizing that in comparison your offering makes more sense."

How do you do that? By putting the math in front of them and helping them to see that you *are* the best choice.

Are you putting the math in front of your brides and showing them that you are the best overall value? If not, you are making a big mistake. If not, brides are only looking at the total price of the dress (which is never an indicator of the best total overall value).

For example, you can offer an incentive if a bride buys on the first visit, she can receive over $1,000 in coupons from local wedding vendors she can't get anywhere else (that you have set up for her), give her the opportunity to get all of the money she spent on her dress back minus sales tax and also get great incentives on accessories and bridesmaid dresses with the purchase of a dress at your store. The overall value is amazing since they have the chance to get their dress for free.

That type of contrast helps brides decide emotionally AND rationally since it makes all of the sense in the world to buy from the place that will save you money and time and give you a chance to get back the money you have spent.

Big box retailers can't put together packages like that with local vendors and the logistics of a referral program with 300 + stores can be so staggering that they'll never be attempted.

JetBlue is an example of a company that understands the lifetime value of a customer and is willing to do the unthinkable while making the inconvenient argument that their airline is the best one as they gain loyal customers.

Stephen Denny explains:

"[JetBlue] is aggressive about introducing the experience to as many people as it can. 'The cheapest marketing tool we have is an empty seat. We can't make money doing that in the long term, but what we think we can do is make new customers who will come back again. The strategy from the very beginning is to sell the seats first. Get people hooked on the experience.' Pricing, therefore, is a very strategic competitive weapon, driving the company's weekly promotions—the $9, $19, $29 fares that give those air travelers sitting on the fence that final push to try JetBlue for the first time. 'If we were a brand that didn't pull people back, this would be a lousy strategy. We love doing things that customers would say, 'I can't imagine anyone doing this except for JetBlue,' like our $31 fares on Halloween.'" –*Killing Giants*, p. 126-127.

He continues:

"A vivid example of how JetBlue samples its experience is its All You Can Jet Pass promotion, the $599 all-access pass that the company first offered in September 2009, giving customers unlimited flights for thirty days. While at first glance, you'd assume this would be an expensive and risky move, even in a risk-tolerant culture, it turns out that the promotion was a calculated bet with little downside. September is JetBlue's worst month for load capacity. The company anticipated having empty seats during this time period, and knowing that the marginal cost of flying one more customer on a flight that was going to take off anyway was minimal, filling these seats in creative ways—preferably with flyers who had yet to experience JetBlue's level of service—was smart and on strategy. Further, the JetBlue team surmised that the offer would only be bought by those travelers who planned on flying more than three times during that thirty-day promotional period....JetBlue's $599 pass was very successful in filling the usually empty seats during their seasonally lightest period and delivered strongly on their goal of bringing in new customers. Importantly, though, it also delivered an avalanche of positive exposure for the JetBlue brand." –*Killing Giants*, pp. 127-128.

Not only did that promotion spread like wildfire through social media and traditional media outlets, it also created tremendous testimonials from the contest they did afterwards asking, "How did the pass change your life?" and "How did the pass change someone else's life?" They now use those testimonials to invite other new prospective customers to experience their competitive difference.

Here are two great questions for you to ponder (as an assignment): 1) What things could you do or offer during slow times at your store that would get the attention of the social media channels or traditional media channels you are in (or aren't in yet)?

2) What can you do to eliminate fine print or worries that brides may have that can help you make the argument that buying a wedding dress from you is the best choice a bride could ever make?

Think about these two questions. Put the math in front of brides and you'll be amazed at how they'll respond. Letting brides know how much they'll save if they buy on their first visit before they even arrive at their first appointment is a big part of this strategy that you can use and it will help you compete and win against the big box retailers.

7. Thrive by drawing attention to your differences. Help brides make the decision to buy from you now by polarizing these differences.

Denny says:

"Think of what words your customers use to describe your brand. What is your brand's 'controlling idea,' its distillation? Once you've defined who you are at your core, what does this require you to do? What associations are now possible because of the choices you've made?...Once you've distilled your message, you can draw your hub and extend the spokes outward into just those associations that are believable, credible, and ownable for you and your brand." –*Killing Giants*, p. 158.

Unfortunately, this is not how most bridal retailers think. Instead, they try to be the same and then offer a twist to what they sell (like a lower price) that they feel will help them get the sale.

Part of being different is knowing what you stand for and eliminating everything that doesn't match that. Emphasizing your difference is an exercise in subtraction—where you prune out anything and everything that no longer matters. This kind of discipline is difficult, especially when you are operating out of fear due to watching your business shrink when a new David's opens in your town.

What should you do when a David's or Alfred Angelo opens in your town? Here are ten suggestions as detailed in Guy Kawasaki's book *How to Drive Your Competition Crazy*. The book details an analysis about Bob Curry, an owner of a small independent retail hardware store and how he dealt with Home Depot moving in a ½ mile from his store. I think there are many lessons that can be learned from how he dealt with this mammoth competitor in ways that we experience when David's opens up near us. Here is what he has to say followed by my comments in italics:

"Lesson #1: Don't Panic. We were petrified of Home Depot because of the things we had read in the trade magazines and because we had talked to stores in Long Island, Atlanta, New Orleans, and Florida (His store is located in Quincy, Massachusetts). Sales were dropping 20 to 25 percent in the first year!

We told ourselves we had to get our act together. We had to find a way to beat Home Depot and stop being afraid of it. Instead of going on defense, we were going on the offense. We were just going to do what we knew how to do, do it right, and not worry about it.

We didn't want our people to be nervous wrecks. And we didn't want them to see that we were nervous wrecks! Everywhere we went, everybody was afraid for us. It was something that we heard several hundred times a day, seven days a week, for a year and a half before Home Depot opened.

We even had one person suggest that our store would be a nice chicken restaurant. Hardware stores all around our area—up to fifteen miles away—would call us and ask us what we were going to do because they figured we were going to be gone."

Because David's does a great job promoting a new store when they have a grand opening, you will see shifts in your business as well. You'll also see shifts when they begin promoting their $99 sale on their television commercials throughout the year. When you see these shifts, it is hard not to panic, but getting your act together and going on offense is the approach you need to take on. When David's has their promotion of their $99 sale, you could have an $88 sale and have a couple of dresses that are discontinued or damaged in some way in your store as well. Promote this in a number of creative ways to get brides into your store. The goal is to divert traffic away from David's and into your store. Most of these brides will buy your regular price gowns. Some of them are only looking for a deal and so you can move some of your old merchandise this way. You will have to decide what will work best for you, but the key point is that you can't panic when you see sales drop. You have to have your own approach to getting your sales back on track. But panicking and doing nothing is a sure recipe for stalling the growth of your store.

Lesson #2: Competition is Good

"Home Depot really got us off our rear ends. It got our blood boiling again and got our entrepreneurial juices flowing. We started scheming and figuring out what we had to do in pricing, advertising, and service.

We had to figure out a way to keep our key people and to find a niche. These were things that we hadn't really done for a few years because we'd been busy while the economy was great all through the 1980s. Why weren't we doing it five or ten years ago? Because sometimes we all need a boot in the rear end, that's why? We needed something to wake us up, I'll tell you.

How has Home Depot affected us? Other stores told us our sales would be off 25 percent the first year. The first few months sales were flat, and then they jumped up 4 or 5 percent. That first spring, which was only six months after the opening, our sales were up 12, 13, or 14 percent. Our sales for the first six months of this fiscal year have been up over 35 percent."

Competitors do make us better. As much as you would love to operate your business in a vacuum without any competitors, you become a better retailer because of the big box retailers like David's and Alfred Angelo. You are forced to think about your businesses differently and this makes all of the difference in the world. Positioning yourself against the competition allows you to compete and grow against them. You have to find your niche and specialize instead of trying to be all things to all people. To some, this seems counterintuitive, but it is the best strategy for beating a big box retailer at their own game. Study what successful businesses in other industries do to compete with their giants. Smaller retailers can adapt quicker and can succeed by doing the things I've been discussing in this book.

Lesson #3: Maintain Morale

"We try to have a lot of fun here. We kid and fool around all day long. We pay well, and we've got a pension and profit-sharing package that most small businesses don't have. We try to have all those things to show our employees that it is worthwhile to work here.

Also, you can't have a staff with high morale if they're not trained. They have to be comfortable and know what they're doing, so we have a training room in the basement of the store where we show the videos…

Finally, we thank them. Thanking employees isn't all about money. There isn't a week that doesn't go by that when I'm handing out the checks, I don't thank them for what they've done for us."

It is no fun to be stressed out all of the time. Brides can sense this. It is much better to laugh, to have fun, and to truly enjoy the experience of working with the brides who come into your store. When your bridal consultants are excited and happy, you'll sell more. Part of being a great leader is to recognize when the morale of your bridal consultants is down and do whatever it takes to get it back up and soaring again. Let your bridal consultants know how much you appreciate their efforts and what they contribute each day.

Lesson #4: Be Realistic

"At hardware-store seminars where I spoke, we had guys come up and say, "Our customers are loyal." Baloney. Customers are loyal to nothing but their wallet. If you had to work real hard for sixty hours a week, are you going to give a guy $49 when you can buy something for $29?

Customers won't be loyal for very long. They think the same way you and I do about our money. They're just as careful spending it, so you've got to create the right mind-set with people and show them that you can be competitive, and you can be fair."

I think Bob Curry is right on here. Brides want to know that they are getting the best deal and the best overall value. Are you putting the math in front of your brides and helping them see the inconvenient argument about why buying from you is the best overall value? If you don't aggressively promote your difference, your brides won't know. If they don't know, they can't contrast what they see at your store versus what they see at another competitor or big box store. This is the same for Internet vendors who compete with you. If you are trying to compete on price, you will lose that battle. The reality is that you can't sell the same product for the same price (because they can always beat you with no sales tax, no shipping, and some other special offer they have) even if the dress is sold at the same MSRP. Build your value in other ways above and beyond price. Carry lines that protect your territory and that aren't sold online. It is a lot easier to build value if brides can't compare apples to apples.

Lesson #5: Do What's Right for the Customer

"We try to get to know as many customers as we can in a personal way. Home Depot cannot do that. You can't have 150 employees in the store and 120,000 square feet of store and expect them to know their customers.

We never opened on Sundays because we had strange blue laws. Then, when stores started to open on Sundays, most of the small stores still didn't follow suit. Only the large stores did, but when Home Depot came in, we had to change.

It was a traumatic thing because we were used to having our Sundays off, but we're getting used to it now—or most of us are. I still haven't gotten used to it, but hours are very important. Hours are customer service.

The first couple of weeks we had seven people on because we didn't know what to expect. For maybe ten Sundays in a row, we did double what we'd done on any Saturday. During the summer things quieted down a little bit, but even now in July and August it's still very, very busy on a Sunday, so there was a need for it.

The most important thing is just servicing and servicing and servicing. A guy brought in an old wooden floor lamp. He wanted to put in a new socket and rewire the lamp, but the wooden part of it was all falling apart. We asked if he wanted us to fix it. He asked, "Can you do that?" You bet your life."

Your ability to get to know a bride on a personal level is what will always set your independent bridal store apart from the big box retailers. Employees of David's or Alfred Angelo will never be as invested as you are in taking care of them and providing that little bit extra that goes a long way in the bride's mind. What are you doing to get to know brides better? Do they sense your commitment to them and helping them create the wedding of their dreams? When you are committed to doing what is right for the brides you serve, they'll sense the difference and do business with you over a big box retailer who doesn't offer the same level of attention to detail.

Lesson #6: Be Flexible

"Pricing was a big thing. We wanted to make sure that people saw us as competitive. They didn't have to see us as being cheaper than Home Depot. It does $10 billion a year in sales (today $90.8 billion a year), so people didn't expect us to be cheaper, but they expect to get a fair deal.

We took four hundred or five hundred items and gave them away. We picked all the most price-sensitive items—for example, Rustoleum, spray paint, and generic things like a gallon of paint thinner or light bulbs. We worked and worked on this for probably a year.

I wished we'd had two or three years to do it. We published lists of our everyday low prices, and we kept changing it. When Home Depot opened, we found we were cheaper on some of these prices, so we immediately marked all our prices up to match Home Depot's.

We didn't try to sell anything lower than Home Depot. We didn't tell anybody we had things cheaper than it—they wouldn't believe us anyway, so we just got our prices up to the same price, and we kept watching it.

One of the ways we showed people we had competitive prices was to use private labels. First, we priced General Electric's bulbs at almost zero margin to match Home Depot's prices. However, all the Ace private label light bulbs are made by General Electric, so we tell customers where they come from and then push the Ace brand. We make 25-30 percent margin on these bulbs yet they still retail for less money."

You have to decide what you will carry in your store. You can choose to carry things that you lose money or break even on, but why? Why not invest in dresses that give you a better margin and that aren't available anywhere else? Set yourself apart from your competitors by finding your specialty and your niche. Remember, it is your store and you can be as flexible as you want by how you choose to buy and sell your merchandise. No one is forcing you to carry dresses that you can't make a healthy margin on. Only you can decide what you will carry and what you won't. At the end of the day, that decision will make all of the difference in how successful you are at competing against and winning against the big box retailers of our industry.

Lesson #7: Develop Niches

"We came up with different niches. We read and researched every trade magazine we could get our hands on to see what other people were doing in different niches, why some of them worked, and why some of them didn't. Long before the customers really wanted something, we felt we had to come up with the right thing.

For example, we never sold propane before because we couldn't get a license, so we fought and fought for a license. Now we probably do $100,000 worth of sales in propane, and we've only been doing it about a year and a half.

We really opened up a paint department. We always had a lot of paint, but the paint was in the basement, on the first flood, and in the warehouse upstairs. We brought it all together and made it look like we were a paint store even though we probably didn't increase our volume of inventory that much.

We do a tremendous amount of servicing of Makita, Black&Decker, and DeWalt power tools. We're authorized to do some warranty work on them. Now we even job out the repairs because we do so much of it.

Also, we have probably tripled the amount of inventory we have in our fastener department. We still don't have as much as Home Depot, but it doesn't have anybody to wait on customers. Fasteners are a department that you need people to help you through—even the tradesmen need help.

On the other hand, we don't have everything that Home Depot has. We don't have a line of 200 faucets. We just don't have it, and we never will, so that's something we have to concede. We don't have a big lighting department either, so we're going to lose some of that business too."

This is a great example of specialization. You have to choose which battles you will fight. Trying to carry everything that David's carries is a recipe for disaster. You'll never be able to compete with them on that level and with that kind of overhead in inventory expense. Instead, you have to look at profitable areas you can focus on that can give you the edge you want and need. Look again at what the giants are unwilling to do and see if you can offer things to your brides that they can't or won't and that can be profitable for you. This is so important. Deciding what you will stand for and sticking to this is as important as a strategy as any to successfully competing with the big box bridal retailers.

Lesson #8 Know Thy Enemy

"When Home Depot first opened, we were there at least once a week. They don't like you shopping their store for prices, so we carried voice activated tape recorders and we would take any kind of literature that we could find in the store.

Any time the managers saw us take stuff, they'd just smile. This stuff is not something top management wanted us to have, but the managers knew who we were so they'd just smile."

How often are you looking at the web site and social media outlets for David's and Alfred Angelo? Do you know what they are doing? Since you don't operate in a vacuum you had better be aware of what they are doing. As the old saying goes, 'Keep your friends close, and your enemies closer.'

Sun Tzu, an ancient Chinese general made this statement in The Art of War:

"Know the enemy and know yourself; in a hundred battles you will never be in peril. When you are ignorant of the enemy but know yourself, your

chances of winning or losing are equal. If ignorant both of your enemy and of yourself, you are certain in every battle to be in peril."

Be aware of what is going on. Get their promotional flyers at bridal shows. Study what they are doing. Put together an outline of their marketing calendar to help you plan your offensive attack against them. Study what they do and think about how you can and will respond.

Lesson #9 Do Something for Your Community

"I've been involved in the Rotary Club in Quincy for a long time and another small group—we call ourselves the Quincy Partnership. There's about fifteen of us. We try to do things to spruce the city up, and we've probably raised a hundred grand in the last couple of years to put up nice signage welcoming people to Quincy.

All of this got me some good connections, and the connections were with people who I didn't really rub shoulders with that often, such as the president of the bank in the city. One small publication called *The Quincy Business News* is probably the best-read paper here in Quincy. We started getting big write-ups because John Graham, the publisher, is a customer.

He saw that a lot of the things we were doing were successful, and he liked those kinds of things because he was doing the same things in his own business, so he started writing about us. When Home Depot opened, the first issue had an article about Home Depot, and 75 percent of it was about Curry Hardware. It seems like every single issue has something about Curry Hardware."

I've already talked at length about this principle. Invent media if you have to promote your difference to the community and your contribution back into the community. Big box retailers typically don't have this type of involvement in the local communities in which they are located. Choose instead to stand out in this area.

Lesson #10 Make the Competition into a Friend

"About a week ago, the new guy that's in charge of power tools at Home Depot came in and checked all of our prices. He said our pricing was really good. The reason he came in, though, was that he was looking at how well we serve our customer. He told us that from now on they're probably going to send anyone with any kind of service problem to us!

Customers who buy a gas grill at Home Depot ask employees there where they can get propane. Home Depot sends them right down to us. Hopefully, we capture them as customers. We make the customers go in the store to pay for the propane, which is stored outside, so they're forced to learn more about us.

We work hard to build some kind of a bond between Home Depot and us rather than try to fight. Most of the people that we've talked to in other parts of the country wanted nothing to do with Home Depot. We felt we'd be better off if we worked with it. If Home Depot wanted to, it could swallow us up, and we prefer that it doesn't do that." — *How to Drive Your Competition Crazy*

When we first opened our store, I introduced myself to the manager at the closest David's and told her that we specialized in sleeved wedding dresses (which they didn't carry). We got a lot of referrals from that store manager who would send brides who were looking for sleeved dresses simply because I had the courage to introduce myself and tell her of a service we offered that brides in our area are looking for. I encourage those in my coaching groups to do the same. Make a goal that you will introduce yourself to your competitors at your next bridal show. Now, you may feel that you could never imagine having that kind of conversation with any of your competitors. You can and you should. Sometimes, a fresh approach can yield big dividends. Look for ways to make friends out of your competitors.

I think those ten suggestions are great ways to respond when you hear that David's or an Alfred Angelo is opening in your town. Get to know what your competitors are doing and it is much easier to point out your differences and help brides see why you are the best choice.

8. Lead the conversation. Step up and lead. Brides are looking for a leader.

Stephen Denny refers to this principle as "seizing the microphone." He says: "Who is the personality in your market? Who speaks the loudest and has the most to say? Who is unavoidable? You. You take up all the oxygen in the room. It doesn't matter if you have one or more giants in your market. They may be big, but it doesn't mean they are leading the conversation. Their size doesn't make them nearer or dearer to the hearts of your core customers. Revenue doesn't equal personality, nor is market share equivalent to emotional connection. You don't have to accept that you're not big enough to be the industry spokesman, so naively grab the microphone and speak up for the whole industry. The giant hates this, but your customers love it. You understand that it's not enough to be polite and participate. So go ahead and step up. Seize the microphone. Your audience is waiting." –*Killing Giants*, p. 161.

Here are some questions for you to reflect on:

- What are you doing to capture the imagination of brides? Is the atmosphere of your store fun (so that brides get emotionally caught up in what they are doing)?
- Are you pointing out your differences? If you don't know what they are, your brides don't either. Step up and seize the microphone so that brides know how fun the experience of shopping at your store will be.
- Are you building your celebrity? Are brides drawn to your comments (blog posts, video posts, special reports) and do they believe that you are an authority in the industry? What can you do to be the conversation and take up all of the oxygen in the room?
- Are you appearing everywhere that brides are looking for help with their wedding planning?
- What have you done today to seize the microphone and let brides know about you and your store?

In most areas, there is no designated spokesperson for brides. You need to become that person. This will set you apart from the big box retailers and let brides know that they must come visit you and your store. David's Bridal and Alfred Angelo are mostly chasing each other and are watching each other more than they are paying attention to the questions that brides are really asking and what the brides in your are *really* looking for. Be the spokesperson that brides trust to get the information to plan their wedding. When you do that, you'll lead the conversation and the market.

You can do this through special reports and articles that you write and share with brides. Once you have these articles written, expand into video articles or a podcast that can be located throughout your web site. There are so many tools today that make is so easy to pick up the microphone and speak directly to your brides. You can be the dominant spokesperson in your market by making the decision to direct and control the conversation in a way that promotes you and your store.

9. Be a fearsome competitor and no one wants to fight you. Choose your battles carefully by specializing in areas only you can win. This makes you more fearsome to battle in the future.

Denny says: "There's always an opponent even the giant doesn't want to fight. The southpaw who can throw an uppercut, the scrapper who messes up their timing, or maybe the accessories brand that owns four feet of linear space in too many of their national retailers. When natural ability and dedication have forged a pair of specialized weapons, you become an opponent the giant is reluctant to face." –p. 179.

One of the ways you can be even more fearsome to your competitors is to be more in tune with what the market wants. Do the dirty work that will give you clues into what is happening in the market. Ask: What are you doing to make yourself indispensible to brides in your area? Are you in the room when the bride is thinking about what she'll do next in her wedding plans? If not, how can you be there?

If you have what brides are asking for, you'll be able to draw brides into your store better and close the sale. How well are you staying on top of what is happening in your market? Remember, listening closely to what your customers are saying can give you the edge. Here are some suggestions to help you do this better:

- Stay in touch with what is going on in your market. "Listening is the way to gain wisdom because everything you say you already know."
- Don't trust your instincts more than what brides are asking for.
- When you lose the sale, find out why. Find out if you had something similar in the store or if it was a type of dress that you don't even carry. By continually interacting with your customers, you'll have a much better sense of what you should buy when you go to markets.
- Stay on top of prom trends by watching what celebrities are wearing to award shows such as the Golden Globes, the Grammy Awards, and the Academy Awards. Listen to what people say about these dresses. Post pictures of gowns you may question on your Facebook or Twitter pages. Get feedback from your blog about what people are looking for.
- Ask your customers what they saw at their proms. Find out what colors were mostly worn by girls, what dresses people were talking about, and any other type of information about trends that can be helpful to you before you go to market to buy.
- Have a prom fashion team to help you gather this information. Encourage your fashion team to bring you pictures of their favorite styles that they've seen. By staying on top of what the customer wants you can beat your competitors (especially if you are more in tune with what the market is asking for).

Stay close to your brides and you'll always have an edge. I like what Stephen Denny says about this. He says:

"No one ever loses because they were too close to the customer. How well do you listen? Is your market telling you something different than you want to hear? Are they buying based on something you never thought was important?" –*Killing Giants*, pp. 195-196.

10. Show your teeth. Promote why you are the best choice loud and clear.

A big part of any fight is the psychological one. Most fighters try to psyche out their competitors long before they get in the ring. If you are going to fight a competitor, you have to let them see your teeth once in while. You have to let them know that you are confident that you will win the battle.

Stephen Denny says in *Killing Giants*:

"In the back of every giant's mind is a nagging fear. The fear is that they'll be called out in public and forced to fight against an upstart who they know, in their heart of hearts, is better than they are. The giant has more people, more money, and more market clout, but there's a hole in their confidence that the right kind of competitor keeps making bigger. When you know you're better—and can prove it—say it early and often. Give the giant's fear a name and a very public face." –pp. 197.

Here are six specific areas where you should be showing your teeth:

1) Your web site

Put written and video testimonials in different areas of your web site. Your testimonials are your best way to instill fear into your competitors, especially if they don't have any on their site. Great testimonials are the best way you can show your teeth. It proves to the bride that you are the real deal because she believes what her peers say about your store more than she'll believe what you have to say.

2) All of your direct personal interactions with the bride (phone calls, postcards, emails, referrals, etc.)

Do your promotions have teeth? How do they stack up and compare with what the big box retailers are promoting to their brides? Be creative and aggressive. Let your competitors know that you are showing up with your "A" game by how you market and promote your store.

Shock and awe your brides with your pre-sales materials. Let her know that she isn't dealing with a novice, but a bona fide expert who can help her find the perfect wedding dress.

How can you better show your difference and show your teeth with the next marketing piece you send out?

3) Your print ads

I once had a very successful print ad that had to be redone twice before our local publication would print it. The publication had to rewrite their rules for their entire publication because my competitors were complaining about our ad to them. If your ads aren't creating controversy like this, your ads don't have teeth. When competitors complain, it means that they are scared and that you are winning the battle. Ads that tell brides only where you are, when you are open, and what lines you carry are wimpy. They don't show any teeth. They don't show why you are truly different. Remember, your location, hours, and what you carry (especially if you are a generalist trying to be all things to all people) are rarely persuasive in and of themselves.

4) TV, Radio

If you do TV or radio advertisements, be sure to infuse them with your own personality and a clear differentiating idea that can set you apart from your competitors. You want your competitors to hear your ads and get scared a little bit. See if you can't lower the cost of doing advertising in these mediums by joining forces with other wedding vendors or prom vendors to offer contest prizes that the radio can give away and promote.

5) PR opportunities

It takes persistence to get well placed publicity. But, there is little that can scare your competitors and show your teeth better than having great articles written about you and your store. Be on the lookout for inexpensive and creative PR opportunities to promote your store. If you don't have any publicity being done at your store, my guess is that you don't have the phone numbers and email addresses of the local paper and television producers handy and that you aren't actively working to develop a better relationship with these contacts. Remember, this is an area where you can beat big box retailers who take this kind of coverage for granted when they first move into town and do little to continue it after they've opened their doors. Don't ever take this for granted. You have to work at it if you want to be newsworthy and promoted in this way.

6) Bridal shows

When your competitors see you show up and set up your booth and signs, how do they respond? If they start copying you, your booth and your promotions have teeth. If not, and you are copying them, you are running from them. Go on the offensive. Get out there and let brides know why they should come see you. If you can't or aren't able to do this effectively before the show, look for creative ways to grab attention to make your booth the talk of the show and the place to be. This excitement will carry over to your store and bring brides into your store to buy if you do it right.

One last area I'll mention is your sales effectiveness. The most powerful thing you can do to show your teeth is to show how much better you are than your competitors by getting really good at closing sales. If brides come into your store and leave with a dress, you've shown your teeth and you are taking back your market one bride at a time. If the bride leaves without buying, you haven't shown that you are a good fighter. Fight for every sale. Get good at building trust, presenting gowns, and closing sales.

If you are going to beat a giant in a battle, you have to study their weaknesses and fight them in ways that will allow you to win. I hope these ten strategies have been helpful to show you the areas you must focus on if you are going to successfully compete and win against the big box retailers who are coming into your area with the goal to take your customers away from you.

Choose to be nimble and fight on thin ice, win with speed, with in the last three feet, fight back by refusing to be content with losing, do the unthinkable, make the inconvenient argument about why buying from you is better, draw attention to your differences, lead the conversation by seizing the microphone, be a more fearsome competitor, and show your teeth. You can successfully compete and win against big box retailers if you focus on the right areas. Be more proactive about your success. You may not be able to be bigger than the big box retailers but you can be better, faster, and more creative than they are. Study the gaps. Where are the giants in the bridal industry weak? Where do they not currently participate? At what point do they assume the sale is already made? Is this a point in which you can enter and dominate the conversation? Choose to get on the offensive and play to win AND you will.

CHAPTER 8

AVOID DESTRUCTIVE MANAGEMENT MISTAKES THAT WILL HINDER AND STOP GROWTH

"There is nothing so useless as doing efficiently that which should not be done at all."
—Peter F. Drucker

L arry Bossidy, the former CEO of Allied Signal and author of *Confronting Reality* and *Execution* recently made this statement:

"The question is often asked, 'How am I doing as a leader?' *The answer is how the people you lead are doing.* Do they learn? Do they manage conflict? Do they initiate changes? You won't remember when you retire what you did in the first quarter of [a specific year]. What you will remember is how many people you developed."

John Maxwell outlines four questions to find out how you are doing as a leader in his book *Leadership Gold.* I've adapted these questions for the purpose of our discussion. These questions are:

Are your bridal consultants following?
Are your bridal consultants changing?

Are your bridal consultants growing?

Are your bridal consultants succeeding?

Basketball coach Pat Riley, who has led two different teams to NBA Championships, observed:"I think the ways a leader can measure whether or not he or she is doing a good job is (1) through wins or losses, (2) through the bottom line, (3) through the subjective and visual analysis of how individuals are improving and growing. If individuals are getting better results, I think the whole product is improving."

As I've mentioned before, there are four types of learning: 1) What to do, 2) What not to do, 3) How to do it, and 4) Why you do it.

This chapter will focus on what not to do or the biggest management mistakes managers and leaders make and how you can avoid them so that your store can grow and succeed.

Obviously, one of the biggest challenges with teaching on the topic of management mistakes and how to be a better manager or leader is the tendency that people have to think that the information they are hearing or reading is better suited for someone else since they are already possess the skills being covered at a higher level than those around them.

The tendency to do this, to overestimate one's achievements and capabilities in relation to others, is what has been coined "The Lake Wobegon Effect."

"It is named for the fictional town of Lake Wobegon from the radio series *Prairie Home Companion*, where, according to the presenter, Garrison Keillor, "all the women are strong, all the men are good-looking, and all the children are above average."...This phenomenon has been observed among drivers, CEOs, stock market analysts, college students, police officers and state education officials, among others [including owners and managers of bridal stores and wedding professionals]. Experiments and surveys have repeatedly shown that most people believe that they possess attributes that are better or more

desirable than average. One College Board survey asked 829,000 high school seniors to rate themselves in a number of ways. When asked to rate their own ability to "get along with others", fewer than one percent rated themselves as below average. Furthermore, sixty percent rated themselves in the top ten percent, and one-fourth of respondents rated themselves in the top one percent." --
http://en.wikipedia.org/wiki/Lake_Wobegon_effect

Have you seen this phenomenon in your life?

Have you observed bridal consultants who rate themselves as better salespeople than they really are, but when you closely observe their skills (overcoming objections, asking questions, closing, etc.), you find that they are weaker than they are.

How about you? Do you or your managers believe that you are better than average managers? When you look at the skills of management do you really rate as above average **or** are there areas where you need improvement? That is the purpose of this chapter – to help you see what mistakes you may be making that are holding you and the other members of your team back and how you can overcome them.

Most people have known individuals and have had bosses who thought they were really good at management or leadership. However, the reality is that they weren't that good at it. Many of the lessons I've learned that I'll share with you are gleaned from the study of great leaders and observing lots of bad ones (especially learning from the mistakes that I personally have made).

Kim Clark, former dean of Harvard Business School once observed:

"How you deal with failure determines part of your success as a leader—not only in your own life, but also in the lives of people around you." --Fast Company, 9/2003

If you've felt any sense of frustration lately with those around you, the ups and downs of the economy, and the brides who are coming into your doors each day, think about this statement from mutual fund founder John Templeton:

"Tough times build character. The best thing that ever happened to me was when the Great Depression hit, and my father couldn't give me one more dollar for college. In order to return to school, I had to learn to be self reliant, resourceful, and diligent....When dealt a bad hand, you learn to play smarter."

In this chapter, I want to discuss 21 specific management mistakes that you should avoid so you can become a better manager and leader.

Management Mistake #1: Not paying attention to indicators or feelings of staff members.

Sam Walton, founder of Wal-Mart once observed:

"Appreciate everything your associates do for the business. Nothing else can quite substitute for a few well-chosen, well-timed, sincere words of praise. They're absolutely free and worth a fortune."

It is so important to pay attention to the moods and attitudes of everyone around you at your store. Great bridal store managers know that most people's motivation buckets leak like a water bucket full of shotgun holes.

They know that they need to be constantly aware of the moods and attitudes of all of their staff members. They go around and are constantly filling people's motivation buckets with encouragement, praise, and helpful assistance. In other words, you let your bridal consultants and members of your team know how they are doing and offer to help them where and when they need a helping hand.

The key is to be sure that you are filling his or her bucket with things that are important to each individual person. This also means that you have to constantly be filling your own bucket or you won't have anything to pour into people.

Ineffective leaders, who have lots of turnover are like big, long dippers that reach in and constantly drain people's buckets. They do this by taking credit for the success of others and a long list of other behaviors that de-motivate rather than motivate.

Most of the frustrating experiences I felt when working for others came from this management blunder: taking credit for what I had contributed and constantly draining my motivation bucket.

Are you ever guilty of this?

Do you pay close attention to the feelings of the bridal consultants at your store?

Do you know when you need to be encouraging and give a motivational training session and how to balance that with hitting the targets and goals you need to achieve?

This distinction is a fine line, but it is the difference between accomplishment and defeat, the difference between high morale and low morale.

If you don't do this well, you will find that you are likely losing those around you.

John Maxwell in his book *Leadership Gold* makes this point:

"As leaders, we'd like to think that when people leave, it has little to do with us. But the reality is that we are often the reason. Some sources estimate that as many as 65 percent of people leaving companies do so because of their managers. We may say that people quit their job or their company, but the reality is that they usually quit their leaders. The company doesn't do anything negative to them. People do. Sometimes coworkers cause the problems that prompt people to leave. But often the people who alienate employees are their direct supervisors." --p. 145.

Pay more attention to the mood and feelings of each staff member.

Management Mistake #2: Not understanding what motivates or inspires your staff.

If you're going to get better results from each member of your team, you've got to understand what drives or motivates them. Dwight Eisenhower once observed: "Leadership is the art of getting someone else to do something you want because he [or she] wants to do it."

Here are several ways you can motivate and inspire those around you at your store:

- Involve your bridal consultants in major decisions.
- Listen to them—they often have the best ideas.
- Know about them and members of their families.
- Listen more to what is important to them. Many times people will motivate themselves if you just ask great questions and listen.
- Give thank you notes and gift cards out to bridal consultants who really go the extra mile. Notice the little things that steamers, receptionists, and seamstresses do make the brides coming into your store smile and reward them accordingly.
- Assign your best sellers to become mentors to those who may be struggling. Let them help your struggling consultants fill their motivation buckets by helping them succeed.
- Give your bridal consultants access to helpful sales training materials. Training is an ongoing process. Have a library at your store of books, training CDs, online training courses, and articles that can inspire them to fill their own motivation buckets.
- Let your team know how they are doing towards achieving your goals. Have group prizes when you reach your goals on a monthly, quarterly, or yearly basis.

One of the best things you can do to inspire and motivate your bridal consultants is to catch them doing things right. You can do this by making up a "Caught Ya" form that anyone can fill out and put in a designated box so that:

- Any bridal consultant or staff member at your store can catch any other employee doing something well.
- When any bridal consultant or staff member witnesses someone else doing something right, they should fill out a "Caught Ya"

Nomination Form and puts it in a Caught Ya Box which is located at the front desk of your store.

- Once a month or once a week, go through the Caught Ya Box and select the best Caught Ya.
- Remind everyone on your team what was done and reward the winner in front of your entire staff with a cash bonus or gift card.
- If you want, you can post the past winners of the Caught Ya Super Star award each month or throughout the year.

As you encourage and recognize the accomplishments of your bridal consultants, morale and performance will improve, especially if you tie the recognition to the accomplishment of critical success factors that will help you reach your store goals.

As Thomas Jefferson once said: "Nothing can stop the man [or woman] with the right mental attitude from achieving his [or her] goal; nothing on earth can help the man [or woman] with the wrong mental attitude."

Catch your team doing things right and reward them accordingly.

Management Mistake #3: Failing to plan the details of how you will accomplish your goals and vision.

How often do you spend time planning your day?

How well do you think through what needs to be done in advance?

Everyone can benefit from spending more time planning, yet it is easy to make excuses about why you don't have time to do so. You <u>must</u> make the time. Come in before anyone else is at your store, don't answer the phone, and think on paper about the upcoming bridal shows you have, the challenges you're facing with your staff, how to bring more brides into the store, how to help your staff sell more, etc.

When people get busy, they tend to wing things. And the first thing we stop doing is taking time to think and to plan. Yet, this is the vital skill that will help you be a better manager and leader. Don't start your day until you've finished it on paper first. Of course, you are going to get distracted from the plan you've written, but it is a lot easier to get back on track when you have a plan written down and goals to achieve than when you don't. There are 1,440 minutes in each day. You can spend 14 minutes or less than 1% of each day thinking and planning out your day.

To be a great leader and manager, you need to set your store vision and articulate it to others. Bob Boylan in his excellent book, *Get Everyone in Your Boat Rowing in the Same Direction* says this:

"Leadership is like love. It's something you do, not just think about. It must be *talked* about, not just *thought* about."--p. 7.

His book outlines 5 principles that are at the very essence of what leaders do in order to get others to follow them (and thus be a leader):

1) They talk about *what's important around here.*

If you don't articulate what is important to you, you will get distracted and lose focus. You may know what your priorities are and they may be something you think about all of the time, but if you don't talk about them and help those you work with understand <u>what</u> is important, they likely won't act on your priorities.

Bob Boylan tells this story:

'Walt Disney was walking through Disney World before its completion, with a small group of his department heads. Suddenly he stopped, pointed to a specific area, and said, 'I want 10,000 fireflies over there!'

The head of construction asked, 'When?'

Notice that the man did not say, 'But, Walt, where could I possibly find 10,000 fireflies?' or 'Wouldn't 5,000 be sufficient?'

He then makes this point:

"Perfection, absolute top quality, was the value here. Just do it, please. The man said, 'When?' No second guessing, just 'when?' He understood that for Mr. Disney, perfection was the value—a value the man himself obviously also bought into.

In order to have this fit, however, it's important that your potential followers understand your values—what's important to you. You need to clearly define this for them. That's the first step." --pp. 15-16.

How do the members of your team know **what's important to *you*?**

Do you clearly articulate your vision so everyone understands their priorities or **is this vague and confusing to those who work in your store?**

2) They talk about *where are we headed*.

Bob Boylan makes this interesting observation:

"In most organizations, few employees can answer the question, 'Where are we headed?' In fact, a recent Booz, Allen & Hamilton study revealed that only 37 percent of senior officials think other key managers clearly understand business goals.

"Well, that's not so good. However, it's normal. How does this happen? Because no clear direction has been established by the leader.

"Or if one has been established, it hasn't been communicated forcefully, or memorably, enough for people to know where they are headed." --p. 45.

He continues:

"Vision is the second step to leadership. Without it, there is no focus. A good vision grabs. Its passion helps transform purpose—where you want to be—into action almost automatically."--p. 50.

Do you know where your store is headed in the future?

Have you communicated that vision with everyone around you or do others feel that you are just trying to hold on to what you've currently got?

That is a brutally tough question – but one that is important to ask – because it *really* indicates what you are communicating about where you are headed.

3) They talk about *what we stand for*.

If you bumped into a person on an elevator who could help you achieve your goals, how would you describe your business and what you stand for in thirty seconds? How would *you* respond? Would you mumble out an answer or clearly articulate:

- The name of your company

- What you stand for/ believe in

- The benefits of what you sell

If you can't clearly articulate what you stand for, your prospective brides won't be able to either. Know and clearly articulate what you stand for.

4) They talk about falling in love with risk. Doing things differently and making changes requires risk. Great leaders help others embrace risk and change as the way to get to the next level. Are you embracing risk or running from it?

5) They learn to motivate people. Tom Landry, former football coach of the Dallas Cowboys made this great observation:

"Leadership is a matter of having people look at you and gain confidence, seeing how you react. If you're in control, they're in control."

To succeed as a leader, you've got to know how to motivate yourself before you can really understand how to motivate others.

Robert Gallant observed in his book *How to Be a Manager*: "The best person to practice on is yourself because the most difficult person to properly manage and to develop is yourself."

Management Mistake #4: Mistaking activity for accomplishment.

I think one of the biggest examples of how common this problem is can be found in Stephen Robbins excellent book, *The Truth About Managing People*. He says:

"A management consultant specializing in police research noticed that, in one community, officers would come on duty for their shift, proceed to get into their police cars, drive to the highway that cut through the town, and speed back and forth along this highway for their entire shift. Clearly this fast cruising had little to do with good police work. But this behavior made considerably more sense once the consultant learned that the community's city council used mileage on police vehicles as a measure of police effectiveness. The city council unintentionally was rewarding 'putting lots of miles on police cars,' so that's what officers emphasized."--p. 60.

Have you made this management mistake? How often is activity mistaken for accomplishment at your store?

Do you reward your bridal consultants based on selling a certain $/hour or for selling over a certain price point?

Being present during a shift is not the same thing as consistently selling at a high dollar per hour figure during a shift.

Remember, the things that get rewarded get done so be sure you are rewarding accomplishment and not just activity at your store.

Management Mistake #5: Taking too long to solve a problem, make a decision, or resolve a conflict.

Waiting too long to solve a problem, make a decision, or resolve a conflict can be disastrous at your store.

I've realized that there are four types of challenges that come up in your bridal store. When you understand what these challenges are, you can deal with them more effectively and get to your decision quicker. The four types of challenges or changes that will come up at your store are:

1) Anticipated Changes - these could include situations where:

- You know you need to add additional inventory at certain times of year.
- You know an employee will be leaving because of a move, pregnancy, etc.
- You know what months are slowest in this business (October, November, December) so you can prepare ahead to market for these slower times in your store.
- You know when you are busting at the seams and need additional space to take care of the new customers coming in (if you're growing at 25% a year or more, you'll will more room soon).

2) Sudden & Unexpected Changes - these could include situations where you have:

- A key employee who decides to leave or has to leave because you've fired them for incompetence
- Your credit card processing company call you to inform you that they will be cancelling your merchant account
- Just realized that an employee has been stealing from you or that inventory has been stolen from you over a period of time.
- A situation where your computer crashes and you lose your computer data.

3) Crisis (Forced on You Changes) - these could include situations where:

- You have a cash flow crunch and discover that you may not be able to make payroll or you'll have to cut your own payroll to make things work.
- Customer service issues come up that cost you money and your reputation.
- You have any type of crisis involving members of your family .
- You discover that you'll have dresses arriving late and then have to deal with the aftermath with brides.
- You get a negative review online from a bride that causes you stress (especially when it is wrong and not true)

- You see your own expenses go up without a corresponding increase in sales.

4) Competitive Changes - these could include situations where you discover that:

- A David's Bridal will be moving into your area.
- A competitor gets a line that you used to have and do well with.
- A key employee leaves to work for one of your competitors.
- A competitor is copying something that you are doing that is working for you.
- A competitor badmouths you online to other brides.

When any of these situations or challenges of any kind (especially when you or one of your staff has made a mistake that will cost you money), it is best to ask yourself the following ten questions so you can get the facts:

1) What is the situation exactly?

2) What has happened from different perspectives?

3) How did it happen?

4) When did it happen?

5) Where did it happen?

6) What are the facts?

7) How do we know that these facts are accurate?

8) Who was involved?

9) Who is responsible for doing (or not doing) the things that set in motion the challenge we are facing today?

10) What can be done to ensure that this situation doesn't happen in the future?

It is helpful to ask these questions because sometimes we make assumptions that get us into trouble before we know all of the facts. It is best to question your assumptions, determine what would happen if they were wrong before making any concrete decisions about doing something different at your store.

When you make a BIG mistake that causes you to lose money or your business experiences something shocking that you weren't expecting, you will likely go through the five stages of grief as outlined by psychologist Elizabeth Kübler-Ross. These are the same stages you go through when you lose someone close to you. When you understand these emotions, you can better bounce back from the disappointment and frustration you feel when something doesn't go your way in your bridal business.

These stages are:

1. *Denial* – basically what happens here is you are shocked because you can't believe what is happening is happening to you because it wasn't supposed to happen and it will now seriously disrupt you and your business. In denial, you mentally try to shut out what you are feeling and pretend that it really isn't happening.

2. *Anger* – once you realize that the situation is indeed happening (such as losing a valuable employee or finding out about a mistake that will cost you money, the natural tendency is to lash out in anger against someone else that you feel is responsible for the setback that you are experiencing). When you do this to members of your bridal staff, you may say things you really don't mean and which you can't take back.

3. *Blame* – anger turns into blame very quickly where you try to track down the person that caused the problem in the first place. Sometimes in really bad situations, someone may end up getting fired.

4. *Depression* – when the reality sets in that you can't avoid the setback and that it will take place, it is common and easy to get depressed and tremendously discouraged. You feel let down, cheated and betrayed by someone else. Very often, you may feel sorry for yourself (especially when you look around at others and see that they don't seem to be experiencing the same challenges that you are).

5. *Acceptance* – At some point, you realize that the setback has happened and that it doesn't do anymore good to be angry about what is going on. You accept what happened and start looking to the future again. In some cases, this may take several weeks or months before this feeling is reached.

The thing I would mention about these five stages (and why it is important to understand them) is that when you recognize what stage you are in, you can take control of your emotions and get through the next step. This isn't easy, but it is a lot harder if you don't have a road map to guide you through the challenges.

On more difficult decisions, consult with your inner circle or management team to advise you in the key actions you should take. You may seek help from an outside source on more dramatic challenges that you face. After getting the information together, make and stand by your decision.

If you are still worried ask yourself, "What prevents me from seizing this opportunity or making this decision?" Then, act and do what needs to be done. Leadership is about making tough decisions.

Look for others to help you and move forward. You don't have to face your challenges alone.

Management Mistake #6: Not leading by example.

If you want others to achieve results, you have to show it is possible by what you do. One of the key responsibilities of a manager is to show that the goals and expectations you are asking can be accomplished.

Why? The answer is because bridal consultants will imitate *your behavior and attitudes*. They watch what you as the manager or owner does first and then adapt their behavior to match what they have seen.

When your words and actions aren't congruent, people are more likely to follow the behaviors of what they see. Promote bridal consultants who are your top sellers into assistant manager or manager positions because other bridal consultants on your team see them lead by example and will be more willing to follow.

Management Mistake #7: Losing focus on what really matters and concentrating on the most urgent things instead.

This mistake happens anytime we get bogged down on our biggest problems, not our biggest opportunities.

A great example of the challenge of focus is found in Mark Sanborn's book *You Don't Need a Title to Be a Leader*. He tells of a friend of his named Bill who lives outside Kalamazoo, Michigan. Bill had a terrible problem with squirrels who got into his bird feeder and scared away the birds.

He went to a local hardware store to buy a 'squirrel proof bird feeder,' an odd looking feeder with wire mesh wrapped around it. But, Bill found out that the squirrels were swinging off the bird feeder that night at sunset. Bill took the bird feeder back to the store and talked to the manager who told him:

"I could have told you when you bought it that there is no such thing as a squirrel proof bird feeder.' Bill looked at him in disbelief...[The store manager] asked him: 'How much time on average have you spent in the last two weeks trying to keep the squirrels out of your bird feeder?' Bill thought it over for a moment and responded, 'Maybe ten to fifteen minutes a day.'

'And how much time do you think the squirrels spend each day trying to get in?' The answer, Bill learned, is almost every waking squirrel moment; squirrels spend 98 percent of their waking hours looking for food. In fact, they are unique in the animal kingdom in that they would rather eat than procreate; they prefer foraging to fooling around. This just goes to show the kind of focus the squirrel brings to its mission.

The moral of this story: Focus and determination beat brains and intellect every time. You don't necessarily have to be smarter or better educated to succeed. Your power lies in your ability to focus on doing what is important. If you focus on the right things, and work at them often, you will achieve exceptional results." *-You Don't Need a Title to Be a Leader*, p. 40-42.

The key to being a successful manager is focusing on what matters most at the right times and helping those you manage to do the same. The most important single thing a manager needs to focus on is selling.

If you have the same kind of focus on selling like the squirrels have on getting the food in the bird feeder, you won't have any problem achieving your business goals.

The problem comes when you are distracted by problems instead of focusing on your opportunities (selling). I really like this statement by former British Prime Minister Tony Blair who said:

"The art of leadership is saying no, not yes. It is very easy to say yes."

Make sure you are saying no to the things that can distract you. Your challenge as a manager in the bridal business is this: the things that distract you aren't necessarily bad – but the problem is that over time you drift away from what really matters.

Management Mistake #9: Hiring under pressure.

In his book *Good to Great*, Jim Collins makes this important point:

"When in doubt, don't hire—keep looking....[I had an interview with] Walter Bruckart, vice president (of Circuit City) during the good-to-great years. When asked to name the top five factors that led to the transition from mediocrity to excellence, Bruckart said, 'One would be people. Two would be people. Three would be people. Four would be people. And five would be people. Huge part of our transition can be attributed to our discipline in picking the right people.' Bruckart then recalled a conversation with CEO Alan Wurtzel during a growth spurt at Circuit City: 'Alan, I'm really wearing down trying to find the exact right person to fill this position or that position. At what point do I compromise?' Without hesitation, Alan said, 'You don't compromise. We find another way to get through until we find the right people." --p. 55.

Have you ever made this management mistake? It is easy to get crazy busy at your store and end up hiring the first person you interview because you are under pressure to meet the demands at your store.

When a hiring decision is made under pressure, a mistake will usually be made. It is better to keep looking than to make a hiring mistake.

In *9 Lies that Are Holding Your Business Back*, authors Steve Chandler and Sam Beckford make this point to a small business owner who is having a really hard time finding good people to work at their furniture business. They say:

"In your business there is no commitment right now whatsoever for building a great team. Not that there isn't a wish and a hope, there's just no commitment. There is reaction to crisis, and choosing to have your hiring be in the 'reaction' mode, rather than the 'creation' mode has caused almost every problem you have. It has tied everybody up, including yourselves." --pp. 27-32.

It is easy to get caught in this trap. When you are busy, your efforts to recruit new bridal consultants are disorganized and frantic at best and if you have enough staff, you probably aren't recruiting at all.

The most important time to be hiring and recruiting great people is when you don't need them. Be creative or proactive about how you hire instead of reactive and hiring under pressure because you have to help now.

Don't make this management mistake: be proactive and hire the people you want, not reactive when hiring the individuals you need.

Management Mistake #10: Managing everyone the same way.

In his book *13 Fatal Errors Managers Make and How You Can Avoid Them*, author W. Steven Brown identifies the four managerial styles. These are:

1) **Autocratic Management** – "As the word autocratic implies, this manager draws from his [or her] own strength. He [or she] says, 'Do it this way...' 'I said so...' 'If you work here, this is the way it will be handled.'"

Most managers utilize the management method that works best on themselves. However, autocratic management only works in certain circumstances and can backfire with certain personality types. I had a manager at our store several years ago who was very autocratic and unfortunately, not very diplomatic at the same time. I ended up getting a new manager because it was her way or the highway and many times she didn't represent what I wanted to our bridal consultants. In reality, I made Management Mistake #9 that I just discussed. I hired under pressure and made a mistake that caused a lot of problems at the store.

Autocratic management can be helpful when you have a younger staff who isn't sure what to do or in particular situations where the circumstances warrant it, but typically it is not how most people prefer to be managed.

2) **Bureaucratic Management** – "This means management by the rule book. The policy and procedural manual calls cadence. As with autocratic management, when it works, it's good. When it doesn't, it's bad....With people mature enough to accept what the rule book says, bureaucratic management works. Others feel totally dehumanized when you drag out a policy and procedure book. They feel as though they are being treated as a robot, a computer, a pawn. Also they may decide that you aren't creative enough in your management to adapt to special situations." --p. 71.

The other challenge with bureaucratic management is that you have to think through every situation in the world in order to come up with an effective rulebook. No one likes to have the rules waved over their head, especially if they have been found violating them.

It is important to have standards and rules (as we'll talk about in management mistake #13), but the most important thing about management is finding what works, not sticking to something no matter what.

3) Democratic Management – This means that you let others participate in the decision-making process. The biggest advantage for this style of management is to get a number of opinions and perspectives other than your own. When you include your bridal consultants in the decision making process at your store, it helps them feel more a part of what you are doing. If you haven't already, take staff members on buying trips based on their performance. When they participate in the ordering process with you, they are much more committed to and sell the inventory when it comes in.

4) Idiosyncratic Management – This type of management refers to the "extremes of personalities (extremes that are literally idiosyncrasies)." What this means is that you manage people based on a one-to-one relationship. In other words, you manage them based on how they would like to be managed. You find out what motivates them and help them achieve their goals.

The best thing you can do is discover which management method works best with each member on your staff. When you know what motivates each member of your team, you will be a much better manager, and you won't violate management mistake #2!

I've found that management style #4 is the most effective in motivating our team members. Be firm in your expectations of what you want but look to others on your team for creative ideas on how to achieve specific goals.

I like what General George S. Patton observed about leadership. He said: "Never tell people how to do things. Tell them what to do and they will surprise you with their ingenuity."

Management Mistake #11: Condoning incompetence.

Why do bridal store owners or managers allow incompetence? It is usually because of one of two reasons:

1) They hope it will go away if it is ignored.

2) They are afraid or unwilling to confront others who have made a serious mistake.

If you see someone doing something that you don't like in your business, here are seven steps to how you should confront the problem:

1) Bring it up immediately. If you ignore it or wait to get to it later, you probably never will. Inaction will condone the behavior you don't really want. Dick Vermeil, former coach of the Kansas City Chiefs once observed: "To not confront poor execution and behavior is to endorse it. To not reinforce good execution and behavior is to extinguish it."

2) Discuss the issue in private. Never, ever confront someone in a public area where other bridal consultants are privy to what you are discussing. The basic rule is this: criticize in private, praise in public.

3) Control your own emotions. When we are angry, our blood leaves our brain. This is a natural instinct since the flight or fight response reroutes blood to the limbs to run away or fight. When the blood leaves our brain, we don't think very well. As a result, we may say things that we don't mean. If you get upset, step away from the situation until you can regain control of your emotions.

4) Be specific about the behavior or action that you did not agree with. Document the issues that have been on your mind and share specific details about the action you disapprove of.

5) Be clear about the standard (what you expect).

6) Set goals for a new direction. This is the most important part of your discussion. Express your confidence that they can do what needs to be done.

7) Schedule a follow-up visit to review their progress.

Bridal consultants who are competent have the following four characteristics:

1) They are committed to excellence.

2) They never settle for average.

3) They refuse to be mediocre.

4) They pay attention to detail.

Dale Carnegie once said: "Don't be afraid to give your best to what are seemingly small jobs. Every time you conquer one it makes you that much stronger. If you do little jobs well, the big ones tend to take care of themselves."

The best members of your team will perform with consistency. To be successful, you need A players and competent professionals to surround you. Never condone incompetence.

Management Mistake #12: Being a buddy, not a boss.

David Cottrell once observed: "If your goal is to get everyone to like you, you will avoid making tough decisions because of fear of upsetting your friends."

I can't tell you how many times I have heard store owners and managers tell me about difficult problems they have with other bridal consultants at their store because of this issue.

Everyone is watching you to see what you will do. When you act decisively and treat everyone the same, you are much more likely to have long-term effectiveness as a manager. Making exceptions for one individual will soon lead to making exceptions to others and pretty soon there will be absolute chaos with your system of rules and procedures.

One of the worst things that can happen to your authority as a manager is when a bridal consultant becomes a great friend and then starts taking advantage of that relationship. It starts innocently enough, but pretty soon they start showing up late for work, goofing off instead of working, and stretching the standard you have set at the store. They expect you to look the other way since you are friends.

When this happens, you have to get over your personal emotions and do what is best for the business and let that person go. It is okay to be friendly with everyone who works with you and for you, but you can't let others on your staff feel like you give preferential treatment to one person over another.

The longer you prolong such a decision, the tougher it will be on you and on them. Part of being a manager is making tough decisions and making them in a timely fashion. Don't postpone for years what you know you should have done earlier because you are afraid of upsetting your buddy, instead of being the boss.

The most important part of hiring someone is to define the relationship (between you and them) when they are first hired. Many store owners have hired friends, relatives, or family before. If you choose to hire a friend or family member, remember that you will have to choose at some point between being their boss and their buddy. It is very difficult to be both and have a relationship that other bridal consultants and staff members will respect and not resent.

The Bottom Line: treat everyone the same. It does not matter if the employee is a steamer or your star salesperson, a receptionist or the one in charge of your marketing; everyone at your store should be treated the same when it comes to adhering to published store policies and your performance expectations.

Management Mistake #13: Failing to establish standards and sticking to them.

Jim Collins in his book *Good to Great* makes this great point about the importance of standards and sticking to them. He says:

"The good-to-great companies probably sound like tough places to work—and they are. If you don't have what it takes, you probably won't last long. But they're not ruthless cultures, they're rigorous cultures. And the distinction is critical. To be ruthless, means hacking and cutting, especially in difficult times, or wantonly firing people without any thoughtful consideration. To be rigorous means consistently applying exacting standards at all times and at all levels, especially in upper management. To be rigorous, not ruthless, means that the best people need not worry about their positions and can concentrate fully on their work." --p. 52.

One of the benefits of having standards and sticking to them is that everyone rises to the standard or they don't. This makes it easier for you to make adjustments in your personnel if someone is not hitting the standard.

There are two parts of this: one is actually setting a standard and two is making sure that you stick with the standards. If you don't stick with your standard, pretty soon it becomes meaningless and can be demotivating to the people who actually do reach it, especially if there is no consequence for those who don't.

I like what Jim Collins says:

"The only way to deliver to the people who are achieving is to not burden them with the people who are not achieving." --, p. 53.

You can set standards for:

- Sales per hour
- # of dresses sold per week
- # of outbound phone calls made each day (require at least 2)
- Sending out a thank you card for every purchase made
- Getting a testimonial from every bride you sell a dress to
- Any other number that will help you better track results.

The key is to look at the critical success factors that you know lead to a sale and then measure and reward those activities.

Another big area where you need to have standards is to prevent time theft, which is becoming a bigger problem all of the time. Here are a couple of standards that can help you prevent time theft:

- *Mobile phones* – There should be no texting or phone calls during work hours (unless on a lunch break that is off the clock). It doesn't leave a very favorable impression when someone is more interested in what is happening on their phone than they are in you and the conversation you are trying to have. Have employees turn off their phones when they arrive for their shift.
- *Internet usage* – Bridal consultants don't need access to email and access to Facebook, Pinterest, or any other social networking site at your store. If someone does need to send a message, they can do it after work or before work. When you establish a policy or a standard like this, it is often resisted. You must be firm on this or you will be stolen from since hours spent on these personal sites typically aren't helping you market to brides or selling more dresses.
- *Not working all the time that you are working* – if you find that your bridal consultants aren't doing productive things when it is slower, this is your fault. Put together a list of things they can do in slower times. Quiz them on overcoming objection flashcards, make phone calls, or put together their own marketing campaigns to bring brides into the store.

I really like this statement by author and speaker Dan Kennedy:

"In the workplace, people need to grasp that they are there to work...whatever they're doing is your business as long as they are doing it at your business on your business's clock."

I'm not trying to be rude, but the point is that your bridal store is a workplace that should be a place of work and productivity, not spending time on the Internet and texting their friends.

If you have employees who would rather spend time working on their projects rather than working on the business of selling and helping brides and prom customers in the store, it is time to replace those individuals with caring bridal consultants who will help you and the other members of your staff get the work of each day completed.

No one wants to pick up the slack of ineffective or unproductive bridal consultants. Do yourself and your bridal consultants a favor and let go of those who will not comply with the standards you've set at your store.

David Cottrell makes this point: "The single greatest 'demotivator' of a team is to have members who are not carrying their load. It takes courage to address issues honestly and then let people go when that's necessary. Your emotions are involved, the employee's short-term livelihood is involved, and it is a tough conversation to have. But, if you have provided someone every opportunity for success and yet his [or her] performance fails to meet expectations, summon your courage and allow him [or her] to go where he [or she] can be successful. It is not a personal mistake of yours, nor is it the employee's mistake—the job is just not right for him [or her]."--p. 47.

When everyone understands **and** follows the rules, it is amazing how much more productive you really are.

Management Mistake #14: Trying to control results without measuring the critical success factors that lead to the results you want.

Bill Glazer, a mentor of mine who once owned two successful menswear stores in Baltimore, Maryland makes this statement about the importance of measuring everything that is important at your store and then posting it for all to see:

"Think about what happened the last time you went to a professional baseball game. The first batter walked to the plate and the big electronic screen posted his name and all his relevant statistics. It gave you his batting average, how many home runs he had hit, how many games he had played, and a host of other statistical information.

Why did they do that?

For one thing, it is a way for the people in the stands to evaluate the quality of the player.

Also, it serves as a motivation for the batter. Don't you think that he wants to have really great personal statistics up there on a huge screen for thousands of people to see, including his manager, his fellow players, and the team owner? If he has pride, it's got to motivate him to try to do better.

Most entrepreneurs and people in management don't really know how well their employees are doing. For example, when I was in retail, I found that most retail store owners would track each of their salesperson's sales. That's good, but it's not enough.

The only way you are going to find out is by measuring everything that's important.

Some people think that's wrong. They don't measure much of anything. They tell people, "Just go out there and do the best job that you can."

That's wrong.

It's wrong because doing the best job that you can may not be good enough. Just like in baseball. If everyone on the team is batting between .225 and .310, a .115 player is not going to be in the lineup even if he is doing the best job he can.

That's why you need to measure everything that's important.

Think of all of the different things that, when measured, can give the result you want and exactly what is acceptable performance."—*No B.S. Management of People and Profits*, pp. 177-178.

He continues:

"Every day at my retail stores we posted our EPR (Employee Productivity Report). We wanted to know how everyone was doing, and equally important, we wanted the salespeople to know how they were performing."

He listed 15 different categories. These are:

- **% OF TOTAL DAY:** The percentage of the total sales that every salesperson sold for each specific day.
- **$ DAY:** The dollar amount that the salesperson sold each day.
- **UNITS:** How many items the salesperson sold each day.
- **RECEIPTS:** How many different receipts the salesperson generated each day.
- **AVERAGE SALE:** The average amount of each of the salesperson's transactions.
- **UPT:** The average number of units of each transaction.
- **AVG DAILY $:** The average amount of each sale for each day.
- **PROJ. 4 WEEKS:** Based on the salesperon's performance to date, what his projected sales volume would be.
- **KIT PHONE:** How many 'Keep-in-Touch' phone contacts the salesperson made that day with his previous customers and how many appointments he made. (NOTE: More than 30% of our sales were by appointment...in a menswear store).
- **KIT WRITE:** How many 'Thank-You' notes the salesperson wrote that day to customers who recently purchased from her.
- **KIT APPS:** How many appointments showed up for that salesperson that day.
- **KIT APPS $:** How much total sales the appointments generated for that day.
- **EMAIL:** How many email addresses the salesperson gathered that day.
- **REFERRALS:** How many referrals the salesperson received from her clients that day.
- **CC:** How many store credit card accounts the salesperson opened that day.

I modified these for our store and measure fifteen areas of productivity. These areas are:

1) % of Total Day's Sales
2) Sales / Day
3) Sales / Hour

4) # of Dresses Sold
5) # of Accessories Sold
6) Average Sale Amount
7) UPT (Units per Transaction)
8) # of Phone Calls to Brides
9) # of Thank You Notes
10) # of Appointments who Came to Store
11) # of Pre-Sales Activities (preparing the next day's appointments)
12) Email Addresses Gathered
13) # of Referrals Received
14) # of Written Testimonials Received
15) # of Video Testimonials Received

As you implement any version of a measurement program, you will probably have the experience that he and I and most likely you have had as well. He says:

"When we first put this program into effect, it met a lot of resistance. Salespeople told us that it wasn't right for other people to see their performance. Funny thing was that these were the same salespeople who had lower performance.

We found that in a short period of time, two very interesting things happened.

First, we experienced some turnover by the underperforming salespeople. These were the same people who should have gone. They were not the right fit for the job.

Second, the performance of the salespeople who remained rose significantly. What we discovered was that good salespeople are naturally competitive. They'll try to be the top in each category measured. The chart that we posted showed each of the 15 categories of statistics was updated daily and was right outside my office. Every day our sales associates walked by, stopped, and studied the chart. They liked it because they knew exactly how they were doing and where they stood."--p. 179-181.

Remember, you must inspect what you expect. Measuring performance in key areas will help you achieve your goals faster than trying to control results.

Management Mistake #15: Failing to evaluate performance and train for improvement.

One of the most important things you do as the manager of your store is to help your bridal consultants evaluate how well they are selling every day.

Jim Collins in his book *Good to Great* says: "Managing your problems can only make you good, whereas building your opportunities is the only way to become great."

One of the most important opportunities to manage is the performance of each of your bridal consultants. Part of this is setting a standard of performance for the job you hire them to do. People will rise to your expectations. What do you expect? Do you expect that each bridal consultant will sell $150 in sales per hour? In other words, if one of your employees works for 8 hours, you expect her to make $1,200 in sales. It is so important to create an expectation and hold bridal consultants accountable to reaching their daily goal.

As the old saying goes, "If you can't measure it, you can't manage it."

A great model for teaching and evaluation uses the acronym IDEA:

Instruction – being taught and trained
Demonstration – watching the skill be modeled
Execution – using the skill
Accountability (evaluation) – what could be done better

If you want to help your bridal consultants sell more, you should take time to coach them often using the IDEA model and it is best if you can provide such coaching right after they have an interaction with a bride. You spend a tremendous amount of money each year on inventory. Be sure you're investing in the training of those who will help you sell that inventory and who make your store work day in and day out.

Even if you are a small store and you are the only person who works at the store, it is vital to ask yourself: How much do I invest in myself, my training, and my development?

Many store owners and managers justify not putting much time and effort into training by asking: "What if I train this bridal consultant and they *leave*?"

Instead, the question that should be asked is: What if I don't train this bridal consultant and she *stays*?

Here are four things to consider when putting together your store's training program:

1) Identify the training that they need. An effective training process begins by identifying the specific areas in need of training. "Generic" training is helpful, but has dramatically less impact and bottom line results. It is like the difference between taking tennis lessons with 19 people in the class and taking private lessons. The former is helpful, but the latter can truly improve your game. Spend time each month on sales training. This is the most important area of training in your store.

2) Commit completely to the training process. No short cuts! Do not attempt to find the "add water and stir" method, or hand out one book or watch an online training class or DVD and think your bridal consultants are trained. It is a never-ending process.

3) Have a budget for training. The best, most innovative, and fastest growing stores have a generous budget for training their management personnel and their bridal consultants. Invest in books and training CDs and DVDs to help your staff improve their performance.

4) Insist on application. This is where the rubber meets the road. You need to resist a merely academic experience (going to a class or reading a book). The key to successful training is application.

Training and developing your bridal consultants especially in the area of selling is the best way to ensure improved sales, profits, and market share. Poorly trained bridal consultants often want to be more effective but just don't know how. When you give employees the tools they need to be more effective—through training—you help them, but you also help your store.

Here are several benefits of training. Training can:

- Improve loyalty of your bridal consultants. When you train your staff, you show that you care about them. Train members on your team with the belief that the things you are teaching and training them will help them through their lives, not just at your store.

- Improve morale at your store.

- Reduce turnover since bridal consultants who are better trained and equipped to sell will make more and will be even more excited about being at your store

- Reduce sales costs because you have a higher close ratio

- Reduce hiring costs over time

- Improve communication at all levels (everyone will know what to do)

- Improve a bride's loyalty because of the experience she has with her bridal consultant (who is properly trained)

The only time training is really a cost (instead of a powerful investment) is when:

- It isn't done very well. Sophocles once said, "One learns by doing a thing; for though you think you know it, you have no certainty until you try."

- It is done too late

- When there isn't enough training (you touch on a subject, but don't really provide lasting tools)

- When it doesn't help everyone

- When it is not reinforced – it is so important to evaluate what has been learned and then to reinforce it through repetition. The stark reality is that less than 15 percent of any new idea is retained after two weeks of learning it. As the saying goes, repetition is the mother of all learning.

- When it doesn't relate to your long-term goals and direction

I go into great detail about how to choose who you will train and develop into leaders in my online 9-week Bridal Management Mastery course. If you would like more information on how you can train your manager or leaders with this course, please email me at info@bridaltrainingsystems.com. Please include the subject line: "Bridal Management Mastery Course".

Management Mistake #16: Having ineffective training meetings that don't motivate, inspire, teach, or train.

How do you know if you have had an effective training meeting? The answer can be summed up in two words: **Performance improves.**

Here is an example of the format of how we do our training meetings on Saturday mornings in a 30 minute format. I would recommend including some practice of overcoming objections in every training meeting (especially with new hires and during the busy season).

Saturday Morning Staff Meeting Schedule

9:30-9:35
Review Sales per hour and Saturday goal and progress towards monthly goal

Discuss and Set Saturday Goal:
Today's Goal: _____

Reward for Achieving Goal: _____ (Individual or Team)

9:35-9:45
Watch training video module or review training information

9:45-9:55
Practice resolving concerns / handling objections with role plays.
First have your top selling bridal consultant demonstrate what to do
and then have consultants split into pairs and practice correct
technique. The store owner or manager can observe and offer
encouragement and suggestions.

Concerns Practiced this Week

_____

_____

It is a good idea to spend time practicing the most common objections
that seem to be holding the majority of your consultants back). In
particular, you can track these by asking your consultants to write
down the reasons why they didn't make a sale on a daily report so you
can practice the most common challenges.

9:55-10:00
Review policies that need to be talked about or store concerns, new
programs or items for previous week.

_____

_____

Other Reminders and Comments (List issues you need to discuss with
the entire team regarding policies or procedures):

_____

_____

Meetings tend to be very ineffective and uninspiring if:

- You try to cover too much in a short period of time.
- The meeting is too long and there seems to be no end in sight.
- There is no agenda and thus little to no leadership during the meeting.
- If you have too many meetings (people tend to get burned out).

Here are five suggestions to help you have better training meetings at your store:

1) Stay focused on the topic at hand. If you are training on overcoming objections, don't get caught up in another area that could confuse or overwhelm your bridal consultants. Don't let discussions or practices get out of hand with off topic conversations.

2) Control distractions, side conversations, and interruptions. Don't answer your cell phone or store phone while you are having your training meetings. Have the meeting before brides start coming in the door. You don't want to be in the middle of a training meeting and have a problem come up that does require your immediate attention and then not be able to continue with what you are training on.

3) Let your bridal consultants know what the meeting will be about in advance. Ask them to contribute in some way. Involvement goes a long way to making training meetings more effective and powerful.

4) Make your training meetings mandatory. It is difficult to have a training meeting if everyone from your store is not there. Start and end on time. Have monetary consequences for individuals on your staff who are late.

5) Evaluate how effective your meetings are. Are you getting results after the meeting? How are your bridal consultants responding to the meeting? What is their reaction? Are they implementing what they are being taught?

One of the greatest teachers I have ever met, Gene Hill, once taught me this. He said, "Great teachers don't just cover material. They uncover understanding."

That is how an inspiring training meeting should be. It should uncover understanding. When your bridal consultants leave one of your meetings, they should be fired up, motivated, excited, and confident because they have been trained and inspired. You will know if you have had a good meeting because performance will improve.

Coach K said in his book *Leading with the Heart*:

"How much I speak to players on our team is important, but they'll forget a lot of what they hear. It's also important to make sure they watch and observe through action and videotape. Usually, the team will remember more of what they see. But the most critical aspect of our team training is what the guys actually do and what they understand.

So we perform all kinds of gamelike drills over and over again. Such repetition is designed to refine physical habits. And it is key to ensuring that a team will perform well in a real-life situation—because the group will not only hear and see what we tell them, they'll actually execute what we tell them."

Then he says this: "Whenever I go into a practice session with my team, I go in fully prepared. I put together a one-page handwritten lesson. I decide not only what points I want to get across, I also pick different places where I will talk to them—in the locker room, in the middle of the court, on the bench, under the basket, and so on. I choose a variety of spots in order to change the environment so the guys will stay attuned and aware. That way they'll be more likely to retain some of the things I tell them. I also determine how I will talk to the team. If I have a seven-minute drill planned, I can't take four minutes to explain it. And while I don't want to rush my explanation, I want to get it done in about a minute so they spend six minutes 'doing' rather than only 'hearing.'

He finishes with this thought: "A leader may be the most knowledgeable person in the world, but if the players on his team cannot translate that knowledge into action, it means nothing. In other words, it's not what I know, it's what they do on the court that really matters." --Mike Krzyzewski, *Leading with the Heart*, pp. 88-90.

Isn't that great? You have the responsibility to transfer what you *know* into what your bridal consultants *do* by how well you train them. Have effective training meetings that uncover understanding and inspire and motivate your bridal consultants to do what needs to be done.

Management Mistake #17: Catching the fatal and very contagious pronoun disease (or 'disease of me').

The fatal pronoun disease we are talking of is the one that begins every sentence with the word: "I."

Don't let this mistake happen to you. Remember what Vince Lombardi, NFL Champion coach of the Green Bay Packers once said:

"The achievements of an organization are the results of the combined effort of each individual."

Everyone at your store makes a difference. No one person is any more important than the other on the team. When someone starts feeling and acting that way, it will dramatically affect the environment of your store.

Here are ten ideas to help you get rid of the 'disease of me' and encourage your team members to work together:

1) Encourage members of your team. Your bridal consultants need genuine, sincere, and authentic encouragement. People will follow you when you encourage them. Choose by live by the 30 Second Rule where you say something encouraging to everyone you come into contact within 30 seconds of seeing them each day.

2) When you hire a new bridal consultant, learn her name quickly.
As Dale Carnegie said, "A person's name is the most important thing in the world to that person."

3) Be more interested in making people feel good about themselves, than making people feel good about you.

4) Smile more and live with a positive attitude.

5) Listen more than you talk and learn to ask excellent questions.
Part of good listening is the ability to ask good questions.

6) Learn to read people correctly. Learn to be observant. Study what people do, and then ask yourself why they do it. Discover what motivates each of your bridal consultants. Make correlations between their behavior and their motivation.

7) Be willing to say "I'm sorry" first. When is the last time you sincerely apologized to someone above you, at your level, and someone below you? I once heard Brian Tracy teach that we should always be willing to say: "I'm sorry. I was wrong." Many people are afraid to say these words, yet they will help you get past the disease of me faster than anything else.

8) Always go for the win/win scenario. Never make a deal unless both sides win. Never.

9) Share the credit and the praise. When there is success, share the rewards with members of your team. Be sure to give the praise publicly so that everyone at your store can hear you (especially when one of your bridal consultants has a great sales day).

10) Adopt a windows/mirror philosophy of life. Look out the window when others succeed and point out those who have made a difference instead of introspectively looking at the mirror and thinking about how good you are. The only time you should look in the mirror is when things don't go well and you are looking for what to change.

Finally, to get rid of the disease of me, remember that the letter "I" is not found in TEAM.

Management Mistake #18: Only telling certain people about what is going on.

Rumors can be a major distraction for employees. Keep your bridal consultants updated with changes that are going to affect your store. Share your passion and enthusiasm, not your worries and stresses.

Management Mistake #19: Not delegating tasks, not delegating tasks to the right person, and not delegating tasks properly.

How effective are you at assigning the right job to the right person in the right way?

Do you define the job clearly in terms of the results expected?

The more time you think through the job before you delegate it, the more successful it will be done. Determine the best person to do the particular task you are going to delegate out.

Once you've delegated a task, ask the person to write down what you've just asked them to do and then ask them to tell you back what they were just asked to do. This will help you make sure that you are on the same page that what you want done is clearly understood.

Set up a time to review progress. Delegation does not mean abdication. You are still responsible for what needs to be done. If it isn't finished correctly, don't take it back. Instead, invite feedback, reassess what went wrong, and invite the individual to whom you've delegated the task to focus on the task at hand *until* it is finished correctly.

Coach those you delegate through the process. No one knows how to do things the first time.

Management Mistake #20: Recognizing only top performers and doing little to improve mediocre performance.

Recognize everyone, but reward top performers for the results they are bringing in. Everyone matters. While rewarding top performers is important, you've also got to make changes if you have those on your staff who aren't selling. Train and invest in those who show a willingness to learn and do what is being taught. Let go of those who aren't willing to study, learn, and become better.

Management Mistake #21: Getting overwhelmed, frustrated, and discouraged and taking this out on others around you.

There are so many things that you are responsible for as a manager that it is easy to get overwhelmed. When you consider all that you have to do, it is understandable that you will get frustrated and discouraged. This typically happens because you have too much to do and too little time to do it in. As a manager, you must wrestle with the following seven challenges everyday:

1) There is too much to do and too little time to do it in. You may feel that it is difficult if not impossible to catch up on all that you have to do. It is like there is a conveyer belt of challenges coming at you all the time. It doesn't stop. The only way to succeed is to decide what you won't do. Break up your tasks and work on them in 90-minute blocks of focused effort.

2) There is continuous pressure for results. This will never go away, but you can share the load with those around you when they are determined to help you achieve your goals.

3) You need to find and recruit good people. Learn to be proactive and look for these individuals when you don't need them, not when you do.

4) You need to manage and motivate staff. This is a constant battle, but it is much easier if you hire motivated people.

5) You need to continuously upgrade your skills and those of your staff. Last year's training won't help you deal with this year's challenges. Look to others who can give you valuable perspective, training, and encouragement.

6) You need to remain flexible in the face of continuous and unexpected change.

7) You need to balance all of the roles that you have in managing the store.

When you are overwhelmed with all of these responsibilities, remain positive and tackle one challenge at a time. If you are frustrated or disappointed, the brides you work with shouldn't be able to tell. A bride should only see enthusiasm, excitement, and the professional demeanor of someone they can trust and who they know has her best interests at heart. Everyone on your team should see the best from you as well.

My hope is that you will use what you've learned here to develop a great team of leaders around you while avoiding the pitfalls I've outlined in this chapter. If you recognize and understand these blunders, you'll be able to successfully navigate your way through challenging times so you can help you manage and lead your team onward towards greatness.

CHAPTER 9

RESOLVE TO OVERCOME RESISTANCE AND STAY PRODUCTIVE ON WHAT MATTERS MOST

"Amateurs sit and wait for inspiration, the rest of us just get up and go to work."
—*Stephen King*

I t is easy to lose focus and drift away from what matters most. To assist you in accomplishing your goals, I've decided to share several resolutions that I hope you will carefully consider and implement at your store. If you've been experiencing the resistance that comes from struggles and disappointments, my hope is that your renewed focus on these areas can help you get back on track or accelerate the speed at which you accomplish your goals. This approach is so important because you are either doing things or not doing things every minute of every day that will bring you closer to what you have set out to do. You are either fighting for your own goals or are you surrendering your time to people and pursuits that are different than your own. At the end of every year, you'll know how committed you were to accomplishing your goals by what you've done, not by what you planned. Here are five areas of resolve that you should focus on now.

1. Resolve to sell more and sell better to every bride who comes in your doors.

There is no question that the dynamics of selling have changed as a result of the changing nature of brides and the shifting new economy that has emerged. These changes require that you have much more focus and that you work harder to overcome the resistance that the bride has built up to why she can't buy from you now. The only way you'll get better at your sales effort is to carefully measure it and work to improve the skills that are holding you back from successfully closing sales.

Often, this just means that you have to be more persistent. You won't close sales if you don't ask. A larger percentage of brides today say that they've found their dress, but they just can't go ahead and buy it now (because they have to think about it) or any other myriad of reasons. They are very stubborn with going ahead, even though they know they like that dress and want to get it. The following question works wonders in getting to the heart of the objection or nudging the bride to go ahead with what she's already decided to do:

"Now that you've decided this is the dress, what (if anything) would prevent you from going ahead and getting the dress you love now?"

Are you and each of your bridal consultants daily practicing the skills required to be exceptional at selling? If not, you shouldn't be surprised when you aren't as successful at closing sales as you would like. In order to be excellent at selling, you have to continually prepare and practice. You can't expect the preparation of six months ago to prepare you for the challenge of today's sale. As an analogy, there is a reason why sports teams practice individual skills each day prior to the big game. They know that in order to be sharp in execution, they have to practice relentlessly for hours on end in order to ingrain the skills necessary for success when snap judgments are required. The same goes for selling bridal gowns or anything else in your business. You can't expect to be effective in closing the sale if you aren't properly prepared for any and every objection that could come up. It is okay to let an objection stop you once or twice, but there is no excuse for letting an objection stop you more than that. It is your personal responsibility to figure out what needs to be said in order to overcome what is holding you back from hitting your goals. Making excuses or blaming the poor economy isn't something you see top companies doing. Companies like Apple are shining and succeeding in the same economy because they have become masters at marketing and selling. You must do the same.

Jill Konrath, sales strategist and author of two sales books (*SNAP Selling* and *Selling to Big Companies*) makes this observation about salespeople who refuse to analyze what went wrong after an unsuccessful attempt to close the sale. She says: "Only one out of seven salespeople will self-assess, and those who do are top sellers. They should constantly be in learning mode." Sales trainer Blair Singer says: "Debrief every sale immediately. What worked and what did not—and write it down. You will correct faster, and it will keep you attitude high." If you aren't already writing down what you could have done to make the sale after any sale isn't made, you should start immediately. Doing so will help you see trends and which objections you need to overcome so you can rise up to be the most successful salesperson.

To help you assess how well you are doing with your sales skills, consider the following classifications of objections from brides. Have you experienced any of the following in recent days?

- A bride who finds a dress she likes at your store, but just won't commit to buy it now.
- A bride who brings in a large party of friends, but it is obvious their intent is only to try on and have fun together (without an intent to buy).
- A bride who just has to 'think about it' and isn't swayed by your most persuasive attempts to get her to buy now.
- A bride who tells you that she just can't decide now because she has plenty of time.

If you've experienced any of these scenarios, take heart. You are not alone. The marketplace has shifted and brides have changed their approach to how they are shopping. That said, there are ways to overcome these objections and convert brides to buyers now (instead of later).

In order to help the growing number of bridal stores who are extremely frustrated with how to overcome this heightened resistance, I created an eight week Bridal Sales Blueprint training course where I unveil how to overcome each of the above scenarios and all of the newest and latest sales strategies to create urgency that have been utilized by the top bridal retailers all over the United States and Canada to close sales far into the future. The training classes are broken down into weekly training segments (and each class is broken down into 15 minute training modules) with assignments for you to work on before the next class. If you would like more information about how you can be a part of this training program, please email me at info@bridaltrainingsystems.com.

Resolve to master the art of selling. Tom Frese, author of the book *Sell Yourself First* makes this statement:

"There will be very few times during the course of your lifetime when an idea gets introduced that is so new and innovative that it truly changes the way people think and do business. In mathematics, for example, long division has been around since the days of the abacus, and in much the same manner, the rules of proper English grammar have changed, but only slightly in the last couple hundred years. Meanwhile, the nature of the strategic sale continues to change dramatically, and it's all happening right under our noses." –*Sell Yourself First*, pp. 26-27.

Are you on track to hit the sales targets you set for yourself at the beginning of this week, month or year? If not, please let me help you and each member of your team to get the results you want now. It's not what you want to accomplish this year that matters. It's what you DO day in and day out. I have put together this eight class Bridal Sales Blueprint specifically for the purpose for you to learn what to

DO and to give you the tools and assignments to help you and each member on your team do what needs to be done to make your sales goals a reality. I hope you'll choose to utilize this training in your store so you can make more sales now.

2. Resolve to make decisions more quickly and to choose what's right for the store over what's comfortable.

It is much easier to let things slide than to address them head on because of the conflict you may feel and wish to avoid.

I really like what Tony Hartl of Planet Tan (a chain of tanning salons) says about this in his book *Selling Sunshine*:

"No one likes conflict, and most people will go to great lengths to avoid it. But running a successful business requires making tough decisions, and that's often uncomfortable. Our philosophy at Planet Tan was that you can be comfortable, or you can be right. In other words, you can either do what is comfortable at that moment—knowing deep inside—that you're going to pay for that decision later—or you can do the right thing from the start. Doing the right thing creates energy and momentum."

He continues:

"In certain situations, you've got to make a conscious decision to do the right thing, even though that's more than likely *not* the path of least resistance. This is where the 'comfortable versus right' choice must be made. The popular decision or the easy decision is not necessarily the right decision. We adopted this philosophy from our COO, Nick, who had used a decision-making process when he had been COO at a major restaurant chain. Nick further distinguishes between comfortable decisions and right decisions: 'Comfortable decisions create incremental degradation that kills an organization in small, seemingly unnoticeable chunks, until one day it is too late. It's much like taking a tiny drop of arsenic each morning, which in itself would be uneventful, but will eventually kill a human being. Right decisions create a firm foundation of trust, deep belief in core values, and loyalty for all the correct reasons. Simply making the right decisions consistently raises the bar for everyone, because it becomes expected and indeed demanded, weeding out the imposters.' –pp. *Selling Sunshine*, 117-118.

Conflicts where you must do the right thing instead of the comfortable thing will likely be:

- Letting someone go who isn't hitting their sales goals.
- Telling a sales rep that you can no longer carry their line because you're losing sales to Internet vendors and other competitors who are cutting prices and don't allow you to make a healthy margin.
- Letting a bridal consultant consistently show up late and not doing anything about it (because she is a good salesperson).
- Letting an employee conduct personal business while working in yours or doing personal business when they are on the clock (Internet, email, texting, etc.).
- Failing to eliminate advertising mediums that are no longer working (yellow pages, traditional magazine print ads, etc.) because the sales people who visit with you are persuasive.

Are you willing to do the right thing instead of the comfortable thing? Have the guts to confront what isn't working. If you don't, you'll continue with the status quo (which is comfortable) to a breaking point that will be neither pleasant, nor fun. When you postpone tough decisions, you'll eventually find that these issues will come up *when you least expect them and when you really don't have the time to deal with them.* Then, decisions that could have been managed become much tougher and the consequences are much farther-reaching than they would have been if you would have confronted the same issues much earlier. Choose to make the tough calls in your business and do what needs to be done *now*, not later.

Are there issues at your store that you need to face up to?

Are there things that will cause conflict that you haven't addressed that you need to? If so, you need to take action and do what needs to be done.

Resolve to make decisions more quickly. Choose what's right for your store over what's comfortable. Take action and do it now.

3. Resolve to beat your greatest competitor, yourself: by beating your own benchmarks and exceeding your own numbers. Seek to blow away averages and blow past your best previous best efforts.

To be the best, you have to be willing to learn from those who are better than you. You should be willing to share what you are doing to get your results and then seek to learn from those who can share what they are doing with you. Many bridal retailers are afraid to do this because they fear their competitors will use this information to beat them. Never allow yourself to think that you are the only one that has great ideas. There are great ideas you can learn from other bridal retailers and other great retailers in other industries. I really like the attitude that Tony Hartl has about this. He says:

"I never really worried about sharing ideas with the competition, as long as we could learn from each other. After all, if you take the best team in the NFL and give their playbook to the worst team in the NFL, the losing team isn't suddenly going to become the number one team in the league. There are too many other factors at play: talent, discipline, execution, etc. It's not the ideas—it's the implementation of the ideas."

He continues:

"I always felt that there was something I could learn from everyone—competitor or not. For example, just one simple idea from Suntan City's Rick Kueber saved my company thousands of dollars....I was generous in sharing my knowledge and ideas because I knew I'd receive knowledge and ideas in return. So, when my competitors asked me how we were able to pull in such large numbers, I'd tell them, 'We've got long hours to make it convenient for our members; we have fifty beds so people don't have to wait; we've got three computers in the lobby for quick check-ins; we're extremely selective about the people we hire; and we do a really thorough job of training those people.' They'd always ask, 'But what else?' and I'd say: 'That's it!

That's what we do!' I think they were always looking for some silver bullet or magic idea, but our success was due to one thing: a consistently developed plan that was executed well, day in and day out. The key, of course, was being completely diligent in a few meaningful areas that had the highest impact in business." –*Selling Sunshine*, p. 168.

Bridal retailers need to overcome this adversarial relationship that they have with one another. A lot of problems exist in this industry brought on by technology and utilized by brides that are far more dangerous than your competitors across town. Resolve to better befriend your competitors and offer information that can help them in their business and ask them questions that can help you. Find out who the best bridal stores in your region or other regions are and seek them out and ask questions that can help you. Ignoring the great resources of others prevent you from expanding and learning what you need to in order to grow and become even more successful. The key to this is that we all have to be willing to share ideas for mutual benefit. Be the first to offer help and encouragement. Pick up the phone and make a phone call and see if you can't sit down over lunch to help one another. This doesn't have to be a direct competitor in your town, but can be a very successful store owner in another state or area. Remember, the key is to share ideas for mutual benefit. No one wants to share solely without getting any kind of benefit in return.

4. Resolve to celebrate your successes and have more fun and reward those who are an instrumental part of making your goals a reality.

Tony Hartl's book *Selling Sunshine* features Hartl's approach to how he grew his tanning salon business named Planet Tan. The book contains many great insights and comments in particular about how he rewarded his staff for great accomplishments. Here are five things he mentioned in the book that you may want to consider integrating into your store environment followed by my comments in italics:

1) Celebrations for new hires – Hartl says: "Once we hired new team members, we welcomed them with open arms as part of the Planet

Tan Team. They were greeted at the store with balloons and a huge cardboard sign that the entire staff had signed. The manager of their location would take them to lunch or for coffee to welcome them. We'd give each team member two picture frames and ask them to bring in pictures of people and places that inspired them." –p. 32.

What do you currently do to celebrate those you have just brought onto your team? Recognizing those who will help you hit your sales goals will help them realize their importance to you and they will work harder to accomplish the goals as a result. Resolve to better recognize those you invite to be a part of your team from the first moments they are in the store.

2) Rewards for your top salespeople each month – Hartl says: "In the early days of the company, we'd go each month to a restaurant to celebrate the top salespeople. We'd have a nice award made, call the top salespeople up to the front of the room, recognize them in front of their peers, and then hand them a cash bonus. Everyone had a blast, and, of course, every member of the team would work even harder for a shot at the 'top grosser' award the following month...One way we continued to acknowledge high achievers was to hang plaques with the names of our award winners on Planet Tan Wall of Fame at the corporate office for all to see. The wall was just one more way to publicly acknowledge our team leaders." –pp. 33-34.

Do you publicly recognize and reward your top performers in front of their peers? Most people are motivated by recognition and this drives them to accomplish even more. Never underestimate the power of recognition and rewards for a job well done at your business.

3) Go to great lengths to create a positive, supportive work environment. Hartl says: "Encouragement, recognition, and rewards were provided as often as possible. Our goal was to ensure that our staff was motivated and inspired to achieve excellent results. We worked hard at finding reasons to celebrate. I maintained a personal goal of sending out at least five thank-you or encouragement letters every week. The letters were mailed to the employee's home so that the person receiving the note could share it with his or her family. I'd even send letters to team members' parents or spouses. In fact, I was at a long-time staff member's home recently, and I noticed one of the letters from years ago. The note, proudly displayed on the wall, was further proof to me of the importance of demonstrating appreciation of an employee's efforts." –p. 34.

Do you tell those who work with you that you value their hard work and their accomplishments? Commit to write thank you notes to your bridal consultants or management team to thank them for the good work they do. I know that I treasure the Thank You notes I've received over the years. Your bridal consultants will treasure your positive encouragement and feedback as well.

4) Celebrate store accomplishments or milestones. Hartl says: "To celebrate a store reaching a milestone, we began a company tradition of sending the team a cake along with our congratulations. Every year, I'd also send out a Mardi Gras King Cake to each store as another fun company ritual. Celebrations became a part of the culture at Planet Tan."—p. 36.

Are celebrations a part of your store's culture? If not, what milestones could you celebrate when reached? What fun traditions could you incorporate at your store to make it an even more enjoyable place to work?

5) Offer contests for exceptional results – Hartl says: "After we had been in business for a few years, I launched an annual contest that we ran for three months during our peak season. Everyone on the staff had a chance to win an all-expenses paid trip to Cancun, Mexico. The team members loved the idea and got really excited about the possibility of winning an all-inclusive vacation with some of their co-workers. Most of the employees were young and Mexico was close by, so they were thrilled with the opportunity....We based the contest on sales, clean stores, and teamwork. Each store could accumulate points based on those criteria, along with 'secret shopper' scores. We'd send a secret shopper to each location to report on the experience at the store. This kept our team members on their toes and also helped us discover any areas that needed improvement. If individuals surpassed their numbers by thirty percent or more, they were also allowed to bring a guest to Cancun with them."—p. 36.

Offer rewards for your top seller during the busy season and to thank those who accomplish exceptional results. Hartl's idea of extending the contest to everyone who hits the goal and an additional bonus for surpassing the target goal by thirty percent or more could be an exciting motivator for members of your team. How could you incorporate such a bonus reward system into your store?

Hartl makes this statement: "In your business, there are more than likely many reasons you can begin celebrating today. Think of someone who has gone above and beyond her normal responsibilities and write her a note—not an email, but a handwritten note. Also, come up with an idea for a celebration ritual that reinforces the values of your company and tell your staff it will be taking place at the end of the week. Remember: What gets reinforced gets achieved." –p. 38.

Have more fun at your store by celebrating your significant achievements. Set target and optimal goals and get everyone's commitment behind their successful completion. Reward and recognize those who make significant contributions at your store. Doing so will make working at your store a place where others want to be and work hard.

5. Resolve to better market and create more interactive experiences with your customers that will help you stand out from your competitors.

Tony Hartl makes this statement about his chain of tanning salons which I think has a lot of merit for bridal stores today. He says:

"We had the same equipment as the tanning salon down the road— the thing that made Planet Tan truly distinctive was the experience created by our team. The truth is that we could have automated the entire process with swipe cards, bar codes and technology. In fact, some tanning salons in Europe do just that. In effect, those tanning salons become self-serve facilities—high tech, low-touch. But our unique selling proposition was the polar opposite. Not only did we have the human interaction, but our team members also developed a real relationship with our members and created an emotional connection that enhanced the member experience.

"We were able to constantly exceed expectations because we provided a relationship and an experience, not just a transaction. Our team really cared about our members and showed genuine interest in them. We created a culture at Planet Tan that was designed to support our members and build rapport with them. We made sure that we knew our members personally and that we took an interest in their lives. We went out of our way to make sure that our members knew how much we appreciated them. Because we took the time and effort to build real relationships with our members, it became impossible for competitors to replicate the Planet Tan experience. Our experience couldn't be commoditized or replaced by a 'bargain-price' strategy, because we offered something much more than a transaction based on price." –p. 181.

Some ways you can work on enhancing your experience are:

- Make sure your marketing and experience are consistent – be sure there isn't a disconnect between what you are advertising and promoting and what you actually deliver. Conversely, having a great experience and not promoting it is a cardinal marketing sin.
- What do brides tell you they love most about their experience at your store? Seek to enhance this. When you have a great experience at another business, think about what happened to you that enhanced the experience. Look for ways you can incorporate the best of what you see into your bridal business.
- Enhance the atmosphere and cleanliness of the dressing rooms. Do brides feel like when they arrive at their dressing room that it is just like arriving at five-star hotel where they feel that everything is brand new and simply waiting for their arrival (or do they see threads on floor, wedding gowns hanging up that aren't bagged or with trains lying on the floor)?

- Change any signs so that they reflect your brand (not the brand of the designers you carry).
- Play music that transports the bride into a setting where she can relax and enjoy the bridal experience. On the prom side, play music loudly so that there is a tremendous amount of energy and excitement.
- Strive to have every bride tell you that her experience at your store has exceeded her expectations. Ask yourself: When was the last time a bride told you that her expectations at your store had been exceeded?

A fascinating web site that you should check out is www.polyvore.com. It is the beginning of what will likely be more interactive experiences that will drive how fashion is purchased in the future and may even be a new trend in bridal in years to come where a bride can mix and match her accessories with the dress she wants right on a web site.

According to Harry Beckwith: "In 2010, a huge buzz and over $8 million in venture capital funding surrounded the website Polyvore. The bright idea behind the site is that women would welcome the mix-and-match clothes and accessories from different sites and create new looks from them. It's easy to understand the site's appeal. Isn't it simply an electronic version of a favorite girls' play activity of decades ago—paper dolls—and a grownup version of dressing Barbie?"

He continues:

"Today's great marketers ask the question: 'Should we add an element of play here—and if not, why not?' Several manufacturers are asking that right now. They looked at their iPhones and asked, 'What if our washing machine looked and felt like that and made doing laundry more fun?" –*Unthinking*, p. 23.

Resolve that your sales and marketing will help you achieve the results you want by implementing these five strategies at your store.

CHAPTER 10

ATTRACT BRIDES TO YOU THROUGH THE POWER OF STORY

"Every great love starts with a great story..."—Nicholas Sparks, The Notebook

One of the most important secrets in marketing is that it is propelled by excellent storytelling. The combination of your story with your star power as the brand behind your business and combined with the solution you provide to a starving crowd will propel you to marketing success. The equation could also be written Star + Story + Solution + Starving Crowd = Success.

People love stories and in this chapter I'll discuss how you can improve your ability to craft your story in a way that attracts brides to your business. To grab attention in today's cluttered marketplace, you must tell your story in a new and big way so that you arrive at the decision point in the bride's mind in a way that no other competitor can. When you begin incorporating more stories into your marketing, you'll find that resistance will drop and that your trust will soar. The future will be bright for those who master this skill and learn to pre-sell themselves to brides through engaging and magnetic stories.

Blake Mycoskie makes this point about the power of stories in his book *Start Something that Matters*. He says:
"Stories are the most primitive and purest form of communication. The most enduring and galvanizing ideas and values of our civilization are embedded in our stories, from those of Homer, whose preliterate epic poems united the Greek's national spirit, and Virgil, whose poems did the same for the Romans, to those told by Jesus, who used parables to teach his disciples. It seems to be in our genetic makeup to capture our best ideas in stories, to enjoy them, to learn from them, and to pass them on to others.

"According to renowned storyteller and author Kendall Haven (author of *Super Simple Storytelling*), 'Human minds rely on stories and story architecture as the primary road map for understanding, making sense of, remembering, and planning our lives—as well as the countless experiences and narratives we encounter along the way.' Smart, future-oriented companies use this ancient impulse in new ways, by telling stories that people can watch on YouTube and share on Facebook.

"When you have a memorable story about who you are and what your mission is, your success no longer depends on how experienced you are or how many degrees you have or who you know. A good story transcends boundaries, breaks barriers, and opens doors. It is a key not only to starting a business but also to clarifying your own personal identity and choices.

"A story evokes emotion, and emotion forges a connection. This is why the way companies introduce themselves to customers has changed. They can no longer rely on simple, straightforward ad campaigns, the kind portrayed on the television campaign *Mad Men*. The *Mad Men* style of advertising was effective during an era when there were only three channels on your television. Back then, major brands controlled the conversation by bombarding consumers with pitches such as: *Ford trucks are the toughest; Crest toothpaste makes teeth their whitest; Coca-Cola is the most refreshing soft drink.*

"I don't believe these work today. The media are much more fragmented and the attention of consumers more divided.

"People are no longer all listening to or watching the same few radio or TV stations each week—they're following their own carefully curated Twitter feeds, commenting on and creating blogs, channel surfing among more than 500 TV stations, watching Hulu on laptops, clicking on YouTube, reading Kindles and Nooks, and surfing on iPads. Sometimes all at the same time.

"It may seem counterintuitive, but because so many product claims and consumer opinions are a click away, it's actually more, not less, difficult to base purchasing decisions on this information. Not only is there too much to sift through, but much of it is contradictory: Chevrolet is the best car—or the worst—depending on which you follow. Crest cleans teeth their whitest—or does Colgate? An article on the Web says one thing, but the stream of comments under it says something different.

"And unless this information is presented in an emotionally compelling fashion in the first place, you'll probably forget most of it almost immediately." –pp. 25-27.

He continues: "Seth Godin is one of my favorite business gurus and is especially astute in describing the value of storytelling in business: 'People just aren't that good at remembering facts,' he wrote in his book *Meatball Sundae*. 'When people do remember facts, it's almost always in context. Patagonia makes warm coats. So do many other companies, almost all of which sell their coats for less money, do less volume, and turn a lower profit. Is it because Patagonia coats are more beautiful or warmer? Not at all. It's because the company has created (and lives) a story that has less to do with clothing and more to do with environment. Their mission statement is: Build the best product, cause no unnecessary harm, use business to inspire and implement solutions to the environmental crisis. And the company totally adheres to that mission." –p. 28.

Author Lauron Sonnier in her book *Think Like a Marketer* offers this powerful advice about why you should shift your focus in your marketing efforts to that of telling stories and building your brand. Sonnier says:

"I have come to observe that there are essentially four strategies for standing out. Like most marketing tenets, they are somewhat intertwined. While you're accomplishing one, you gain the compounding effect and benefit of another. Use each and all of these methods to help you stand out as an individual and as a company.
1. Do different things.
2. Do things differently.
3. Stir emotions; spread happiness.
4. Be consistent." –p. 106.

In this book and in my other books I've talked at length about numbers 1, 2 and 4. Yet, I've never really discussed the concept around #3 although I've alluded to it. The reason that stories are so powerful and so important in your marketing now is that they get to the heart of stirring emotions. Stories, simply put, help you build your brand around what you are passionate about in order to accelerate the speed at which brides talk about you and promote you to their friends and family.

Sonnier says: "The power of emotion cannot be underscored enough. Emotion is energy in motion, and when you stir intense feelings of happiness, you will definitely stand out. In fact, targets will beat a path to your door.... The benefit goes even deeper. When you stir positive emotions, be that joy or inspiration or peace of mind, you send a message that there's more where that came from. Targets will think that if you are considerate here, you'll be considerate elsewhere and, until you prove them wrong, they will attach that perception to you. Spreading happiness and stirring positive emotions will always make great things happen for your business."—p. 109-110.

The importance of standing out by standing for something and not just being a store is becoming more and more important today. The way many companies are doing this today is by telling their story and telling their customers what they stand for. Successful companies either create movements or align themselves with movements that are on the rise that speak to the owners of a company and form a big part of their passion and purpose.

When you go about telling your story to the brides you serve in your marketing efforts, be sure that you infuse emotion into them. If you aren't already using stories in your marketing, here are four big secrets you can use to get out *your* story in a new and exciting way to your prospective customers and to give your existing customers a story they can excitedly share with all of their friends and family.

1. You alone are responsible to articulate and share your story. Then, everyone on your team should focus on selling *your* story. In order to articulate what makes you unique, it is tempting for many to look to others for inspiration, instead of looking inwardly and finding the story that makes your story truly unique and inspiring.

Advertising legend and creative genius George Lois once observed: "Teamwork might work in building an Amish barn, but it can't create a Big Idea. The accepted system for the creation of innovative thinking in a democratic environment is to work cooperatively in a teamlike ambience. Don't believe it. Whatever the creative industry, when you're confronted with the challenge of coming up with a Big Idea, always work with the most talented innovative mind available. Hopefully...that's you. Avoid group grope and analysis paralysis. The greatest innovative thinker of our age [was] Apple cofounder Steve Jobs, a modern-day Henry Ford. Jobs was not a consensus builder but a dictator who listened to his own intutions, blessed with an astonishing aesthetic sense. Everybody believes in co-creativity—not me. Be confident of your own, edgy, solo talent. (Once you've got the Big Idea, that's where teamwork comes in—*selling* the Big Idea, *producing* the Big Idea, and bringing the Big Idea into *fruition*." –D--- *Good Advice for People with Talent*, #27.

A great example of this is how Subway has transformed their business from being a fast food restaurant that sells sandwiches to a business that sells weight loss through a transformative story about a guy named Jared Fogle.

"In the late 1990s, the fast-food company Subway created a new line of healthy sandwiches and, along with it, an advertising campaign centered on an impersonal numbers-based product description: They were introducing seven subs that each contained less than six grams of fat.

"Few consumers cared. But then, in 1999, Subway accidentally discovered Jared Fogle, a one-time 425-pound college student who had been diagnosed with edema, a condition that can lead to diabetes, cardiovascular disease, and other severe health problems. Jared, who at the time had a sixty-inch waist, knew he had to lose weight to avoid serious illness; to do that, he started eating what he called 'The Subway Diet'—a low-fat sub for lunch and another for dinner. "Three months later, Jared had lost almost one hundred pounds and was on his way to losing more—so much that newspaper and magazine articles began to appear about his counterintuitive diet of sandwiches. A Subway franchise owner read one of these articles and sent it to Subway's ad agency; they in turn tracked down Jared. Some company executives weren't convinced that Jared's story, memorable as it was, would sell sandwiches, so Subway tried a Jared-based advertising campaign in select locations as an experiment. The results were spectacular. Subway eventually rolled out a major national campaign built around the story of Jared.

"The seven-under-six campaign had gone nowhere, but the Jared story gave the company an 18 percent increase in sales its first year and another 16 percent the year after that, at a time when other chains were growing at less than half that rate." –*Start Something that Matters*, pp. 28-29.

Subway found its story literally by accident, but everyone at their company has helped to sell the story. Jared himself has been selling the story for years.

To help you write your story, here are a list of seventeen questions that should help you find your unique angle so you can tell your story in a compelling way:

1) How did you get into the bridal business? How did you become interested in it in the first place?

2) When you go to market to pick out dresses, how do you narrow down your choices from the hundreds you see to the few dresses you'll actually bring into your store?

3) What is your approach to helping a bride find her wedding dress?

4) I understand you recently dressed ___*a celebrity or well-known person*___ in your area. Can you tell us about the wedding dress she chose?

5) Is there an area that you consider to be your specialty?

6) What attracted you to specialize in that area in the bridal business in particular?

7) What services do you offer to brides and prom girls in your region that are unique to you?

8) What's been the secret to your success in the bridal business? What do you bring to the table that others in the industry don't? In other words, what makes you unique and different?

9) What are the current trends in bridal? What trends are on the horizon? How do you spot these trends?

10) What is the best piece of advice you give to brides who just got engaged?

11) What is the biggest mistake that brides make when planning their weddings?

12) What is the best part of working with brides? What do you enjoy most? What is the most difficult thing about what you do?
13) What do you see for yourself professionally in the future in the bridal business?
14) Are there any other comments or things you would like to let brides know about you and your store?
15) What are the biggest concerns brides have when shopping for their wedding dress and preparing for their wedding?
16) What unforeseen obstacle usually surprises brides when they go shopping for a dress? What should a bride do to avoid this obstacle?
17) What one thing have brides told you that they have learned from you or from your store about how they should know what dress is best for them?

Take the time to answer these questions. They'll help you discover your story and then you and every member of your staff can work together on selling your story.

2. Look for a unique angle to tell the truth about you and your story.
My favorite example of this is the "Think Small" Volkswagen campaign created by Julian Koenig.

The copy on one of these "Think Small" ads promoted this unique angle. There are many lessons you can learn from reading the copy in this ad and thinking about the specific message it articulated to its specific audience:

"Ten years ago, the first Volkswagens were imported into the United States. These strange little cars with their beetle shapes were almost unknown. All they had to recommend them were 32 miles to the gallon (regular gas, regular driving), an aluminum air-cooled rear engine that would go 70 mph all day without strain, sensible size for a family and a sensible price-tag too. Beetles multiply; so do Volkswagens. In 1954, VW was the best-selling import car in America. It has held that rank each year since in 1959, over 150,000

Volkswagens were sold, including 30,000 station wagons and trucks. Volkswagen's snub-nose is now familiar in fifty states of the Union: as American as apple strudel. In fact, your VW may well be made with Pittsburgh steel stamped out on Chicago presses (even the power for the Volkswagen plant is supplied by coal from the U.S.A.). As any VW owner will tell you, Volkswagen service is excellent, and it is everywhere. Parts are plentiful, prices low. (A new fender, for example, is only $21.75.) No small factor in Volkswagen's success. Today, in the U.S.A. and 119 other countries, Volkswagens are sold faster than they can be made. Volkswagen has become the world's fifth largest automotive manufacturer by thinking small. More and more people are thinking the same." –#85.

George Lois once said that "Sometimes the big idea is hiding in the truth."

What is your unique angle?

Is there a way you tell your story about how you got into the wedding business that will help you stand out in a category of one?

You may feel like you don't have a very exciting story, but as you can see in the example above with Volkswagen, sometimes the simplest facts about how they got started can be fascinating in the way that they are told.

Blake Mycoskie tells about when he realized that the story of TOMS was spreading and that his story was as important as his product. He says:

"Back in November of 2006, I was checking in to a flight at New York's JFK airport on my way to Los Angeles. At the time, I wasn't wearing any TOMS because I had come directly from the gym, in a rush to catch the plane, and still had on my sneakers. That was very unusual for me—I almost always wear TOMS.

"The trip had been difficult. At the time, TOMS was a very young company, and the tough and jaded buyers at the major New York fashion retailers didn't yet understand our mission. I hadn't made one sale in the city that week and was leaving feeling a little deflated. "While I was checking in at the American Airlines automated kiosk, I noticed that the woman next to me was wearing a pair of red TOMS. Now, at this early point in TOMS' history, I still hadn't seen a single person outside of friends, family, and interns wearing our shoes. This was a big moment for me.

"Containing my excitement, I said, 'I really like your red shoes. What are they?'

"It was as if I'd pushed a button on the kiosk; the response was automatic. The woman's eyes widened, her face came alive, and she said boldly, 'TOMS!'

"Trying to be cool, I kept watching the ticketing kiosk, but the woman became so excited that she grabbed my shoulder, pulled me away from the machine, and, in an animated voice, told me the TOMS story.

" 'You don't understand,' she said. 'When I bought this pair of shoes, they actually gave a pair of shoes to a child in Argentina. And there's this guy who lives in Los Angeles who went to Argentina on vacation who had this idea—I think he lives on a boat and he was once on the *Amazing Race* TV show—and the company is wonderful, and they've already given away thousands of shoes!'

"At this point I was getting embarrassed and knew I had to tell her who I was—I couldn't walk away from such excitement. So I said, 'Actually, I'm Blake. I started TOMS.' She looked me right in the eyes and said, 'Why did you cut your hair?'

"This wasn't the question I'd expected. But it turned out she had seen the YouTube videos we'd created on a TOMS Shoe Drop—when I had much longer hair, which is why she didn't recognize me. But it also showed how much attention the woman paid to the video and to our company.

"I gave her a hug and proceeded to my gate. Only when I was seated on the plane did the magic of what had just happened dawn on me: This woman was passionate about telling the TOMS story to a complete stranger. How many other people had she already spoken to? If she was willing to talk like this to me, she'd probably told her family and friends as well. She might even have uploaded a photo of her shoes to Facebook and shared the YouTube video with her friends. How many people had she influenced?

"I wondered, 'What happens when we have ten thousand or one hundred thousand people wearing TOMS? If they all tell the story to only three or four others, and then those people tell the story...' Well you can do the math.

"That's when I fully realized the power of our story. And we've been focused on it ever since." –*Start Something that Matters*, pp. 30-31.

Do you have a story that your brides are telling all of their friends and family about? If not, it is time that you got over your feelings of shyness and that you get out there and tell your story. Others will spread a fascinating story, so look for ways you can promote how you got into this business to everyone around you.

Study other great companies for inspiration. I would suggest you study Disney, Pixar, Patagonia, Ralph Lauren, Vera Wang, TOMS, and others to get a better sense of how to tell a great story. The only thing that is limiting you from telling your story is your own willingness to open up and share. You've got to get over feeling that no one really cares about your story and begin to realize that this is the one reason why brides and prom customers *really* will care about you and your bridal store.

3. Use facts, but don't let them overwhelm your story. Tell your story in a way that is easy to understand and easy to explain.
Blake Mycoskie makes this point in his book, *Start Something that Matters*:

"A barrage of facts is simply not as powerful as a simple, well-told story—and science offers proof. In 2009, Carnegie Mellon University researchers compared how our behavior is affected by abstract facts versus a concrete story. The team offered students five dollars to complete a survey about various technological gadgets. Unknown to the students was that the questions had nothing to do with the study. Instead, the research focused on what happened when they got paid for their participation. At the end of the 'study,' students received five one-dollar bills and one of two letters asking them to donate some of their newly earned money to Save the Children, a well-known international charity.

"One of the letters was studded with facts about food shortages in Malawi and statistics correlating severe rainfall deficits with fewer crops. The other told the riveting story of a desperately poor seven-year-old Malawian girl named Rokia.

"The students who received the letter filled with statistics contributed an average of $1.14. The students who read the story of Rokia contributed $2.38. That's more than twice as much!
"The researchers then gave a third group of people both letters—one of full of statistics and one with the story of Rokia. These students gave almost a dollar less than the people who saw only the story about Rokia.

"Facts are important, but the story matters. Poorly presented facts can even get in the way of the story's impact." –p. 28.

Are there any facts that you include in your story that confuse or overwhelm brides? Sometimes stores can share how long it takes to make a dress and create a concern when a bride would be perfectly fine to buy a dress off the rack. The story you tell about the dresses you have in your store is another example of overwhelming brides.

For example, some stores refer to the dresses they sell as 'samples' which diminishes their quality and likelihood that a bride could or should actually wear *that* dress on their wedding day. In other words, bridal stores actually inadvertently train brides to want to order dresses by how they sell their merchandise! Don't make that mistake. Tell the stories that will help you sell more in a way that grabs attention.

Chip and Dan Heath explain that there are six elements that make an idea powerful enough to grab and hold your attention in their book *Made to Stick*: "A sticky idea is a simple, unexpected, concrete, credible, emotional story. Lots of sticky ideas have only a few of these traits, but some have all six, like John F. Kennedy's famous call to put a man on the moon and return him safely before the end of the decade. It's **simple**—easy to understand, easy to explain. It's **unexpected**—in 1961, putting a man on the moon sounded like science fiction. It's amazingly **concrete**—notice how easy it is to visualize the moment of success, the moment when a human being sets foot on the moon. It was **credible** because it came from the mouth of a popular president. It's **emotional**—it appealed to our yearning to reach the next frontier (and, let's not forget, our desire to beat the Soviets). And it's the **story** of a journey, in miniature."

A great example of all of these elements is found in the story of Dr. Henry Heimlich, who invented the Heimlich maneuver. He was a successful surgeon specializing in the chest and throat in problems with swallowing. One day, he read (in the early 1970s) that choking was the sixth most common cause of accidental death.

He recalls, "I had thought choking to death was a rare occurrence. I said this is something I should become aware of." The recommended procedure at the time to help someone who was choking was to hit them on the back (which was really useless) since as Dr. Heimlich explained, "It drives objects tighter into the airway. If you were able to breathe before, you're now not able to breathe. Backslapping was worse than useless. Being a chest surgeon, I knew there was enough air in the lungs [and] that if you could compress the lungs, you would get a flow of air that would push the object toward the mouth."

Robin Spizman and Rick Frishman explain how Heimlich developed the method he became famous for in their book *Where's Your Wow?:* "Through continued research and experimentation, he created a method focused on compressing air in the lungs and then pushing the air up through the windpipe, forcing the lodged object up and out of the mouth. In 1974, he published an article in a medical journal announcing his discovery. He called his method the 'abdominal thrust.' Not exactly a catchy name. The American Medical Association, in an article published later that year, christened the method the Heimlich maneuver.

"Of course, in saving a life with this maneuver, timing truly is everything. Wait too long, and the person chokes to death. But timing also was crucial in spreading the word. The sooner people learned to use the Heimlich maneuver, the more lives would be saved. "The key, says Dr. Heimlich, was simplicity. 'I spent a lot of my research time simplifying so that anyone can learn it,' he says. 'You have to keep it simple. Otherwise, people would keep dying. It had to be easy to learn. The simplicity was imperative.'

"Dr. Heimlich notes that the youngest child to save someone using his now world-famous method was a four-year-old who saved a two-year-old. Because he kept it simple, more than 30 years after the first published report, tens of millions of people a year have learned how to use the Heimlich maneuver." –pp. 121-122.

A big lesson from this story is how important simplicity is in spreading a story quickly. If you look at most ideas that become big quickly, the key to their success is really that they are designed to keep it simple.

By sticking to a simple narrative, you can put a unique spin on what you do that will help you stand out and be different. Keep your story simple enough to remember and share, but engaging enough that brides will want to share what they've discovered about you and your unique difference.

4. Use the six elements that push people's buttons and start conversations in the story you tell. These elements help a story to be more memorable.

Mark Hughes says that there are six buttons you can push to create buzz with any story in order to start a conversation in his book *Buzzmarketing*. He says: "Creating buzz sounds very tough. But it can be easy if you know which buttons to push. Time and time again, these six things push people's buttons and start conversations:

- **The taboo** (Clairol's Herbal Essences campaign showcases a woman in the shower in sheer delight as she washes her hair with Herbal Essences shampoo)
- **The unusual** (David Letterman did this with "Stupid Human Tricks" and his "Top 10 Lists"; Pepsi vs. Coke in the Pepsi challenge; Ian Klein and his OverweightDate.com web site for overweight singles vs. Match.com)
- **The outrageous** (Don't just be outrageous like Outpost.com with their promotion of shooting gerbils out of a cannon. Look for a connection to what it is that you do. Trash the dress shoots are a good example of something outrageous that is done with wedding dresses.)
- **The hilarious** (Humor isn't easy, but when it works, it works well).
- **The remarkable** (Have you won awards that you can promote that show what a great job you do at your store?)
- **The secrets** (both kept and revealed) "Secrets are currency. Revealing a secret is a definite conversation starter. People love to talk about secrets, and when they do, they become 'in the know.'" What secrets do you know about wedding dresses that you can share with brides in a fascinating way?

"Push any one of these buzz buttons and you'll give people the currency to start a conversation." –p. 29.

I think these six steps are critically important to telling a story that is fascinating in a way that will allow you to arrive in a big way in any bride's mind. You just have to make sure that your story matches up with what it is that you are promoting.

Mark Hughes explains: "Word-of-mouth marketing ain't easy. You've got to create a story....ready-made for watercooler conversation. It's got to be entertaining, fascinating, and newsworthy. You've got to give 'em something to talk about. Connections count, impressions don't. When people begin talking about your brand, you'll break away from the pack in no time." –*Buzzmarketing*, p. 38.

Allen P. Adamson makes this point in his book *The Edge: 50 Tips from Brands that Lead*:
"It's an absolute truth that talk value in building a brand is significant. The Internet and every device with an app have put the power of branding into the hands of anyone with a digital connection. Word of mouth has become supersized. The stories in this chapter are about brands that have gained an edge because they know how to use this power to their advantage and to the advantage of their customers. To ensure that you have the same advantage, here are a few tips to guide you:

- Word of mouth will happen with you or without you. Use it to learn what you're doing right. Use it to learn how you can improve the brand experience.
- Short jokes are easier to tell than long ones. Consumers can only tell your brand story the way you want it told if you've sharply defined it for them.
- Always remember that when something impacts a customer's life on a personal level they're more likely to share it.
- For people to want to pass along a brand experience it must be extraordinary. Make sure you give them something to talk about.
- Make it easy for consumers to share your brand story with others. Give them a platform or forum to pass along their input.

- Consumers like to be recognized and thanked for their loyalty. Acknowledge consumers who have something nice to say about your brand. Reward their support.
- Consumers vote with their wallets. Treat your brand's advocate like the shareholders they are." –p. 156.

You must do a better job of telling your story and getting the word out about your store and your business so your customers can help spread the word. You may be thinking: "I don't know where to find any good stories to tell." Nonsense. Everyone has a story they should be telling.

Here are five suggestions to help you get started:

1) Recall stories from your past. Create a database of great stories that you and your staff can access and tell to brides when they come in.
- Your greatest successes and failures
- How you learned to do what you do
- What caused you to get into the bridal business
- Unexpected lessons

2) Tell stories you've seen happen or that brides have told you about. Brides who've had a bad experience at a big box store and why that tragedy wouldn't have happened at your store.
- Nightmare scenarios of brides who have purchased wedding gowns online and the stress it caused before you were able to help them get the *right* dress.

3) Have a contest with your staff to compile the best stories from brides.

4) Have a contest on Facebook asking brides to share their stories with you. Then, post them on your website and all around your store.

5) Write an article about yourself or hire someone to do it for you. Michael Stelzner wrote why story and great content is so powerful in his book: *Launch: How to Quickly Propel Your Business Beyond the Competition.* He said:

"Content is the ultimate fuel for launching your rocket ship into space. Why? Outstanding content attracts people in ways that ads, billboards, or commercials never could. Great content is food for the mind. It feeds the deep desires of people. It enriches lives, solves problems, educates, and even entertains. Great content has a magnetic quality that points the internal compasses of people directly toward your business." –p. 107.

One of my favorite examples of the power of story is told in the ad that Apple ran a few days prior to the opening of their first retail store. The headline read: "5 Down. 95 to Go." The ad read as follows: "Apple currently has 5 percent market share in personal computers. This means that out of one hundred computer users, five of them use Macs. While that may not sound like a lot, it is actually higher than both BMW's and Mercedes-Benz's share of the automotive market. And it equals 25 million customers around the world using Macs. But that's not enough for us. We want to convince the other 95 people that Macintosh offers a much simpler, richer, and human centric computing experience. And we believe the best way to do this is to open stores right in their neighborhoods. Stores that let people experience firsthand what it's like to make a movie on a Mac. Or burn a CD with their favorite music. Or take pictures with a digital camera and publish them on a personal web site. Or select from over 300 software titles, including some of the best educational titles for kids. Or talk to a Macintosh Genius at our Genius Bar. Because if only 5 of those remaining 95 people switch to Macs, we'll double our market share, and more importantly, earn the chance to delight another 25 million customers. Here we go…" –*The Apple Experience*, p. 208.

Here are seven lessons you can learn from this ad and that you can use as you tell your own story:
- Be clear, easy to understand. Never forget what it is that you are trying to say.
- Use comparison and contrast for others to understand and to frame your point in a positive light.
- State what you've already accomplished.

- State your goal clearly going forward: Here's why we're opening stores.
- Define clearly what's in it for the reader to come into the stores (learn how to make a movie on a Mac, burn a CD, take a picture and publish it online, etc.)
- Be positive in your invitation. Here their goal was to delight another 25 million customers.
- The goal is clear and the invitation is inclusive (using the word 'we').

Story is so important. But, it isn't the only thing. One caution I would offer is that great story doesn't matter if you can't deliver on your promise.

Camine Gallo makes this observation in his book *The Apple Experience*. He says: "Cosmetic [or story] changes don't matter if you have people who don't like their boss, don't like their job, and can't communicate with their customers. I decided to return to a hotel for a second time even though I didn't enjoy my first experience. It was pricey, dated, and dirty. Most of the staffers were also unfriendly. I stayed again for only one reason—it was the closest hotel to the place where I had to be the next morning and I would be arriving late the night before. When I walked in, I noticed something new. The hotel had recently added a signature scent, which seems to be a trend among some hotel chains. The Westin hotels have a signature scent, but they also provide a nice experience to complement the scent. That was the problem with my hotel. The scent was nice, but the staff was still unfriendly, the hotel was dated, and the rooms were still dirty! On a trip to Las Vegas we stayed at a beautiful smoke-free boutique called Vdara. It, too, had a signature scent. The scent was so nice I actually bought scent sticks to put in my office. But, the scent was simply a bonus that capped a memorable experience. The scent didn't make the experience—the people made the experience. But the scent reminded me of the experience. I hesitate to use the hackneyed expression 'It's like putting lipstick on a pig.' But in this case it works. No amount of lipstick is going to make up for unfriendly people delivering poor service. But if you have the people and the communication right, poor packaging will actually detract from the experience you worked so hard to achieve. Ron Johnson said all great customer service experiences start with great products and a clearly defined and concise vision. Once you have the products in place, the vision, the people, and the communication, it's time to pay attention to the details of design and packaging to create a place where people feel comfortable returning again and again."--pp. 181-182.

I totally agree with this assessment. You can't just tell a good story and expect that your business is going to skyrocket to success. The combination of having a star (you), telling your story, and offering a solution to a starving crowd means that you have to deliver on your promise. Because if you don't, your starving crowd will wait and go somewhere else before they buy their wedding dress.

Take the time to articulate your story AND ensure that your experience delivers on the experience you've promised with the story you've crafted. Otherwise, you will arrive in the bride's mind in an old and repulsive way that will do nothing to help your business thrive. Instead, craft your story so that it helps you arrive in a new, fresh, fascinating, and exciting way that makes each bride who walks through your doors grateful that she has an opportunity to do business with you.

Epilogue

Getting Unstuck:
What You Can Do Now to Accelerate and Rise Out of Plateaus in your Bridal Business

"Organizations that are out of balance become stuck—unable to move forward. What's more...those organizations that remain stuck, become dead."
–Keith Yamashita & Sandra Sparo

I t is easy to get stuck in business. When you get stuck, you may feel trapped and not sure what to do to get out of the rut you find yourself in. Things may have been cruising along just fine for a long period of time and then all of the sudden or gradually over time, something happens that causes you to lose your momentum, get stuck on a plateau, and nothing you do seems to allow you to break free from the feeling that you are stuck where you are.

I want to share with you several lessons from authors Keith Yamashita & Sandra Sparo in their book *Unstuck* and in Bob Sullivan and Hugh Thompson's book *Getting Unstuck: Break Free of the Plateau Effect* that will be very helpful to you if you've felt any of these emotions in your business and aren't sure what to do now.

Bob Sullivan and Hugh Thompson make this observation in their book *Getting Unstuck: Break Free of the Plateau Effect*:

"A real plateau means you have stopped growing. It means your mind and senses are being dulled by sameness, by a routine that sucks the life and soul out of you, by getting less and less out of life while doing more and more. Plateaus ultimately force you to make bad decisions and feel desperate. Understanding this force, and tapping into it, will let you get more from less effort and feel more in tune with the reasons you were put on this planet."—pp. xvi-xvii.

They continue: "Any business school teacher will tell you that companies either contract or expand—there's no such thing as standing still. This is true in all areas of life. Think of a shower drain clogged with hair. Running more water won't help, that's for sure. But leave it untreated, and you're soon standing in a puddle of water every morning in the shower. Plateaus are a sign—a tangible warning—that your life, your relationship, or your business is clogged. Ignore such clogs at great peril.

"When humans shared the earth with predators and were under constant threat of being eaten alive, 'getting used to' the familiar—and reacting only to the extreme—was a matter of life or death. Today, however, 'getting used to' your job, your spouse, your exercise routine, or your local deli has become a matter of dying a very slow, boring death. The force of acclimation means even the strongest odor, or the prettiest girl, or the most amazing new rock band will soon become routine and dull for you. This is why so many things you do seem exciting at first, but within a few weeks, the thrill is gone. It's why most exercise and diet plans fail at around the two-week mark."—pp. xvii.

This is why you always get really excited when you start the busy season, but can get discouraged if it starts off slow or be completely burned out by the time you get to the end of May. Everyone gets stuck from time to time. The key is being able to bounce out of those moments and build the momentum that will help you experience continual growth.

Why do people and businesses experience plateaus? The biggest reason according to Sullivan and Thompson is acclimation or tolerance. The authors explain several ways in which this tendency happens:

- Not being able to smell a bad smell after a period of time.
- The decline of American Idol over the past few seasons because it was always the same (no criticism like was experienced in earlier seasons from Simon Cowell – judges only had positive things to say about everyone).
- Car alarms going off often cause people to ignore them (as a result, less than 1% of people would call police if they hear a car alarm).
- Going with the flow so long that you lose your competitive edge.

Sullian and Thompson say: "Acclimation desensitizes us to consistency...In the battle of signal versus noise, noise has a decided advantage. It's a human reflex to tune out information channels that get flooded by noise. The downside is that there are a few messages in those channels that we really care about. Cars do get stolen. Some alarms are legit, but the communications channel has been burned. Car thieves actually use oversignaling to their advantage. A common yet brazen technique when stealing a car is to set off multiple car alarms in a lot at once if your goal is to only steal one particular car. Car alarms lost their effectiveness because they stopped being unusual. When we go numb, we miss really important signals—and this can lead to some pretty major mistakes."—pp. 26-27.

When talking about how Netflix completely destroyed entrenched competitor Blockbuster, Sullivan and Thompson ask: "How did David and Goliath switch positions so quickly? More important, why did Blockbuster burn out while Netflix burned bright? Why were analysts armed with simple tools able to predict the flameout while those titans of industry seemed powerless to stop it? And what can Netflix's success teach you? Blockbuster failed for precisely the same reason that movie theaters lost favor and that Netflix almost wrecked its own dominant position in the marketplace—they all plateaued when they stopped providing value to their customers and instead focused on short-term gains. We call that the greedy algorithm. These firms and industries got distracted and stopped listening, which meant they ignored the obvious warning signs. They were victims of missing the just noticeable difference. And while they all had an impeccable sense of timing on the way up, that same sense betrayed them when trouble began. When these things happen, a plateau is unavoidable—as unavoidable as the impact an apple makes on the ground after falling from a tree.

In this chapter, I want to talk with you specifically about how to get unstuck and how you can build momentum to reach your goals.

First, let's talk about what is causing you to feel and be stuck. Keith Yamashita & Sandra Sparo in their book *Unstuck* call the causes of getting stuck The Serious Seven.

They say: "Let's move from symptoms to causes. Symptoms vary quite a bit—no two teams feel stuck in quite the same way. But a great majority of 'stucks' results from at least one of seven primary causes—what we've termed the Serious Seven. In the following pages, we describe each cause. If you suffer from one or more of the Serious Seven, you'll very quickly recognize yourself in these descriptions. Then, knowing which causes apply, you can craft a plan of action.

1) **Overwhelmed** – You're stuck because your team doesn't know what to do next. You used to be so certain about where to go, but here you are now, rudderless. It all seems like too much work. Or you feel like you're under too much scrutiny. Or there are too many moving parts. Or you don't have enough people or time to get it all done.

Tell-tale signs: It's procrastination city. You can't figure out why you can't get started—you may even have many of the elements to succeed, but you're still stuck. The task ahead feels huge.

Sound familiar?

- "We know what to do, but we have no idea how we're going to get it done."
- "Is it just me, or does the boss look like a deer in the headlights?"
- "Failure might not be an option. But it doesn't look like success is either."
- "Does it seem like we spend more time talking about how to scale back the project than actually doing the work of the project?"

If left untreated: You'll fail to tap into the great talent of your team. It's like having a car with a turbocharger that never gets used.

2) **Exhausted** – You're exhausted because it's been rough sailing recently. Perhaps your original intent—your North Star, if you will—was clear. But as the team sailed on, the sextant was thrown overboard. Once a brilliant crew, the team is now paralyzed by politics, wasted efforts, opinions arising from fear, and even the occasional mutiny. Progress is slowing to a standstill.

Tell-tale signs: Team burnout. Resentment over new projects. Waning interest or involvement in team get-togethers and meetings.

Sound familiar?

- "It's not like things are broken, but it doesn't feel right either."
- "I'm pooped."
- "If it's not one thing, it's another."
- "Once we get one thing fixed, something else springs a leak."

- "Have you ever noticed the boss is too chicken to ask for help?"
- "Hey, where did all the fun go?"

If left untreated: Exhaustion slowly gives way to cynicism. Shutdown, then backlash, may not be far behind. It's like losing the other runners—and even the course—halfway through the marathon."

3) **Directionless** – You're stuck because your team is all thrust, no vector. People are busy, but aren't necessarily effective. Everyone is obsessed about their to-do list, yet there is no 'big picture' to guide their actions. Decisions are made with little regard for the context of the day—let alone what tomorrow might bring.

Tell-tale signs: It may seem like there's a lot of good action taking place, but there are few tangible results. Often, team members are unable to connect their work to the larger context of what must be done. What's more, judgment calls about what's important often turn out to be wrong later.

Sound familiar?
- "I'm so busy, I don't have time to think."
- "We get to good, but rarely to great."
- "Why doesn't the boss tell us why we're doing this?"
- "Luck is our biggest salvation."

If left untreated: The outcomes are often mediocrity and a failure to reach desired goals. The team may arrive somewhere, but it is not likely to be the correct destination.

4) **Hopeless** - You're stuck because your team lacks a central purpose. A kind of general defeatism has set in. The team is spinning. All the hard work seems like exactly that—just hard work. There is no feeling of reward, no sense of achievement.

Tell-tale signs: Your team used to have tons of purpose—but where'd it all go? There's no rallying cry, especially when the going gets tough. It takes an awfully big dose of success to get the same rush you used to.

Sound familiar?

- "We have no idea why we exist."
- "We all have our own agenda and no one is on mine."
- "I get a certain joy when there's a rumor I'm going to be transferred to a different team."
- "I'm outta here."

If left untreated: A lack of inspiration can be contagious. One person's uncaring attitude soon becomes the mood for the group. Before long, motivating your team, rather than doing the work, is how you spend virtually all your time. And you feel like a cheerleader with laryngitis.

5) **Battle-Torn** – You're stuck because your team can't get along. This syndrome leads to a group so torn by its own foibles that it never even gets to fight the outside enemy. This is friendly fire at its most disturbing. It can bring even the toughest to their knees.

Tell-tale signs: Team members with hurt feelings, bruised egos, or political agendas. Team interactions characterized by unresolved conflict, defensiveness, lack of communication, and high levels of inhibition. Factions, cliques, bullies, and desertions.

Sound familiar:

- "We spend more time fighting than working."
- "You don't dare speak up in meetings because someone will take your head off."
- "Psst. Collude with me and you'll be okay."
- "I never said I'd protect you."
- "Emotions are for wimps."
- "Let's take this offline." (And all the real decisions are made in the hallways after official meetings.)
- "People are only comfortable offering ideas one on one."

If left untreated: The team never turns its attention to the real task at hand. It's like a dysfunctional family trying to throw a wedding.

6) **Worthless** – You're stuck because your team is unable to recognize what success looks like. Moving targets. Muddy expectations. The right actions aren't rewarded. Even when the team does something amazing, it's overlooked. Before long, the team feels its contributions don't matter.

Tell-tale signs: You don't know what victory looks like—so you wouldn't know if you achieved it. The metrics of performance seem vague. Team members are puzzled over which goals to pursue. Management has little credibility—when they request that work be done, employees don't always listen. Commitment wanes.

Sound familiar?
- "The boss asked me to do this. Should I even bother?"
- "Do you think when they said it was due Friday they meant Friday?"

  "It seems like we're all just going through the motions."
- "Okay, I'll do your project—but what will you give me if I do?"

If left untreated: Team members spend their time thinking up ways to sabotage progress—except for the few martyrs who continue working when neither the expectations nor the rewards are clear. Imagine a whole team of Dilberts.

7) **Alone** – You're stuck because the team has lost its own religion. It used to feel like a close-knit unit, but somewhere along the way the sense of belonging was replaced by the haze of an identity crisis. Your crew lacks a culture to unite it, so it is far less than the sum of its parts.

Tell-tale signs: Individual team members make up their own rules. The team never seems to be in sync. Every meeting feels like the first time the team has worked together. Lots of new leaders pop up, but they don't seem to last very long.

Sound familiar?

- "Unless the boss tells me what to do, nothing gets done."
- "New team members can't seem to master the ropes."
- "It's just chaos, chaos, chaos."
- "You can get away with pretty much anything you want."

If left untreated: The costs of coordination go through the roof. The group has no natural pattern of success, and methods are invented anew every time. Visionary leadership is replaced by the need to command-and-control authority. "Herding cats" doesn't even begin to describe it."–Keith Yamashita & Sandra Sparo, *Unstuck*, pp. 30-45.

Isn't that a fascinating analysis of what causes people to get stuck? The reality is that none of the symptoms of the Serious Seven are any fun. It makes movement at your store feeling like moving through an ocean of tar or molasses on a cold day. It is easy to see why such behaviors and attitudes can cause you to feel and to get stuck. But, let's not just dwell just on what has caused you to get stuck. Let's talk about how to get unstuck—how you accelerate out of business plateaus by building momentum in your business.

First, let's evaluate how stuck you may be now. To do so, consider this diagnostic quiz in Keith Yamashita & Sandra Sparo's book *Unstuck:*

1) Do you have a clear, inspiring purpose?	*Yes*	*No*	*Hmm...*
2) Do you have the right people, in the right positions to make a difference?	*Yes*	*No*	*Hmm...*
3) Do you work effectively as a team? Can you always get the right stuff done?	*Yes*	*No*	*Hmm...*
4) Does the team truly get the most from diversity—in skills, geography, gender, age, ethnicity—to broaden its thinking?	*Yes*	*No*	*Hmm...*

5) Do you know how to make decisions?	*Yes*	*No*	*Hmm...*
6) Do those decisions stick?	*Yes*	*No*	*Hmm...*
7) Is your team capable of radical ideas?	*Yes*	*No*	*Hmm...*
8) If your team leader quit today, could the team carry on?	*Yes*	*No*	*Hmm...*

--Unstuck, pp. 26-27.

Regardless of where you are now, you want to be unstuck. Here are six specific actions you can take when you feel stuck to accelerate and gain momentum to grow your business to new heights.

1. Be very clear about what you want. You usually get stuck when you start drifting and aren't clear about your destination. Spend 14 minutes each morning planning where you want to end up at the end of each day.
Drifting with the status quo or just going with the tide can give the false appearance of ***motion without direction***. Drifting is dangerous because you feel as though you are making progress (and sometimes you are), but you will never get to your desired goals with the speed and momentum you could if you focused in on the actions required to get you to where you want to go.

You have to cause results to happen by deciding to have them happen. When you are clear about what you want, you will do so much more and stop being stuck.

Are you clear on the result you want to create? When you are, you will do the work necessary to put the systems into place to make sure that the results you want will happen. When you are clear about what you want, and you build a plan and then you go out and do the work, you will gain more and more confidence in what you are doing.

Author John C. Maxwell in his book, *The 21 Most Powerful Minutes in a Leader's Day* says this:
"They say that one of the most difficult challenges for any sports team is back-to-back championships. Getting everyone on a team to come together for a season is an incredible challenge. Making it happen two seasons in a row is close to impossible. Yet occasionally it happens. Recently the New York Yankees did it. So did the Denver Broncos. But more often, a team reaches the pinnacle and then fades back into the middle of the pack. Why? Because the players on the team think that once they've made it to the top, they can cruise to stay there. But that's not the way it works. Momentum never sustains itself."-- *The 21 Most Powerful Minutes in a Leader's Day*, p. 268.

To sustain the momentum you need, be clear about what you want to happen with each day. Here is your new rule: Spend 14 minutes planning each day. There are 1440 minutes in each day. By planning for 14 minutes each day (less than 1% of the total day's activities), you will accelerate the rate at which you will able to accomplish so much more. Eric Lofholm, author of *The System*, talks about how important it is to plan your day in terms of results per hour, not minutes per hour. That is an important distinction.

Have you been consistent over the past 30 days with your daily activities that will help you achieve your goals?
- With your time management?
- With your lead generation?
- With your closing ratio?

If not, it is time to step up and do more. Don't beat yourself up. You have influence over your self-talk. Quiet your self-talk by speaking what you want through affirmations. Choose to take action and get better each and every day. Remember, change begins with language. This is what the inner game is all about. You can tell yourself whatever story you want. Are you telling a story about what you really want?

Plan out an optimal day. Block out your first 14 minutes in the day. Ask yourself: What two items (if I do them) will have the greatest impact on my business today?

If you don't do this, don't beat yourself up. But, if you do, you will see a difference in the results you actually get each and every day.

I've talked here about how important it is to have clarity. Those who are stuck will find themselves in what James Kilts, former CEO of Gillette calls "The Circle of Doom" if they don't get clarity about what needs to happen quickly.

He explains this in his book *Doing What Matters*:
"Most business leaders are hardworking and well intentioned. Yet despite their best efforts, they get in trouble because they lack the clarity of vision and certainty of purpose necessary to confront the reality of their business situations. It's often an inadvertent failure to face the truth fully and honestly. It existed at Gillette as well as Nabisco. And from my discussions with other CEOs, I know that this 'doomsday' scenario plays out at hundreds, if not thousands, of companies. Although I will describe the Circle of Doom's manifestations at a corporate level, it is prevalent at all levels within companies."—p. 193.

He continues:
"At times, the slide into the Circle of Doom is the unfortunate by-product of success. A company enjoys several years of strong growth and even stronger earnings. Everything is going right—a bright, motivated management team is in place; the leadership process is functioning well; new products are successful; economic growth is robust; and competitors are quiet. Earnings growth of 15 to 20 percent annually seems like a slam dunk....So a wager is made, and lost, and companies start their descent into the Circle of Doom. It always starts with unrealistic growth targets that are, at best, a long shot to be met....In order to meet the anticipated growth and keep momentum strong for the future, companies must spend capital and aggressively

build overhead structures. Sharp increases in the planned rate of sales mean a larger supply of product will be needed, which in turn means new production capacity will be necessary—a new production line or maybe even a new factory. Since adding capacity takes lead time, capital has to be allocated in advance of the increased sales in order to start the planning and move the organization into high gear.

"...[Then] when it appears that the unrealistic targets are beyond reach, then the companies throw even more money at their problems. Perhaps some high-value cents off coupons will stimulate sales....These stopgap efforts may work for a while. But, ultimately, reality comes knocking. No amount of wishful thinking can create sustainable growth. Sales begin to slide, and so do profits. To increase revenues, prices are raised. But that further erodes sales, and market shares start to drop as consumers balk at the big price gaps between your products and competitive brands. So to prop up the bottom line, marketing budgets are cut. The rationalization goes something like this: Our brand is so strong that reducing the marketing budget by one-quarter and dropping the savings to the bottom line won't even be noticed. We have high consumer loyalty that will carry us through. It is far better to bolster the company's bottom line than it is to have some extra ad impressions. And when that isn't enough, companies start what's called trade loading. They jam products into their customer's warehouses at cut-rate prices with special terms and conditions, which again helps to delay reality. Yet the outcome is never pleasant."—pp. 193-197.

I think this is an interesting phenomenon that happens in the bridal business as well. Here is the sequence of what happens in the Circle of Doom in the bridal industry:
- Unrealistic objections (goals with no strategy to make it happen)
- Invest in additional inventory requiring more capital (and possibly overhead with employees and space)

- When sales targets aren't met, bridal store owners panic and cut prices in order to make whatever sales they can or to create cash flow.
- Profits are down and it is hard to pay the bills so owner invests in a different line with potential of having greater profitability and increasing their prices (also requires more capital outlay) – this becomes an even more severe problem when the addition of a new line isn't also paired with the deletion of another line.
- Amount of money spent on marketing is cut because there isn't enough profit or all additional capital is now tied up on merchandise on the racks.
- Decline in new customer acquisition results in fewer sales.
- Prices are cut through sales to generate cash flow (what Kilts called "Loading the Trade")
- Store owner feels frustrated and stuck – decides to set higher goals without putting the systems in place to make goals a reality – tries to get big wins without making small wins first. As a result, they go back to setting unrealistic objectives of what can be sold.
- The loop continues spirally downward into even lower and lower profitability until the store either goes out of business or is sold to another owner who thinks the business will be fun and enjoyable (who doesn't understand what is required to make the business profitable).

When you get into the Circle of Doom, it is difficult to get out without a clear strategy and a lot of hard work. It takes focus working on the systems that will help you achieve the goals you want to actually stop being stuck with what is going on.

Anyone can get stuck on a plateau and be frustrated with the lack of results they have. What matters is choosing to do something about it and to work on creating more momentum now.

To escape from the Circle of Doom and to get unstuck, you've got to have an escape plan. You've got to have realistic goals, improved organizational discipline (especially in marketing and sales) and stronger financial management.

Kilts says the following about what can be done to escape: "While escaping from the Circle is long and difficult, there are a number of things that can keep you out:

1) Never chase unrealistic, unsustainable growth targets. You must spend the time to identify a rate of growth that is realistic for your sector and business. And not just for a year or two, but for the long run. Setting a sustainable growth target is one of the most important things you can do. Going for a blowout number is a sure way to blowup.

2) Regardless of the business, you must control costs and maintain them at a level that gives you a competitive advantage. So benchmark; find out what other companies, your peers, are doing, and then go them one better.

3) ZOG (Zero Overhead Growth) should be your mantra, not just for a year, or only in bad times. Always. Let your organization know that ZOG isn't a onetime event or a tactical activity. It's a fundamental strategy.

4) Every business sector has a few key metrics that tell you how your business is doing. Learn what they are and focus on them incessantly.

5) In consumer products, a rising market share is a critical measure of a brand's health. While competitive activities will cause deviations, the share trends must be heading up over time, or trouble lies ahead.

6) Half of all advertising expenditures may be wasted. But you must invest robustly in the marketing of your brands. Determine the right ratio of advertising to sales for your

specific product category and then make sure that over time you maintain that level.

7) Avoid trade loading and other bad business practices that result in selling more of your product than the market wants or consumers will buy. Selling excess products in order to meet quarterly earnings expectations is a sure sign that you have one foot in the Circle of Doom. Remember, never chase unreal targets. Facing the short-term rebuke from Wall Street is far better than risking an agonizing plunge into the Circle."—*Doing What Matters*, pp. 208-209.

That is great advice. It is so important to have clarity, but to have realistic goals and real targets. I believe in setting minimum, target, and optimal goals for this reason. The minimum goal is at the minimum the real target, but you incentivize your team to hit the target and optimal goals because those are what we really want to achieve. Yet, even if you have a setback, you know you have still had growth if you only hit the minimum goals.

Being stuck can happen for a number of reasons, but being unrealistic is right up there near the top.

Let me give you an example. I once had a bridal store owner approach me after a seminar and tell me that she wanted to hit the goal of $1,000,000 in sales and she wanted to know what to do. I asked her a few questions and discovered that she was doing less than 10% of that number in her store at the time. She told me that she wanted to hit the goal in a year or two. I asked her about what she was willing to do to hit the goal. She didn't want to change anything but she just wanted the sales to magically happen and asked me what my secret was to making this happen at our store. I told her there wasn't one magic secret and that a lot of work was involved. She wasn't interested in doing all of the work. She just wanted to know the secret formula to making the goal happen. I think this is what Kilts means by not setting unrealistic, unsustainable growth targets. You aren't going to hit targets without working hard at all of the fundamentals of business.

Jim Collins talks about this principle in his book *Good to Great*. He calls the process of building momentum The Flywheel Effect and he calls the Circle of Doom, the Doom Loop. Here is how both of these cycles work in the process of achieving a goal. First, you decide to achieve a goal (financial goal for the store, improve customer service issues, build a web or email strategy, sell more dresses, etc.)

Then, you take a specific action towards achieving the goal. The first gains seem incremental. It takes tremendous persistence to keep on going when you are not seeing an immediate result or very little improvement or benefit for the store or your bridal consultants.

Obstacles come up and threaten to derail your forward momentum. You are about ready to break through to a new level and increased momentum. Keep going. This is the worst place to give up, yet this is sadly where many people do lose the momentum they've created.

Then, finally over time, you break through to the next level and start gaining momentum to grow even more. Then, you start over and continue the cycle.

Be clear about what you want. When you find yourself drifting away from your clear objectives, stop, regroup, and get back on track.

2. Change your focus from goal orientation to systems implementation.

I read a really interesting statement about the power of systems in *How to Fail At Almost Everything and Still Win Big* by Dilbert artist Scott Adams. He said: "Throughout my career I've had my antennae up, looking for examples of people who use systems as opposed to goals. In most cases, as far as I can tell, the people who use systems do better. The systems-driven people have found a way to look at the familiar in new and more useful ways. To put it bluntly, goals are for losers. That's literally true most of the time. For example, if your goal is to lose ten pounds, you will spend every moment until you reach the goal—if you reach it at all—feeling as if you were short of your goal. In other words, goal-oriented people exist in a state of nearly continuous failure that they hope will be temporary. That feeling wears on you. In time, it becomes heavy and uncomfortable. It might even drive you out of the game.

"If you achieve your goal, you celebrate and feel terrific, but only until you realize you just lost the thing that gave you purpose and direction. Your options are to feel empty and useless, perhaps enjoying the spoils of your success until they bore you, or set new goals and reenter the cycle of permanent pre-success failure.

"The systems-versus-goals point of view is burdened by semantics, of course. You might say every system has a goal, however vague. And that would be true to some extent. And you could say that everyone who pursues a goal has some sort of system to get there, whether expressed or not. You could word-glue goals and systems together if you chose. All I'm suggesting is that thinking of goals and systems as very different concepts has power. Goal-oriented people exist in a state of continuous pre-success failure at best, and permanent failure at worst if things never work out. Systems people succeed every time they apply their systems, in the sense that they did what they intended to do. The goals people are fighting the feeling of discouragement at each turn. The systems people are feeling good every time they apply their system. That's a big difference in terms of maintaining your personal energy in the right direction.

"The systems-versus-goals model can be applied to most human endeavors. In the world of dieting, losing twenty pounds is a goal, but eating right is a system. In the exercise realm, running a marathon in under four hours is a goal, but exercising daily is a system. In business, making a million dollars is a goal, but being a serial entrepreneur is a system."—pp. 31-32.

He continues:

"For our purposes, let's say a *goal* is a specific objective that you either achieve or don't sometime in the future. A *system* is something you do on a regular basis that increases your odds of happiness in the long run. If you do something every day, it's a system. If you're waiting to achieve it someday in the future, it's a goal.

"Language is messy, and I know some of you are thinking that exercising sounds like a goal. The common definition of goals are a reach-it-and-be-done situation, whereas a system is something you do on a regular basis with a reasonable expectation that doing so will get you to a better place in your life. Systems have no deadlines, and on any given day you probably can't tell if they're moving you in the right direction.

"My proposition is that if you study people who succeed, you will see that most of them follow systems, not goals. When goal-oriented people succeed in big ways, it makes news, and it makes an interesting story. That gives you a distorted view of how often goal-driven people succeed. When you apply your own truth filter to the idea that systems are better than goals, consider only the people you know personally. If you know some extra successful people, ask some probing questions about how they got where they did. I think you'll find a system at the bottom of it all, and usually some extraordinary luck."

"...Consider Olympic athletes. When one Olympian wins a gold medal, or multiple gold medals, it's a headline story. But for every medalist there are thousands who had the goal of being on that podium and failed. Those people had goals and not systems. I don't consider daily practices and professional coaching a system because everyone knows in advance that the odds of any specific individual winning a medal through those activities are miniscule. The minimum requirement of a system is that a reasonable person expects it to work more often than not. Buying lottery tickets is not a system no matter how regularly you do it."—pp. 33-34.

What a great insight! When you view what you do at your bridal store everyday in this light, it shifts your focus on building and acting on systems that you can control that produce the results you want. In reality, both goals and systems are required. You need to have a direction, but you also need to have a specific plan of attack for what you will do to make the goal happen.

For example, consider two bridal store owners. One focuses on setting goals and the other focuses on setting up systems for achieving a specific target of a sales revenue number of $3000/day. Look at the difference:

1) Bridal Store Owner A is **goal oriented**. She sets a goal for $3000 in sales each day. *She is frustrated every day her goal isn't hit.*

2) Bridal Store Owner B is **systems oriented**. She sets a goal for $3000 in sales each day and has the following systems in place:

- She has a Lead Generation System that brings in 6 brides / day so a minimum of 3 dresses at an average of $1000/day can be sold with a 50% close ratio. She has a training system to work at getting her close ratio to 70-75%.
- Each of her consultants makes 2 outbound phone calls/day and she has 5 consultants. That equals 10 calls / day which equals 5 appointments/day; 30 appointments/week in a 6 day week.
- She has a system that generates inbound leads by mailing out at least 5 postcards / day. With her 5 consultants, that means she could theoretically have 25 possible appointments scheduled. With her system and follow up, she expects at least one qualified lead or appointment/day to result from this system.
- She has a system that generates leads daily from her web site and numerous systems to direct traffic to her web site.
- She generates leads daily from marketing system including utilizing Google Ad Words, her blog, her web site, bridal shows and other events.
- Each sale at her store results in an upsell because of follow up systems (converting every bride buying a dress to a bridesmaid

appointment, tuxedo appointment, wedding gown preservation kit, etc.)

- She has a referral strategy in place to get referrals from past brides (generating 5-10 leads/month).
- She has a system of cross-promotional offers with other wedding vendors that results in new leads every week.

I could go on with more systems that she has in place, but the point is this: ***This business owner is happy when systems are followed because the owner knows this will consistently lead to success. They may have a disappointing day, but with consistent systems in place, the results take care of themselves.***

Are you focused on your goals or on your systems? If you would like more help with systems development, I encourage you to get my book *The System is the Secret* available on Amazon.com.

3. Refocus on your goals, not your problems.
Problems and challenges can distract you from achieving your goals. Some of these problems can keep you up late at night worrying about what to do. The reality is that when you find yourself feeling stuck and discouraged, you are probably focusing on the problem, not the goal. Here are five suggestions for you to reflect on when considering obstacles you face at your store.

1) *Refocus your attention on the goal.* See yourself with the goal already achieved. What does it feel like to have accomplished your goal? Make your mental image as vivid and detailed as possible as you imagine the feeling of accomplishment.

2) *See your problem from a distance.* Make the picture small. See the problem as a challenge—an opportunity to use your creativity. Look down on your problem from a mental mountaintop.

3) *Recall past successes.* Bring the confident feelings back to your mind as you recall these successes. Hold those feelings in your mind as you vividly picture the accomplishment of your new goal.

4) *Review what happened just before you got stuck.* Is there something different you can do at *that* point; is there another direction you can take that will help you get unstuck?

5) *Examine your goal again.* Ask yourself these three questions: a) Is it reasonable? Does it fit your self-image—your talents and training? b) Does it conflict with other goals? (For example, spending more time with your family and doubling your income may be goals that are conflicting— they both require your time. Consequently, it will be very difficult to achieve both.) If it does conflict, modify it or the other goal to resolve the conflict. c) Do you need to be more flexible? If you are stuck on a particular steppingstone, maybe you need to get rid of it and create an alternative steppingstone.

Brian Tracy makes this observation in his book *How the Best Leaders Lead* which I think is great advice for you to follow as you work through your challenges. He says:

"There is a systematic method of problem solving that is used by the most effective executives in almost every organization. It is easy to learn and apply, and it is incredibly effective in helping you overcome obstacles and achieve your goals.

"First, define your problem or goal clearly in writing. Remember, a goal unachieved is merely a problem unsolved. The more clearly you define your problem or goal, the more likely it is that you will find an answer or solution.

"Second, once you have defined your problem clearly, ask 'What else is the problem?' Never be satisfied with a single definition of a problem. As Jack Welch said, 'Continually expand your definition of the problem, and you expand your view of all the different ways that it can be solved.'

"Third, restate the problem to make it easier to solve. If you settle for a quick definition of the problem, it could lead you down the wrong path, to solving the wrong problem and wasting resources for no purpose.

"For example, the biggest problem that a company usually experiences is low sales, leading to low revenues and decreased cash flow. When we ask, 'What else is the problem?' The answers we eventually arrive at change the entire nature of the solution and the proposed action.
What else is the problem? 'Our competitors sales are too high.'
If this is truly the case, this requires changes in marketing, sales, product quality, positioning, and many other things.
What else is the problem? 'We are not attracting enough qualified leads with our advertising.'
If this is truly the problem, new strategies in marketing advertising, and public relations and new choices in advertising media, copy, and advertising material are necessary.
What else is the problem? 'We are not closing enough of the customers attracted by our advertising.'
If this is the answer, then the solution is to train and retrain the sales force so that they are more competent at converting sales leads into actual customers.
This exercise can go on and on. Its importance is simple. If you settle on the wrong definition of the problem, you will go off in the wrong direction to solve the problem and eventually have to come back and start over.

"Fourth, determine all the possible causes of the problem. Ask the brutal questions. Be prepared to accept the very worst scenario. Get your ego out of the way.
Many companies have had to admit that the 'real' cause of their problem is that their products or services are not good enough in comparison with their competitors. Maybe they have to admit that there is no real market or what they're selling, or that what else is available in the market is superior or cheaper than their offerings. They may even have to admit that they made a mistake entering into this market in the first place.

"Fifth, determine all the possible solutions to this problem. Then force yourself to ask, 'What else is the solution?'
As the business writer Ian Mitroff says, 'Beware of a problem for which there is only one solution.'
Creativity, brainstorming, and flexibility—the willingness to entertain all options are key to uncovering and discovering all possible solutions."

"Sixth, once you have done a thorough and complete analysis of the problem and laid out all the possible causes and possible solutions, make a decision! Any decision is usually better than no decision at all.

"Seventh, once you have made a decision, assign responsibility. Who exactly is going to carry out each part of the decision?

"Eighth, set a deadline. Set a schedule for reporting on progress.

"Ninth, implement the plan. 'A weak solution vigorously carried out is usually better than an excellent solution weakly pursued.'

"Tenth, check and review later to see if the solution was successful. Did you get the expected result? Be prepared to implement your Plan B if your first solution doesn't work. Always have a backup."—Brian Tracy, *How the Best Leaders Lead*, pp. 161-164.

4. Start. Get going. Look for little wins that will give you forward progress.

Achieving momentum starts with creating forward progress. Getting started is often the most difficult part. It's like the law of inertia: an object in motion tends to stay in motion, and an object at rest tends to stay at rest. Momentum is what happens when you get moving.

Here are five things to consider regarding achieving momentum.
1) Momentum starts with the leader, and then moves outwards and impacts the entire team. You are responsible for the momentum of your team; you can't place the responsibility on anyone else. You need

to be motivated yourself, before you can motivate others. Develop a vision or goal for what you need to do in sales each day and keep that in front of you. Your early sales successes will motivate you and will give the bridal consultants on your team the feeling that they can sell more as well.

2) Leave the starting blocks quickly and with power. In Olympic sprinting, the most important part of the race is often leaving the starting blocks. In your business you need to leave the starting blocks fast. Even if your bridal business has been in a slump for a while you can turn it around tomorrow morning just by getting out in front with a fast start. Pick up the phone and make some phone calls; come up with a sales promotion that you can do this weekend; get it out in front of brides (via email or up on your web site, etc.) The best way to create momentum is to start doing massive amounts of what it takes to succeed. Start quickly and with power.

3) Follow one success immediately with another one. The best time to sell a wedding gown or prom dress is immediately after you've just sold one. You are confident and have momentum working in your favor. Don't stop to take a break after you reach a goal. Immediately, go after your next sale or goal. If you stop to take a break, you will limit the amount of momentum you can achieve.

It is like a pot of boiling water. It takes time to start boiling. Once it does, if you take it off the burner, it immediately starts cooling down. Momentum can switch so fast in a basketball game. If the momentum starts to switch to the other team, the opposing coach will take a time out to slow things down and so that they can start to regain the momentum that they lost.

4) Help your team create wins by assisting with sales. Get out on the floor and help your bridal consultants close sales. We are all so busy with the administrative details of running our stores, but getting out and selling will help you create momentum faster than anything else you can do. Remember, momentum begins with you. From there it flows over to the rest of the bridal consultants on your team. Help your bridal consultants make sales and they will gain the confidence to continue on to sell and be more successful at selling. When everyone is winning and selling, you will build a tremendous amount of momentum and enthusiasm (which in turn will help you make more sales).

5) Help your bridal consultants overcome barriers that may come their way. When you are first starting to build momentum, it is so easy to lose it. Look for potential barriers that can derail your forward momentum and eliminate them for the members of your team. As momentum increases this will be come easier but in the early stages it may take a focused effort if problems come your way.

For example, a train moving at full speed will smash right through a brick wall and keep moving; however a single rock place properly can prevent a stopped train from getting started. So in the early stages of creating momentum if problems or obstacles come your way, do whatever it takes to get past them and move forward. That same problem will become easier as you see more and more success.

Take some time to write down the obstacles or barriers that may prevent you from gaining momentum at your store in different seasons. When it starts to slow down after the busy season, what kinds of things can you do to continue building momentum?

Creating momentum is not easy. It takes hard work and effort, but once you have momentum, it can change your business. Be persistent. It is easy to lose heart and focus when you are building momentum, but it is the little things consistently done over and over that will take you to new heights.

Momentum is like a chain reaction or dominoes falling. Once the first domino falls, it is hard to stop all of them from falling. Momentum, by its nature, requires a lot of upfront pushing to get the ball rolling. It takes time and effort to build up momentum.

John Maxwell explains: "It takes a leader to create momentum. Followers catch it. And managers are able to continue it once it has begun. But creating it requires someone who can motivate others, not who needs to be motivated. Harry Truman once said, 'If you can't stand the heat, get out of the kitchen." But for leaders, that statement should be changed to read, "If you can't make some heat, get out of the kitchen."--*The 21 Irrefutable Laws of Leadership*, p. 171.

To get unstuck, you've got to understand what creates momentum, what stops it or slows it down and how you can work to maintain and sustain the momentum that will help you rise out of a plateau that you may have been experiencing at your store.

So, how do you get unstuck from lost momentum? Here are five steps:

1) *Recognize that you are in a slump.* Take a time out. Rethink, re-energize and refocus on your business. Talk to those who support you—mentors in the business, friends in other businesses, family members, etc.

2) *Remind yourself of a major accomplishment.* Select a recent month's sales figures, or a notable victory in your life that made you feel great. Replay it vividly in your mind. Talk about it. Look at photos, thank you letters from brides, or comments from others about the success you experienced. Understand that you are a talented person. You've proved it before with your store and you can do it again.

3) *Get back to the basics.* One of the main reasons for breaking momentum is that you're not practicing the fundamentals that got you to where you are in the first place. Take some time to have a reality check about your current situation.

Are you doing the easy things instead of the activities and developing the systems that will guarantee you the results you are looking for?

4) *Take a break if you're physically or mentally drained.* Recapture your energy before you start up again. Don't spend too long here or you'll lose your momentum entirely.

5) Work your way out of the slump. Life and the bridal business are full of cycles. They don't last forever so take one day at a time. Remind yourself, "This too shall pass." The best way out is through. As Winston Churchill once stated, "If you're going through hell, keep going."

5. Take responsibility to steer the momentum. Don't expect anyone else to take the reins and make it happen. It is *your* job to steer and increase momentum.
John Maxwell says: "Momentum always has a direction. Most people in an organization are carried by that momentum and have little impact on it. But leaders cannot afford to surf momentum; they must steer it."--*The 21 Most Powerful Minutes in a Leader's Day*, p. 269.

It is a lot easier to steer momentum while you are in motion then it is when you are at a complete standstill. Do you need to change the direction of your store? Are you gaining or losing momentum?

I've learned that the times of transition at your store are the most critical times for continuing and sustaining momentum. These can happen when you have a change of leadership at your store. They can happen following a really good month where you start to slide into a bad month. Remember, good leaders can *sustain* momentum. Great leaders can *increase* it.
Where are you at in your store right now? Do you need to sustain momentum or do you increase it? It takes a specific set of skills in leadership to increase momentum. You've got to be able to set a new vision, incentivize those who are helping you to achieve the vision, offer encouragement and be willing to get in the trenches and get your hands dirty too. The help of an outside coach or mentor to guide you through such times can be invaluable.

To steer and increase momentum, you often need to break new ground and set new records. You can't just rely on what you used to do in order to sustain what you did last year. There are too many aggressive competitors and constantly shifting parts that this is no longer possible.

Eliot A. Cohen and John Gooch wrote a book called *Military Misfortunes: The Anatomy of Failure in War*. In this book, they identify three reasons for failure in warfare. These three reasons apply to business as well.

1. **Failure to anticipate**. This refers to the inability or unwillingness of the commander to look down the road into the future and think about all of the possible actions that a competitor could take to defeat your forces.

2. **Failure to learn from mistakes.** If you don't learn from your mistakes you are doomed to repeat them.

Thomas J. Watson, Jr. (longtime chairman of IBM): "We don't mind if people make mistakes around here. This is normal and natural. What is unforgivable is the failure to learn from the mistakes, which leads to repeating them."

That's great advice. See failure as sent to you to help you learn what you need to know to be more successful in the future.

3. **Failure to adapt.** Cohen and Gooch say: "No strategy ever survives first contact with the enemy." Accept feedback and make corrections quickly. Be open to the possibility that you could be wrong. Don't close yourself off to thinking that a line that has sold well for you in the past must continue to be a part of your store if it isn't profitable.

If you fall in love with a particular product line or way of doing business you can be unproductive (like straightening deck chairs on the Titanic). In the end, it won't really matter.

You know you have momentum when you run over obstacles in your path like they were nothing. Momentum is when things happen easily, where one success follows another and forward growth comes quickly.

Anticipate the obstacles you will face and your momentum will allow you to move past mistakes quickly. When your bridal consultants learn from their mistakes they will sell more and achieve more, and they will do it at a higher level. If something isn't working don't ride it all the way around the doom loop. Adapt quickly and you can pull out of a bad situation.

When the flywheel of momentum starts to turn, pay attention to clues, connections, and opportunities that are presented to you so that you can anticipate obstacles, learn from your mistakes and adapt quickly to succeed.

Remember, your job as the leader of your store is not just to sustain momentum, but to increase it. It is hard to do this if you are always at the grindstone pushing everything forward. Eventually, you will lose your energy, your drive, your enthusiasm and you will drop out or drop dead. Stephen R. Covey calls this "sharpening the saw."

Abraham Lincoln once said, "If I had eight hours to cut down a tree, I would spend six of them sharpening my axe." Find ways to eliminate the things that drain your energy. Find outlets that inspire you and help put you in a good mood.

Refuse to be bored by the mundane in life. As writer Paulo Coleho observed: "We can become blind by seeing each day as a similar one."

Look for the result you want before you begin. I like this observation about how the process game creator Cranium utilizes to create their products as explained by Sam Harrison in his book *IdeaSpotting*. He says: "Robert Tait, co-creator of the game Cranium, likes to imagine how the wow factor looks as he begins creating games. He calls it 'moment engineering'—visualizing the perfect moment customers will experience when playing the game. For example, before Tait's team began designing a children's game, they drew a picture of a mother sitting around the floor with her kids on a rainy day. She and the children were laughing and high-fiving as they played the game. That image became the team's creative goal."-p. 105.

Think about Robert Tait's exercise for the brides who come into your store and ask yourself the following three questions:

1) What kind of moment engineering could you do at your store to increase your momentum?

2) What does that moment look like?

3) How can you help your bridal consultants have more of those moments every day?

John Maxwell said: "Momentum can make or break your organization. Learn to use it to your advantage and you can take your people anywhere."--*The 21 Most Powerful Minutes in a Leader's Day*, p. 264.

6. Sustain and build momentum. It starts slowly but with consistent focus and time, you can accelerate out of any business plateau that you may currently be on.
The most difficult part of getting unstuck is getting started. Once the ball gets rolling it seems that projects often take on a life of their own and carry themselves through to the finish. Choose to be a person of action.

Sullivan and Thompson sum up how to get unstuck with this observation: "If things are stuck, shake it up. This simple truth lies at the heart of the Plateau Effect. Trying new things literally rewires your brain, forcing it to open up long-closed neural pathways. Embracing diversity is such a profound concept that it actually can be, along with laughter and love, the best medicine. Elderly folks who learn a new language are less likely to suffer from Alzheimer's disease. This same approach—shaking up your mind—can work across every single human endeavor you might undertake."—*Getting Unstuck*, p.253.

If you've felt any of the Serious Seven in your life that have been causing you to feel stuck, I hope you realize that you don't have to be stuck there forever. It is a choice to break free of negative momentum and start doing the things that will help you get back on track.

Don't get so bogged down with your obstacles that you fail to spend time on your opportunities. True leaders see opportunities where others see only problems. Be a leader and look for the opportunities at your store so that you can accelerate out of any business plateaus you may have been on and start climbing again up the ladder of success.

What will you do with the opportunities you've been given? What will you be able to say about what you've done at this time next year? Focus on what matters most. Get good at promoting yourself so brides and prom girls can't wait to come into your store and get to know you and see all of the beautiful dresses you have to offer for their special events. Get so good at selling that the majority of the brides you see purchase from you on their first visit.

There will always be challenges in any endeavor as you grow and move upward, yet there is a tremendous amount of excitement and optimism when you do so. I hope the ideas I've shared with you here will be things that you will act on each and every day. I look forward to hearing of your successes as you implement these game changers in your business. Get in the game and go for it!

ABOUT THE AUTHOR

Jim Butler and his wife Heather started their bridal business in the fall of 2001. They grew their business from $0 to over $1,000,000 per year in sales in three years. Jim has helped some of the most respected and largest bridal stores across the country to grow their sales and shatter their previous sales records. Jim is a recognized marketing authority and provides training and coaching to hundreds of bridal retailers and wedding professionals to help them improve their businesses each year. He is the author of the best selling books *Bridal Profit Explosion* and *Bridal Boosters & Breakthroughs*. Most recently, he has created the *Bridal Sales Blueprint*, which is the #1 best selling sales training program in the bridal industry used by top bridal retailers across the world to increase their sales. He has appeared as a panelist and speaker at the Wedding MBA, Las Vegas, New York, and Dallas markets. He offers a monthly coaching and tele-seminar program to bridal stores offering sales and business insights and is the host of the Bridal Business Success Podcast. He loves the bridal business and really enjoys helping individuals and businesses reach their true potential through his coaching and training. He and his wife Heather have five children. Visit his web site at www.BridalBusinessSuccess.com.

www.ingramcontent.com/pod-product-compliance
Lightning Source LLC
Chambersburg PA
CBHW061006220326
41599CB00023B/3845